INDIANA

GEORGE SAND was born as Amantine-Aurore-Lucile Dupin on 1 July 1804. From her father's death in 1808, she was raised at Nohant in Berry, France, which was her grandmother's home and in which she herself would spend the greater part of her life, although she travelled widely and frequently stayed in Paris. A prolific writer of plays, short stories, novels, and journal articles, she published her first novel, *Indiana*, in 1832. Closely allied with major socialist thinkers in the years leading up to the revolution of 1848, she was distressed by the violence and brutality of the uprisings and sought in subsequent novels to reconcile socialist theory with the harsh teachings of experience. Her interest in music is strongly reflected in *The Master Pipers*, while her love of the countryside in the Berry and Bourbonnais regions of France, together with her desire to give permanence to local customs and beliefs, can be seen in her pastoral novels *Little Fadette*, *The Devil's Pool*, and *François the Foundling*. She continued writing until her death in 1876.

SYLVIA RAPHAEL has taught French language and literature at the universities of Glasgow and London, specializing in nineteenth-century literature. Her translations include a selection of Balzac's short stories and of his *Eugénie Grandet* and *La Cousine Bette*.

NAOMI SCHOR is William Hanes Wannamaker Professor of Romance Studies and Literature at Duke University. Her publications include *Reading in Detail: Aesthetics and the Feminine* (1987) and *George Sand and Idealism* (1993).

THE WORLD'S CLASSICS

GEORGE SAND

Indiana

Translated by
SYLVIA RAPHAEL

With an Introduction by
NAOMI SCHOR

Oxford   New York
OXFORD UNIVERSITY PRESS

Oxford University Press, Walton Street, Oxford OX2 6DP

Oxford New York
Athens Auckland Bangkok Bombay
Calcutta Cape Town Dar es Salaam Delhi
Florence Hong Kong Istanbul Karachi
Kuala Lumpur Madras Madrid Melbourne
Mexico City Nairobi Paris Singapore
Taipei Tokyo Toronto

and associated companies in
Berlin Ibadan

Oxford is a trade mark of Oxford University Press

British Library Cataloguing in Publication Data

Data available

Library of Congress Cataloging in Publication Data
Sand, George, 1804–1876,
[Indiana. English]
Indiana / George Sand; translated by Sylvia Raphael; with an
introduction by Naomi Schor.
p.   cm.—(The World's classics)
1. France—Social life and customs—19th century—Fiction.
2. Man—woman relationships—France—Fiction. 3. Marriage—
France—Fiction. 4. Women—France—Fiction. I. Title. II. Series.
843'.8—dc20   PQ2404.A4   1994   94-6215

ISBN 0-19-283075-9

3 5 7 9 10 8 6 4 2

Printed in Great Britain by
BPC Paperbacks Ltd
Aylesbury, Bucks

CONTENTS

Sir. Ralph Bran   India's cousin   RB

India Delmare (Creole).   I

Noun   I's maid (Creole) mam...

Rayman

INTRODUCTION

Of the many legends attached to George Sand's name, one has particular relevance to the publication of Sand's stunningly successful first novel, *Indiana*. Henry James, Sand's perfidious admirer, puts it this way: 'About this sudden entrance into literature, into philosophy, into rebellion ... there are various different things to be said. Very remarkable, indeed, was the immediate development of the literary faculty in this needy young woman who lived in cheap lodgings and looked for "employment". She wrote as a bird sings; but unlike most birds, she found it unnecessary to indulge, by way of prelude, in twitterings and vocal exercises; she broke out at once with her full volume of expression.'[1] Characterized on the basis of her remarkable achievement—*Indiana* literally launched Sand's career overnight—as a 'natural' writer, Sand was by the same gesture assigned the second rank reserved for writers, particularly female, who are said to serve no apprenticeship, to expend no effort in writing, who like Minerva spring full born from Jupiter's forehead. Not surprisingly, the apparently flattering notion that Sand was not just a bird but a rare one at that, was to mutate in time into other less flattering natural analogies than the ornithological. Most famously, Nietzsche compared the seemingly effortless flow of her prose to that of a milk-cow.

Whether or not Sand was a natural writer, James failed to mark a crucial aspect of what made *Indiana* so exceptional, and its publication such an event: Sand was in no sense a natural *author*. When it appeared in May 1832 *Indiana* bore an unfamiliar and enigmatic signature, G. Sand. Was the author male or female? Did the G stand for George or, as one eminent contemporary critic (Gustave Planche) would have it, Georgina? G. Sand was, as it was soon revealed, the pseudonym of Aurore Dudevant, the recently separated wife of the

---

[1] Henry James, 'George Sand', in Leon Edel (ed.), *French Poets and Novelists* (New York: Grosset & Dunlap, 1964), 162.

Baron Casimir Dudevant. Specifically enjoined by her mother-in-law not to sully her noble married name in her pursuit of a professional writing career, Sand gradually elaborated what was to become her lifelong pen-name and accompanying male persona. Writing first in collaboration with her lover Jules Sandeau under a series of pen names (Signol, J. Sand, J.S.), when she published her first solo effort, *Indiana*, she retained the marginally established and marketable Sand but made it her own by substituting the trace of the lover's name, the vestigial initial J, by a G. It was only when later that same astonishingly productive year she published her second novel, *Valentine*, under the name George Sand, that the process of renaming herself was completed.

Given the peculiar difficulties women encountered in assuming authorship of their writings in both France and England, due to obstacles placed in their paths by a misogynistic social and cultural order buttressed by a legal system which worked to dispossess them of their literary productions, George Sand was hardly the only nineteenth-century woman author to adopt a pseudonym—and of course men too adopted pseudonyms, albeit for different reasons. But she was the first of any standing: breaking with a tradition of anonymity and genteel lady novelist 'Madame de' signatures, George Sand, née Aurore Dupin, was the initiator of a tradition linking women's coming to writing with self-naming, a veritable rebirth: 'In Paris Mme Dudevant is dead. But George Sand is known as a lusty fellow,' writes Sand to a friend in the flush of *Indiana*'s success.[2] Because of her immense productivity—her *œuvre* comprises some sixty-nine novels, twenty-five volumes of correspondence, and other forms of writing—and the international status as a cultural icon she achieved in her lifetime, Sand's use of a male pseudonym was to prove remarkably influential, and nowhere more so than in Victorian England: the English spelling of George—in French the accepted spelling is Georges—finds its ultimate

---

[2] George Sand, Letter to Laure de Decerfz (3, 6, and 7 July 1832), in Georges Lubin (ed.), *Correspondance* 2, *1832–35* (Paris: Garnier, 1966), 120. All translations are mine except where otherwise noted.

justification in the pseudonym Marian Evans explicitly borrowed from her French model; I am referring of course to George Eliot.

Just the sort of demeaning cultural stereotyping that led so many nineteenth-century women authors to adopt male pseudonyms greeted the publication of what was immediately recognized as a major modern work, the literary event of 1832. Confronted by the sexually unmarked initial of the author's first name, contemporary male critics trotted out familiar clichés to ascribe a sex to the author and hence a value to his work. These clichés fall into two familiar classes: according to one, women's and men's writing is essentially different, bodily grounded in man's strength and woman's weakness. Thus Edouard d'Anglemont writes, 'this is a novel written with all the strength of a man's grip and all the grace of a woman's pen'.[3] Because *Indiana* combines allegedly masculine and feminine traits, the critic Jacques Lerond can only conclude that this is a two-handed, doubly authored work: 'this brilliant but unharmonious cloth is the work of two distinct workers.'[4]

A second category of clichés involves the relationship between the author and his or her characters: to the extent that an author projects his or her self into a character, he or she gives his or her sex away. Because of *Indiana*'s extraordinary emphasis on the miseries of female destiny in a patriarchal society, its author could only be a woman; no man could have described woman's estate as Sand does. By the same token, and more to the point, no man could or would have portrayed the cad Raymon in as clinical a way as Sand does. A similar logic is at work in Baudelaire's celebrated essay on Flaubert's *Madame Bovary*. The issue there is not, of course, the sex of the author, which is never in doubt, but the sex of the main female protagonist: for all her femininity, according to

---

[3] Edouard d'Anglemont, review of *Indiana* in *La France littéraire* 4 (Nov. 1832), 457, as cited by Sandy Petrey, 'George and Georgina Sand: Realist Gender in *Indiana*', in Michael Worton and Judith Still (eds.), *Sexuality and Textuality* (Manchester: Manchester University Press, forthcoming).

[4] Jacques Lerond writing in the *Revue des Deux Mondes, Chronique de la Quinzaine* (1 June 1832), as cited by Georges Lubin, *Correspondance* 2. 115 n.1.

Baudelaire, there persists in Emma Bovary a trace of the virility the male author projects on to her, hence her androgyny. An androgynous character can only be the product of an androgynous author. Thus Indiana's androgynous nature—she is a sort of ultra-feminine Amazon—is viewed not as the result of collaboration between a male and a female author, but rather as the product of her author's 'virile character', her own unstable gender identity.

Now whereas Flaubert proudly and famously proclaimed his identification with his fictional creation—'Madame Bovary, c'est moi', he is reported to have said—in her autobiography Sand protests against the widespread implication that her female protagonists are projections of the author: 'I am too romantic ever to have seen the heroine of a novel in my mirror.'[5] Whereas for male authors identification is cause for boasting, for women authors, as feminist critics have convincingly demonstrated, it is cause for concern, because the identification of a male author with his female creation is taken as an emblem of his imaginative powers, while that of a female author is taken as a proof of her creative deficiency. Far better, then, for the author that Sand is in the process of becoming that her text mirror not herself—'Indiana ce n'est pas moi,' she might have cried—but external reality. Of course these are not the same processes of reflection: one involves the public and metaphoric mirror/that the realist writer following Stendhal is said to carry down the road, the other, the private and literal mirror of the narcissistic woman.

Sand came to writing at the very moment when, under the joint impetus of Stendhal and Balzac, the literary movement that has come to be known as realism was rising to the dominant position it was soon to achieve. Seeking to obtain the literary legitimation that being a realist writer bestows, Sand's first edition of and first preface to *Indiana* are replete with protestations of her allegiance to the familiar ideology of realism, namely that it has no ideology: it is pure reproduction, a mirror without a curve, a machine that merely

---

[5] George Sand, in Thelma Jurgrau (ed.), *Story of my Life: The Autobiography of George Sand*, a group translation (New York: SUNY Press, 1991), 922.

registers material phenomena and events without distorting them. 'The writer is only a mirror which reflects them [society's inequalities and fate's whims], a machine which traces their outline, and he has nothing for which to apologize if the impressions are correct and the reflection is faithful.'[6]

What the 1832 versions of the preface and text demonstrate is that for a fledgeling writer realism provided the means for distancing oneself from the sort of unreal or idealistic romantic literature often disparagingly associated with femininity, especially in the heyday of the novel's rise in the eighteenth century. The gendering of the aesthetic categories of realism and idealism is clearly enunciated by Balzac, when in a conversation Sand transcribes in her autobiography, *Story of My Life*, he tells her:

You are looking for man as he should be; I take him as he is. Believe me, we are both right. Both paths lead to the same end. I also like exceptional human beings; I am one myself. I need them to make my ordinary characters stand out, and I never sacrifice them unnecessarily. But the ordinary human beings interest me more than they do you. I make them larger than life; I idealize them in the opposite sense, in their ugliness or in their stupidity. I give their deformities frightful or grotesque proportions. You could not do that; you are smart not to want to look at people and things that would give you nightmares. Idealize what is pretty and what is beautiful, that is a woman's job.[7]

According to this plausible if perhaps apocryphal statement, realism—which is in fact a form of negative idealism—is an unfiltered mode of vision that looks harsh reality in the face, while idealism is a prosthetic device that functions to dim the blinding dazzle of truth. Writing as a would-be realist, which is to say as a man, Sand denies in her preface of 1832 any recourse to the prettifying visual aids of idealism: 'If he [the writer] had felt learned enough to write a really useful book, he would have softened truth instead of presenting it with its crude colours and glaring effects. Such a book would have served the purpose of blue spectacles for faulty eyes.'[8]

---

[6] George Sand, see 'Preface to the 1832 Edition', pp. 5–9 of this book.
[7] Sand, *Story of my Life*, 923.
[8] Sand, see 'Preface to the 1832 Edition', pp. 5–9 of this book.

Despite Sand's strategically placed disclaimer, idealism and not realism came to be her preferred and distinctive aesthetic mode. Hence, just as it is impossible to write about Balzac without writing about realism, no analysis, let alone re-evaluation of Sand's work can proceed without taking account of her (allegedly feminine) idealist aesthetics, without rethinking idealism, idealism being understood here both as the heightening of an essential characteristic (the pretty and the beautiful, but also the ugly and the stupid), *and* the promotion of a higher good (freedom, equality, spiritual love). However, so imbricated are realism and idealism at the outset, so great the influence of Balzac on his peers, that Sand did not come on the literary scene as an idealist in full possession of her aesthetic vision. *Indiana* records the difficult emergence of Sandian idealism from the realist paradigm constituted by Balzacian realism.

Given this state of affairs it is not surprising that *Indiana* opens with a tableau whose realist insignia are so glaring as to have fooled even Sand's curmudgeonly mentor, Henri de Latouche. Quickly scanning his pupil's manuscript he exclaimed: 'Well! it's a pastiche, school of Balzac. A pastiche, what can I say? Balzac, what can I say.'[9] It was only after having spent the night reading the entire manuscript that he recognized the novel's originality, and even its superiority to the chief representatives of the realist school: 'Balzac and Mérimée lie dead under *Indiana*.'[10] What creates the illusion of a pseudo-Balzacian beginning is precisely the tableau-like presentation of the characters. Following the realist descriptive code which, as Roland Barthes has shown, consists of appropriating a pictorial model[11]—in this instance a Rembrandt-like chiaroscuro painting—to mediate the description of brute reality, the initial tableau features three of the novel's main protagonists grouped around a flickering fire. But there is nothing particularly Balzacian about this triangle, which recalls rather *La Nouvelle Héloïse*, an unsurprising

[9] Sand, *Story of my Life*, 931.
[10] Latouche, cited by Georges Lubin in *Correspondance* 2. 88 n.1.
[11] Roland Barthes, *S/Z*, trans. Richard Miller (New York: Hill & Wang, 1974), 55.

literary reminiscence on the part of such a daughter of Rousseau as was Sand. The three figures we find glumly arrayed before the fire in Lagny, a manor in Brie, constitute, however, a bizarre Oedipal triangle: Colonel Delmare, the tyrannical and jealous paternal husband who received Indiana from the hands of her brutal father; Sir Ralph, Indiana's asexual cousin, who watches over her like a brother; and Indiana herself, the oppressed exotic heroine. Soon this static tableau is interrupted by the arrival of the third male protagonist, the dashing aristocrat recently moved to the area, Raymon de la Ramière, the outsider who sets the narrative into motion. Though a stranger to this dysfunctional family circle, Raymon's irruption onto the scene completes the complex triplication of the male protagonist. Thus the initial pseudo-Oedipal triangle is overlaid and energized by a homosocial triangle, where men seek out and engage with each other through the mediation of a mutually desired woman. What Raymon does, in other words, is to set the ambiguous and latent structure of male rivalry and desire into motion. By contrasting Indiana's non-rivalrous relationship with her foster-sister Noun with the rivalrous relationship between men that the seductive Raymon brings to the surface, Sand turns received ideas on their ear; it is the rivalry between empowered men and not that between disempowered women that undergirds the social structure.

It has often been argued that each of the male protagonists represents a specific political position along the spectrum of political possibilities available during the waning days of the Restoration and the early days of the July Monarchy. Delmare is the embittered cashiered Napoleonic soldier, Raymon, the opportunistic legitimist, Sir Ralph, the idealistic democrat. Though historically accurate, this somewhat reductive reading does not account for the interest of the novel. What *Indiana* shows is that politics is not simply the stuff of male debate, it is also the stuff of women's lives. What makes Delmare such a compelling figure is not his adherence to some sort of Balzacian social typology, rather his instantiation of an idea, the Law, which reduces women to the status of objects of exchange, to the abjection of virtual slaves. What immediately

signals Sand's difference from the prestigious models invoked
in her first pages (Chateaubriand for the gloomy decor,
Rousseau for the dramatic personae, Balzac for the pictorial
code) is the pronounced allegorical drift, which is highlighted
in the preface and more fully developed in *Lélia*, which was
published the following year. In Sand's novel each protagonist
incarnates an abstraction; the ideal toward which the idealist
novel tends is always a form of allegory.

Read as an allegorical figure, Delmare represents patriarchal law under the regime of the Napoleonic Civil Code; the
struggle between Delmare and his rebellious young wife is a
struggle between legal oppression and a personal quest for
liberation. The immense difficulty of articulating such a struggle in the first half of the nineteenth century is made clear by
Sand's own (re)reading of the novel during her most politi-
cally radical decade: thus in the preface of 1842 what was
presented as an allegorical struggle between the law and its
victims in 1832 is recast into an even more explicit and
impassioned protest against the inequity of marriage. In retro-
spect it becomes clear to Sand that *Indiana* is the first of a
triptych (the other panels of which include *Valentine* and
Lélia) concerned with the institution of marriage, especially as
it determines the condition of women. As such it participates
in a major trend in nineteenth-century French fiction: like
Eugénie Grandet, her provincial Balzacian contemporary,
Indiana and, following her, Valentine body forth their rejec-
tion of women's subordination to the patriarchal exchange
system by undermining the sexual and reproductive obligations entailed by the marriage contract. Though Indiana's
conjugal sexuality remains shrouded in mystery, the novel is
replete with hints at her virginity; such is the undecidability
that surrounds the consummation of her marriage vows that
critics are divided between those who maintain that Indiana
remains a virgin in marriage, and those who view her as the
victim of the legalized rape that is marriage in nineteenth-
century feminist discourse.

The question that then arises is the extent to which Sand's
novel can be said to be feminist. At least ever since feminist
critics began to rediscover Sand under the impulse of second-

wave feminism, Sand's feminist credentials have been subjected to close scrutiny. The initial response was one of disappointment and condemnation: perhaps because of its
inaugural position and self-styled feminist protest, *Indiana*
was taken to exemplify the deficiencies of Sand's feminism.
The problem, according to these 1970s-style readings, is that
Indiana only seems to challenge prevailing representational
codes of femininity; in actual fact, 'the novel's rhetoric of
rebellion conceals but is an integral part of a novelistic structure which encourages conformity to the feminine stereotypes
then in force'.[12] For all her Amazonian horse-riding and rebellious conduct, in short her androgyny, Indiana's represen-
tation reverts to type; it is no accident that in the novel's
Utopian epilogue, Indiana not only falls silent, is spoken of
and for by Ralph, but moreover does not accede to the sensual
bliss that is the prerogative of a desiring female subject. The
failure of Sand to imagine a heroine endowed with subjectivity
goes hand in hand with her failure to imagine a heroine
endowed with sexual desire. Does this failure, however, be-
token a lack of feminism, indeed of feminist solidarity on the
part of George Sand, or is it rather a part of the contradictory
legacy that Sand, like Mary Wollstonecraft, inherited from the
Enlightenment? According to this essentially Rousseauistic
view of the interplay of citizenship and sexual difference, for
women participation in the fraternal society of rights and
reason can only be purchased at the cost of a deadening of the
senses, a curbing of disruptive sexual desire.

But then what is feminism? Can Sand be described as feminist according to one definition, not feminist according to
another? Can one escape the pitfalls of anachronism? Feminism as such does not offer a stable semantic ground for
deciding these questions one way or another, for feminism too
has a history; there is no univocal and universal sense of
feminism. Whereas in the age of sexual difference—roughly
the 1970s—feminist theory was preoccupied with the existence of female subjectivity, in the age of gender—roughly the

[12] Leslie Rabine, 'George Sand and the Myth of Femininity', *Women and Litera-ture*, 4/2 (Fall 1976), 2.

1980s—it came to focus more on the distinction between what is viewed as essential (femaleness) and what is viewed as cultural (femininity), what is natural, what is constructed. There is thus an oscillation between two voices in *Indiana*: the male authorial voice that echoes the prevailing essentialist discourse on femininity ('women are . . .'), and another voice, the sexually unmarked (and humanist) narrative voice, which asserts that women, and other oppressed human beings, such as the black slaves Ralph and Indiana devote themselves to freeing, are not born naturally inferior; there is no metaphysical essence, no natural difference that marks those that are socially disenfranchised as irredeemably condemned.

And yet this much is certain: Sand and her contemporaries, especially the Saint-Simonians—a highly influential romantic social movement committed to equality between the sexes to which she did not belong but with whom she shared enemies—viewed the institution of marriage as oppressing women; marriage in the French social order instituted by Napoleon's Civil Code was a prime feminist issue in nineteenth-century France. For this reason Sand never stopped rethinking marriage, transforming it in such Utopian political novels as *The Journeyman Joiner* and *The Miller of Angibault* from an instrument of patriarchal oppression into the mainspring of class reconciliation.

Indiana is not of course the only female protagonist in the novel: there is a near-perfect symmetry between the male triangle and the female, which includes Laure de Nangy, the aristocratic heiress to an industrial fortune whom Raymon finally marries, and Noun, Indiana's foster-sister and servant whom Raymon seduces and abandons, and who commits suicide by drowning. The character of Noun is, as psychoanalytically inclined critics have been quick to observe, of particular interest, for it inscribes at the very threshold of Sand's career the theme of doubling which recurs throughout her fiction, notably in such works as *Jacques* and *La petite Fadette*. But the case of the Indiana and Noun dyad represents not merely a first and quite brilliant manifestation of a persistent myth of doubling: it is rather a unique case of a split within femininity which far exceeds the paradigmatic angel/

whore opposition, and renders the very category of woman problematic. The split is inscribed in the very adjective creole—both maid and mistress are identified as 'Creoles'—which has in French a double and contradictory meaning: (1) of mixed or black race (multiracial); (2) a white person born in the colonies (monoracial). No more than it can be ascertained whether Indiana is a virgin or not, can one assert that Noun is black or white. And yet if most readers—myself included—assume that she is black,[13] that is because they are responding to a series of cues in the novel that lead them to read blatant indications of class difference as signs of a repressed racial difference. However blurred the line between black and white in the novel, however minimal the racial difference between Noun and Indiana, class separates them irrevocably. Noun can dress up as the absent Indiana, and Indiana assume the appearance of the dead Noun, but travesty is no substitute for education, and Noun cannot write like Indiana. In a novel where the command of language constitutes both political and erotic power, language is the emblem of their insuperable social differences.

There is no aspect of the novel we have dealt with thus far that does not lead in one way or another towards and then away from what is without a doubt one of the most fascinating spaces in all of Sand's fiction—Indiana's circular-shaped bedroom,[14] the site of the ultimate confusion of Indiana and Noun. It is difficult here to avoid superimposing a symbolic grid over the novel's topography, for everything suggests that the description of this strangely configured bedroom exceeds the constraints of realism and opens the way to the idealism of the novel's surprising and controversial epilogue. But more of that in a moment.

In the first of the three major scenes that will unfold there, Raymon enters this curiously shaped room as though passing from the world of prosaic reality into a dream space and thus

[13] Doris Kadish, 'Representing Race in *Indiana*', *George Sand Studies*, 11/1–2 (1992), 23.
[14] Stirling Haig, 'The Circular Room of George Sand's *Indiana*', in his *The Madame Bovary Blues* (Baton Rouge: Louisiana State University Press, 1987), 29–42.

dramatizes the uneasy relationship between the two compet-
ing aesthetic modes within the novel. It is within this odd
excrescence on the body of the realist novel that the contend-
ing forces in *Indiana*—the *roman de moeurs* and the idyll,
realism and idealism, the colonies and the metropolis, Ralph
and Raymon—are brought into physical contact, and it is
from here that the novel emerges transfigured. Decorated with
prints illustrating Bernardin de Saint-Pierre's widely read tale
of idyllic love in a tropical island setting, *Paul et Virginie* on
the one hand, and the veiled portrait of Sir Ralph on the other,
the secret chamber is a luminous space lodged within the
gloomy frame of Balzacian realism. And at the very heart of
this Utopian space there is a hall of mirrors, and it is through
this specular mechanism that the two female subjects Noun
and Indiana become one, and that the mirror of narcissism is
enfolded within the mirror of realism.

The question in this novel is which mirror shall triumph: the
self-reflecting mirror of narcissism (both male and female) or
the other-reflecting mirror of mimeticism, or whether there is
fictional life beyond the looking glass? Like so many nineteenth-century French novels, *Indiana* is centrally concerned
with the lure of narcissism, the impossibility of escaping the
prison of self-reflection characteristic of the romantic ego and
replacing it with a mimesis that strives to accommodate the
other's otherness, but which more often than not is simply
a more perfect model of the primary mirror of narcissism.
The central issue then is, in René Girard's terms,[15] the
demystification of romanticism and the instrument of that
demystification is linguistic: thus the space most clearly coun-
terposed to the circular bedroom is the all too prosaic hotel
room in which Indiana lodges when she returns from the
Bourbon Island to give herself to Raymon, who has meanwhile, and unbeknownst to her, married. In her humble lodgings, Indiana discovers her place in the world: stripped of the
false identity derived from reading romantic literature target-
ing women, she comes to realize that she is no heroine pos-

[15] René Girard, *Deceit, Desire and the Novel: Self and Other in Literary Structure*, trans. Yvonne Freccero (Baltimore: Johns Hopkins University Press, 1976).

sessed of a private language, but rather a subject bound by the common laws of language. In a novel centrally concerned with language, the shabby hotel room which Indiana comes to after a stay in the hospital that has deprived her of some of her proudest marks of individuality—her name, her magnificent hair, so catastrophically fetishized by Raymon—is the common place where Indiana is inducted into the law of the symbolic, which is precisely that subjectivity is a pre-assigned position: 'All these objects belong, as it were, to nobody, by dint of belonging to all comers; no one has left any trace of being there, except to an unknown name sometimes left on a card in the frame of the mirror.'[16] Language, which is described earlier on in the novel as a prostitute, belongs to no one: like the objects in the hotel room, words are merely letted out to the individual speaker and simultaneously the mirror has lost its powers of reflection and been reduced to a mere frame.

Like Emma Bovary, Flaubert's very Sandian heroine, Indiana's response to the loss of a fantasied, self-aggrandizing uniqueness fed by her readings, and flattered by her involvement with the Don Juanesque Raymon, is deep depression and ultimately an attempted suicide. But unlike Emma—and here we must raise the question of the specificity of women's writing—Indiana is saved, indeed twice, and increasingly implausibly saved from drowning by the good angel figure of Ralph, with whom she lives out her days in the idyllic valley of Bernica. Like so many of Sand's heroes and heroines, she must complete an erotic developmental trajectory that takes her from an inappropriate object-choice based on infantile narcissism to an appropriate object-choice based on an adult recognition of the moral and spiritual qualities of the worthy love-object.

But it would be too simple if all that were necessary for the novel to reach closure was for the blind heroine or hero to see the truth, as though the truth was simply lying there, only waiting to be unveiled. Such, however, is not the case: just as the romantic would-be heroine must accept the levelling qual-

---

[16] Sand, *Indiana*, see p. 234 of this book.

ity of the common language, the good lover must overcome the blockage, the linguistic impotence that prevents his true self from shining forth. On their way toward a higher union both Indiana and Ralph must shed the shackles that have encumbered them. There is much to lend credence to the reading of the novel that views Ralph as Indiana's true double, in the sense of a kindred spirit, a spiritual brother. Though their relationship is not strictly speaking incestuous, there is more than a suggestion of incest in what is held up to be the ideal love relationship for Indiana. Like Paul and Virginie's, whose story constitutes their privileged intertext, theirs is first and foremost a fraternal love, even though the brother and sister are not biologically related.

The whiff of incest that pervades the final section of the novel is but one aspect of its problematic nature. Ever since the novel's publication, critics have taken Sand to task for the novel's conclusion, which is judged either as inappropriate for a text that advertises its realism, or unsatisfying for a novel that proposes a Utopian way out of the universe of realism. As the defender of realist orthodoxy, Sainte-Beuve was the first and most influential of the former category of critics, writing:

Indiana is not a masterpiece, there is a place in the book right after Noun's death, after the fatal discovery that pierces Indiana's heart, after that morning of delirium when she makes her way into Raymon's bedroom and he rejects her—there is a point, a line of demarcation where the true, felt, and observed part of the novel ends; the rest, which seems almost pure invention, still includes some beautiful sections, great and poetic scenes, but fantasy seeks to prolong reality, imagination has taken it upon itself to crown the adventure.[17]

For the second category of critics—the pioneering feminist critics mentioned earlier—the Indiana of the epilogue offers scant hope for women in search of a radical transformation of their condition in the post-revolutionary rising capitalist social order: childless and childlike, deprived of all illusions and virtually all direct speech, more dead than alive, in her

---

[17] Charles Sainte-Beuve in *Le National* (5 Oct. 1832) as cited by Béatrice Didier (ed.), 'Notice', in *Indiana* (Paris: folio, 1984), 361.

ultimate incarnation Indiana is hardly a role model for newly born women. And yet one has only to think of the fates of Eugénie Grandet—loveless and sexless marriage—and Emma Bovary—suicide—to know that for all its problematic aspects this epilogue does represent a hopeful innovation. The differences between Sand's fiction and both Balzac's—the admired friend of her debut—and Flaubert's—the dear 'troubadour' of her later years—those gigantic figures who sit astride French realism, are more than stylistic, they are political. To insist on locating Sand merely within the great realist tradition is to participate in the very process that has worked to diminish her achievement—the forgetting that there exists another great tradition in nineteenth-century French literature, one that includes Victor Hugo and Émile Zola, and whose great theme is saving the innocent victims of the new bourgeois social order (the poor, the hungry, the enslaved, the disenfranchised, the persecuted). Love in this socialist and humanist tradition is as inextricably bound up with politics as the public and the private are in Balzac. When Indiana dreams, she dreams not of living the high life in Paris but of helping others; when Indiana fantasizes about falling in love, she fantasizes not about meeting a lady's man, but a messiah. For the idealist woman, and this is perhaps her ultimate and most secretly megalomaniac desire, the ideal lover is a saviour, not to say God.

Allegory is, as we have noted, the trope of idealism, but it is also the trope of exotic primitivism, indeed exotic primitivism is perhaps the most popular form of idealism in early and premodern fiction. The final section of the novel demonstrates that in Sand's Rousseauistic framework the only way out of a contemporary society viewed as hopelessly corrupt is escape to an exotic space, which is imagined in at least two crucial respects as the opposite of the common European social order: there is no social hierarchy—the relationship between Indiana and Ralph and the slaves they free is one of reciprocity and mutual caring—and the prohibition of incest is lifted. Clearly, as the final dialogue in the novel indicates, the flight from society is a last and desperate resort; *Indiana* marks in this sense the end of the primitivist solution. Hereafter, Sand will transfer the Utopian space to Europe: thus in the first of her three Utopian socialist novels of the 1840s, *The Journeyman Joiner*, the circular bedchamber resurfaces but not the wild valley of Bernica.

   Ethics, and with it idealism, can hardly be said to have generated much critical heat in recent decades. The canon, by contrast, has been the object of so much critical ferment that it now appears that the very notion of a classic, let alone a *world*'s classic, is in serious need of reconsideration. Recent writings on realism have done much to demystify the mimetic and mechanical pretences of realism, but they have done little to dismantle realism's aesthetic hegemony. Sand's contemporaries already knew that her fate was linked to that of realism, what they could not imagine was that it was also linked to that of feminism. Greeted as a masterpiece in its own time, *Indiana* has been allowed to go intermittently out of print in ours. If the measure of classic status in France is selection as a text of the *agrégation*—and only precious few texts are—then *Indiana* has still not attained supreme institutional recognition. But in the final decades of the twentieth century, when feminism has profoundly affected the way we read and the canon of great works we study, *Indiana* has attained classic status. If the measure of a classic is that it can be read and reread, then contrary to what James asserts—'George Sand invites reperusal less than any mind of equal eminence'[18]—*Indiana* can, has been, and will be reread.

---

[18] James, 'George Sand', 181.

NOTE ON THE TEXT

INDIANA was published in 1832 by J.-P. Roret and H. Dupuy, by Gosselin in 1833, and in a new edition by Perrotin in 1842. An illustrated edition was published by Hetzel in 1853. The last edition to be published in George Sand's lifetime was by Calmann-Lévy in 1856, and that is the text which has been followed in this translation.

SELECT BIBLIOGRAPHY

There is an edited English translation of George Sand's autobiography: *My Life*, trans. D. Hofstadter (London: Gollancz, 1979). The complete text is also available in a group translation, ed. Thelma Jungrau, *Story of My Life* (Albany: State University Press of New York, 1991). A translation of selected writings is available under the title *In Her Own Words*, trans. J. A. Barry (Garden City, NY: Anchor Books, 1979).

There are numerous biographies of George Sand. The following is a brief list of the best of these:

Barry, J. A., *Infamous Woman: The Life of George Sand* (Garden City, NY: Doubleday, 1977).

Cate, Curtis, *George Sand: A Biography* (Boston: Houghton Mifflin, 1975).

Dickenson, Donna, *George Sand: A Brave Man—The Most Womanly Woman* (Oxford: Berg, 1988).

Maurois, André, *Lélia: The Life of George Sand*, trans. G. Hopkins (London: Jonathan Cape, 1953).

Toesca, Maurice, *The Other George Sand*, trans. Irene Beeson (London: Dennis Dobson, 1947).

Secondary works:

Crecelius, Kathryn, *Family Romances: George Sand's Early Novels* (Bloomington: Indiana University Press, 1987).

Haig, Stirling, 'The Circular Room of George Sand's *Indiana*', in his *The Madame Bovary Blues* (Baton Rouge: Louisiana State University Press, 1987).

Hirsch, Michèle, 'Questions à *Indiana*', *Revue des Sciences Humaines*, 165 (1977), 117–29.

Kadish, Doris, 'Representing Race in *Indiana*', *George Sand Studies*, 11/1–2 (1992), 22–30.

Naginski, Isabelle Hoog, *George Sand: Writing for her Life* (New Brunswick, NJ: Rutgers University Press, 1991).

Petrey, Sandy, 'George and Georgina Sand: Realist Gender in *Indiana*', in Michael Worton and Judith Still (eds.), *Sexuality and Textuality* (Manchester: Manchester University Press, forthcoming).

Rabine, Leslie, 'George Sand and the Myth of Femininity', *Women and Literature*, 4 (1976), 2–17.

Schor, Naomi, *George Sand and Idealism* (New York: Columbia University Press, 1993).

Vareille, Kristina Wingard, *Socialité, sexualité et les impasses de l'histoire: L'Evolution de la thématique sandienne d'Indiana (1832) à Mauprat (1837)* (Uppsala: Almqvist & Wiskell, 1987).

A CHRONOLOGY OF
GEORGE SAND

1804   Birth on 1 July of Amandine-Aurore-Lucile Dupin (the
        future George Sand). Her father Maurice, an army officer,
        was the son of an eighteenth-century financier Dupin de
        Francueil who at 72 married the 29-year-old, illegitimate
        daughter of the distinguished military commander, the
        Maréchal de Saxe, illegitimate son of a king of Poland.
        Aurore's mother, Antoinette Delaborde, daughter of a
        Parisian birdseller, married Maurice Dupin on 5 June
        1804, the couple having had a liaison since 1800.
1808   Maurice Dupin is killed in a riding accident.
1808–18 Aurore Dupin lives with her grandmother at her country
        estate at Nohant. Relations between Aurore's mother and
        grandmother are strained.
1810   Aurore's mother goes to live in Paris.
1818   Aurore is sent as a boarder to the convent of the English
        Augustine nuns in Paris.
1819   Aurore undergoes a mystical experience and wants to
        become a nun.
1820   Aurore returns to Nohant.
1821   Death of Aurore's grandmother.
1822   Her paternal relative, René de Villeneuve, becomes
        Aurore's legal guardian, but she does not agree to break
        with her mother as her grandmother had wished. Aurore
        goes to live with her mother but suffers from her capricious
        and unstable temperament. On 19 April Aurore meets
        Casimir Dudevant (aged 27), the illegitimate son of a
        Baron of the Napoleonic Empire. On 17 September Aurore
        marries Casimir and in October the couple go to Paris.
1823   Maurice Dudevant (later known as Maurice Sand) is born.
1824   The marriage is unhappy; the husband and wife have no
        interests in common.
1825   Aurore meets Aurélien de Sèze, with whom she has a
        passionate but platonic relationship lasting till 1830.
1827   Aurore develops a circle of faithful friends, including
        Jules Néraud to whom the conclusion of *Indiana* is
        addressed. She becomes the mistress of Stéphane Ajasson
        de Grandsagne.

1828	Birth of Solange Dudevant (thought probably to be Stéphane's daughter).
1830	Aurore meets Jules Sandeau.
1831	Having become his mistress, Aurore (with an allowance from Casimir) goes to Paris with Sandeau, leaving her husband and children at Nohant. In collaboration with Sandeau, she writes two novels, signed J. Sand and J.S.
1832	She returns to Nohant and then goes back to Paris with her daughter. Having written *Indiana* on her own, she publishes it under the pseudonym of G. Sand. Then she publishes *Valentine* under the name of George Sand.
1833	Beginning of George Sand's liaison with Alfred de Musset, and journey of the couple to Italy. Publication of *Lélia*.
1834	George Sand and Musset fall ill, and Musset is attended by Dr Pagello, with whom George falls in love. Musset returns to France, while George stays in Venice and writes several novels and the first *Lettres d'un voyageur*. In July she and Pagello go to Paris; in October he goes back to Italy and George again becomes Musset's mistress.
1835	George Sand's liaison with Musset ends and she becomes the mistress of an eminent republican lawyer, Michel de Bourges. Proceedings begin for the judicial separation of George Sand and her husband.
1836	Legal separation of George Sand and her husband confirmed. George and her children join Liszt and Marie d'Agoult in Switzerland and go to Paris.
1837	Liszt and Marie d'Agoult visit George at Nohant. End of her liaison with Michel de Bourges. She becomes the mistress of the painter Bocage and of her son's tutor Mallefille. She comes under the influence of the socialist thinker, Pierre Leroux. Casimir Dudevant takes Solange away, and George has to go to her father-in-law's home to recover her daughter.
1838	Balzac visits Nohant. Beginning of George Sand's liaison with Chopin. They go to Majorca. Chopin falls ill; they settle in a former monastery at Valldemosa.
1839	Chopin and George Sand return to France and settle in Paris. Publication of *Spiridion* and *L'Uscoque*.
1840	Publication of *Le Compagnon du tour de France* and other works. Beginning of George's friendship with the singer Pauline Viardot.
1841	George Sand and Chopin stay at Nohant. Publication of *Horace*.

INDIANA

INTRODUCTION

I WROTE *Indiana* in the autumn of 1831. It was my first novel. I wrote without any plan, without any aesthetic or philosophical theory in mind. I wrote at the age when one writes instinctively and when reflection serves only to confirm our natural tendencies. People wanted to see it as a carefully thought-out argument against marriage. I was not trying to do anything like so important and I was completely surprised by all the fine things that the critics found to say about my subversive intentions. Criticism is far too clever; that is what will be the death of it. It never judges straightforwardly what has been done straightforwardly. It looks for midday at two in the afternoon, as the old saying goes, and it must have done a great deal of harm to those artists who pay too much attention to its opinions.

Under all régimes and at all times, moreover, there has been a race of critics who, bringing their own talent into contempt, have imagined that they ought to ply the trade of denouncers, of suppliers of information to the authorities. What a strange role for men of letters in relation to their fellow writers! Governments' strict regulations against the press have never been enough for these ferocious critics. They would like such regulations to be directed not only against works, but against persons as well, and if they were listened to, some of us would be forbidden to write anything at all. At the time I wrote *Indiana* they brought accusations of Saint-Simonism against everything. Later on they brought accusations of all sorts of other things. Some writers are still forbidden to open their mouths under pain of seeing certain journalist guardians of the law pounce on their work to bring it before the official police authorities. If a writer makes a workman express noble feelings, it is an attack against the bourgeoisie; if a girl who has strayed is rehabilitated after expiating her sin, it is an attack against virtuous women; if a scoundrel assumes titles of nobility, it is an attack against the aristocracy; if a bully behaves like a swashbuckling soldier, it is an insult to the army; if a woman is ill-treated by her husband, it is an argument for promiscuity. And so it is with everything. Worthy fellow writers, critics with pious and generous hearts! What a pity that no one is thinking of setting up a little inquisitorial literary tribunal in which you would be the torturers! Would you be satisfied with tearing the books to pieces and burning them in a slow fire or, at your own request, could you not be allowed to give a taste of torture to the writers who allow themselves to have other gods than yours?

Thank God, I have forgotten even the names of those who tried to discourage me on my first publication and who, unable to say that this humble beginning fell completely flat, tried to turn it into an inflammatory proclamation against the peace of society. I did not expect so much honour, and I think I owe these critics the thanks that the hare addressed to the frogs when, on seeing their alarm, he imagined he was entitled to think himself a warlike thunderbolt.

Nohant, May 1852

PREFACE TO THE 1832 EDITION

IF SOME pages of this book were to incur the serious reproach of a tendency towards new opinions, if strict judges were to think they have an imprudent, dangerous ring, one would have to reply to the criticism that they are doing too much honour to a work of no importance, that to tackle the great questions of social order, one must have great moral strength or lay claim to great talent, and that so much presumption does not enter into the scheme of a very simple story in which the writer has invented almost nothing. If, in the course of his task, he has happened to express cries of pain wrung from his characters by the social unease which affects them; if he has not been afraid to record their aspirations towards a better life, let society be blamed for its inequalities and fate for its whims. The writer is only a mirror which reflects them, a machine which traces their outline, and he has nothing for which to apologize if the impressions are correct and the reflection is faithful.

Consider, next, that the narrator has not taken as his text or slogan a few exclamations of suffering and anger scattered throughout the drama of human life. He makes no claim to hide a serious lesson beneath the guise of a tale; he has not come to give a helping hand to the structure which a problematic future is preparing for us, or a parting kick to that of the past which is crumbling away. He knows too well that we live in a time of moral decline, when human reason needs a curtain to soften the overbright light which dazzles it. If he had felt learned enough to write a really useful book, he would have softened the truth instead of presenting it with its crude colours and glaring effects. Such a book would have served the purpose of blue spectacles for faulty eyes.

He does not give up the idea of fulfilling that honourable, noble task some day, but, young as he is today, he tells you what he has seen without daring to draw conclusions about the great controversy between the future and the past, which perhaps no man of the present generation is very competent to decide. Too conscientious to conceal his doubts from you, but too timid to set them up as certainties, he relies on your reflections and refrains from weaving preconceived ideas and ready-made judgements into the web of his story. He performs punctiliously his job as a story-teller. He will tell you everything, even what is annoyingly true, but if you were to rig him out in the philosopher's gown, you would find him very muddled, for he is only a simple story-teller whose task is to amuse and not to instruct you.

Even if he were more mature and more skilful, he still would not dare lay his hand on the great sores of dying civilization. One must be so sure of being able to cure them when one takes the risk of probing them! He would prefer to try to bring you back to past outworn beliefs, to old vanished forms of worship, rather than to use his talent, if he had any, to knock down overturned altars. He knows, however, that in the prevalent charitable spirit, a timid conscience is despised by public opinion as hypocritical reserve, just as, in the arts, a timid approach is mocked as a ridiculous attitude. But he also knows that in defending lost causes there is honour, if not profit.

On those who might misunderstand the spirit of this book, such a profession of faith would jar like an anachronism. The narrator hopes that, after listening to his tale to the end, few listeners will deny the *morality* that emerges from the facts and triumphs there as in all human affairs. It seemed to him, as he completed it, that his conscience was clear. In short, he flattered himself that he had written of social miseries without too much irritation and of human passions without too much passion. He has put a mute on his strings when they were making too loud a sound; he has tried to stifle certain notes of the soul that should remain unheard, certain voices of the heart that are not aroused without danger.

Perhaps you will do him justice if you agree that he has shown you the misery of the person who wants to free himself from legitimate restraint, the utter distress of the heart that rebels against its destiny's decrees. If he has not shown in the best light the character who represents *the law*, if he has been even less favourable to another who represents *public opinion*, you will see a third who represents *illusion* and cruelly thwarts the vain hopes and crazy enterprises of passion. Finally, you will see that if he has not strewn roses on the ground where the law pens up our desires like sheep, he has cast nettles on the paths which lead us away from it.

That, it seems to me, is enough to guarantee this book against the reproach of immorality. But if you absolutely insist that a novel should end like a Marmontel* story, perhaps you will reproach me with the final pages. You will think it wrong that I have not cast into poverty and neglect the being who, for two volumes, transgressed mankind's laws. To this, the author will reply that, before being moral, he wanted to be true. He will repeat that, feeling too inexperienced to compose a philosophical treatise on how to cope with life, he has limited himself to writing *Indiana*, a story of the human heart with its weaknesses, its violent feelings, its rights, its wrongs, its good, and its bad.

If you insist on an explanation of everything in the book, Indiana is a type. She is woman, the weak creature who is given the task of portraying *passions*, repressed, or if you prefer, suppressed by *the law*. She is desire at grips with necessity; she is love dashing her blind head against all the obstacles of civilization. But the serpent wears out his teeth and breaks them when he tries to gnaw a file. The powers of the soul become exhausted when they try to struggle against the realities of life. That is the conclusion you may draw from this story, and that was its meaning when it was told to the writer who passes it on to you.

In spite of these protestations, the narrator expects reproaches. Some upright souls, some good men's consciences, will perhaps be alarmed at seeing virtue so uncouth, reason so sad, and public opinion so unfair. For what a writer should fear most in the world is the alienation from his works of the trust of men of goodwill, the arousal of baneful sympathies in embittered souls, the poisoning of the already acutely painful wounds that the social yoke inflicts on the impatient and rebellious.

The success which is based on a despicable appeal to the passions of a period is the easiest to attain, the least honourable to strive for. The writer of *Indiana* denies ever having thought of it. If he believed that was his achievement, he would destroy his book, even if he had for it the naïve paternal affection which swaddles the current rachitic productions of aborted literature.

But he hopes to justify himself by saying that he believed he served his principles better by real examples than by poetic inventions. He thinks that, with its quality of sad truthfulness, his tale will be able to make an impression on young, ardent minds. They will find it difficult to mistrust a historian who forces his way roughly through the midst of the facts, elbowing to right and left with no more consideration for one camp than for the other. To make a cause odious or ridiculous is to persecute it but not to fight against it. Perhaps the whole of the story-teller's art consists of interesting in their own stories the guilty whom he wants to reclaim, the wretched whom he wants to cure.

It would give too much importance to a work, destined no doubt to receive little attention, to want to save it from every accusation. So the author gives himself up entirely into the hands of the critics. Only one complaint seems to him too serious to be accepted, that is the one of having intended to write a dangerous book. He would prefer to remain obscure for ever, rather than to build his reputation on a ruined conscience. So he will add yet another word to refute the blame he most dreads.

Raymon, you will say, is society; his egoism is morality, is reason. Raymon, the author will reply, is the false reason, the false morality by which society is governed. He is the honourable man as the world understands it, because the world does not examine closely enough to see everything. The good man is there beside Raymon, and you cannot say he is the enemy of order, for he sacrifices his happiness, he abnegates his own interests before all questions of social order.

Then you will say that you have not been shown virtue in a striking enough way. Alas! The reply will be that the triumph of virtue is only to be seen nowadays at the boulevard theatres. The author will tell you that he has not undertaken to show you society as virtuous but as necessary, and that honour has become as difficult as heroism in these days of moral decadence. Do you think that this truth gives great souls an aversion for honour? I think quite the opposite.

PREFACE TO THE 1842 EDITION

IF I have allowed the pages you have just read to be reprinted, it is not because they sum up in a clear, complete way the beliefs I have reached today about society's rights over individuals. It is only because I look on opinions freely expressed in the past as something sacred which we ought neither to decry nor tone down, nor try to interpret as we please. But today, after travelling further in life and seeing the horizon widen around me, I believe I ought to tell the reader what I think of my work.

When I wrote *Indiana*, I was young; I was obeying very strong, sincere feelings which overflowed into a series of novels, almost all based on the same theme: the ill-organized relationship between the sexes due to the constitution of society. These novels were all more or less blamed by the critics for making unwise attacks on the institution of marriage. In spite of the limited scope and naïve hesitancy of its views, *Indiana* did not escape the indignation of several so-called serious minds whom, at that time, I was very much inclined to take at their word and listen to obediently. But although my reason was scarcely developed enough to write on such a serious subject, I was not so much of a child as to be unable to judge, in my turn, the thoughts of those who judged mine. However simple-minded an accused man might be, however capable a magistrate, the accused has quite enough understanding to know if the magistrate's sentence is just or wrongheaded, wise or absurd.

Certain journalists, who set themselves up nowadays as representatives and keepers of public morality (I do not know by virtue of what mission, since I do not know in the name of what faith), made strict pronouncements against my poor tale and, by presenting it as an argument against social order, gave it an importance and a kind of celebrity which it would not have achieved otherwise. In so doing they gave a very serious and weighty role to a young author barely initiated into elementary social ideas, whose literary and philosophical baggage was only a little imagination, courage, and love of truth. Sensitive to these reproaches and almost grateful for the lessons these critics were happy to give him, he examined the accusations brought before public opinion against the morality of his ideas, and thanks to this examination, which he conducted without any pride, he gradually acquired convictions, which at the beginning of his career were still only feelings and which today are principles.

I have had ten years of researches, scruples, and indecision, often painful but always sincere; I have shunned the role of schoolmaster, which some attributed to me to make me ridiculous; I have loathed the imputation of pride and anger, with which others have pursued me to make me odious; I have proceeded, according to my artistic ability, by analysing life to search for its synthesis; and so I have related facts which have sometimes been recognized as plausible, and depicted characters whom, it has often been agreed, I knew how to study with care. I restricted myself to that work, trying to establish my conviction rather than to shake that of others, telling myself that if I were mistaken, society would be well able to let powerful voices be heard to overturn my arguments and, by wise replies, to repair the harm that might have been caused by my imprudent questions. In fact, numerous voices were raised to put the public on guard against the dangerous writer, but, as for the wise replies, the public and the author are still waiting.

Long after writing the preface to *Indiana*, under the influence of a remnant of respect for organized society, I was still seeking a solution to this insoluble problem: *how to reconcile the happiness and dignity of individuals oppressed by that same society without modifying society itself*. Feeling for the victims and mingling his tears with theirs, making himself their interpreter to his readers, but, as a prudent defender, not trying too hard to excuse his clients' faults, and appealing far more to the clemency of the judges than to their austerity, the novelist is the true advocate of the abstract beings who represent our passions and our sufferings before the tribunal of force and the jury of public opinion. Under its frivolous appearance the task is a serious one and it is quite difficult to keep it to its true path, for one is interfered with at every step by those who think the form is too serious and by those who think the content too frivolous.

I do not flatter myself that I have performed this task skilfully, but I am sure that I tried to do it seriously in the midst of inner hesitations in which my conscience, at times frightened by ignorance of its rights, at times stimulated by a heart enamoured of justice and truth, marched nevertheless towards its goal without deviating from it too much and without taking too many backward steps.

To let the public into the secret of this inner struggle by a series of prefaces and discussions would have been a childish method of proceeding, in which the vanity of talking of oneself would have occupied too much space for my liking. I have had to abstain from that, as well as from mentioning too quickly the points which remained unclear in my mind. Conservatives thought me too bold, innovators too timid. I admit that I had respect and sympathy for both the past and the future, and, in the conflict, I found peace of mind only on the day I fully realized that the one ought not to be the violation and annihilation of the other but its continuation and development.

After this novitiate of ten years, I was at last initiated into broader ideas, which had their source not in myself but in the philosophical progress which had taken place around me (particularly in a few great minds whom I questioned religiously and in the sight of the sufferings of my fellow men). Finally, I realized that if I did well to have doubts and hesitate to make a judgement at the time when, ignorant and inexperienced, I wrote *Indiana*, my present duty is to congratulate myself on the bold ideas by which, nevertheless, I let myself be carried away then and since. I have been greatly reproached for these bold ideas, but they would have been even bolder if I had known how legitimate, honest, and sacred they were.

So today, when I have just reread the first novel of my youth with as much severity and detachment as if it were the work of another, when I am about to expose it to a publicity which the popular edition has not yet had, I have resolved in advance not to retract (one should never retract what has been done and said in good faith), but to condemn myself if I discover that my former opinions were mistaken or dangerous. However, I was so much in agreement with myself as regards the feeling which inspired *Indiana* and which would inspire it again if I had to tell that story today for the first time, that I did not want to change it at all, apart from a few incorrect sentences and unsuitable words. There are still probably a lot left and I submit the literary merit of my writings entirely to the judgement of the critics; in that matter, I recognize in them all the competence I lack. That there is in the daily press today an incontestable mass of talent, I do not deny, and I am pleased to acknowledge it. But that this class of polished writers contains many philosophers and moralists, I positively deny, with all due respect to those who have condemned me and who will condemn me again at the first opportunity, from the heights of their morality and philosophy.

So, I repeat, I wrote *Indiana* and I had to write it. I yielded to a powerful instinct of complaint and reproach which God had placed within me, God who makes nothing without a use, not even the most insignificant beings, and intervenes in the most trivial causes as well as in the great ones. But really! Is the cause I was defending so trivial, then? It is the cause of half the human race, it is that of the whole human race; for the distress of women entails that of men, as the distress of the slave entails that of the master, and I have tried to demonstrate this in *Indiana*. It has been said that I was pleading the cause of one individual, as if, assuming that I had been animated by a personal feeling, I had been the only unfortunate creature in peaceful, joyous humankind. Enough cries of pain and sympathy have responded to mine for me to know now what to think about the supreme happiness of others.

I do not think I have ever written anything under the influence of a selfish passion; I have never even thought of preventing myself from doing such a thing. Those who have read me without prejudice understand that I wrote *Indiana* influenced by a feeling, unreasoned, it is true, but deep and legitimate, of the injustice and barbarity of the laws which still govern the existence of women in marriage, in the family, and in society. My task was not to write a treatise on jurisprudence but to fight against public opinion, for it is that which delays or promotes social improvements. The war will be long and hard, but I am not the first, nor the only, nor the last, champion of so fine a cause, and I shall defend it as long as a breath of life remains in me.

So the feeling which motivated me to start with, I have rationalized and developed as people opposed it and censured me for it. Unjust or ill-disposed critics have taught me more about it than I would have discovered in the calm of impunity. So in this connection I give thanks to the incompetent judges who have enlightened me. The motives for their judgements have cast a bright light on to my thoughts and injected a deep sense of security into my conscience. A sincere mind benefits from everything and what would discourage vanity doubles the ardour of devotion.

These reproaches which, from the depths of a heart serious and calm today, I have just addressed to the majority of journalists of my time—let no one look on them as any kind of protest against the right of control that public morality invests in the French press. That the critics often fulfil badly, and understand even worse, their mission in present-day society is obvious to everyone. But that the mission in itself is divine and sacred, no one can deny, unless he is an atheist as regards progress, unless he is an enemy of truth, a blasphemer of the future, and an unworthy child of France. Liberty of thought, liberty to write and speak, sacred conquest of the human spirit! What are the petty sufferings and the fleeting cares occasioned by your errors and abuses compared to the infinite blessings you bring to the world?

PART 1

I

ON a chilly wet autumn evening, in a little manor house in Brie,* three people, lost in thought, were solemnly watching the embers burn in the fireplace and the hands make their way slowly round the clock. Two of these silent individuals seemed submissively resigned to the vague boredom that oppressed them. But the third showed signs of open rebellion; he moved about restlessly in his chair, half stifled a few melancholy yawns, and struck the crackling logs with the tongs, obviously trying to fight against the common enemy.

This person, who was much older than the other two, was the master of the house, Colonel Delmare, a retired army officer, who had once been handsome but now was heavy and bald with a grey moustache and a fierce look; he was an excellent master who made everyone tremble, wife, servants, horses, and dogs.

At last he left his chair, having obviously lost his patience at not knowing how to break the silence, and began to tramp up and down the room. But he did not for a moment relax the stiff movements of an old soldier, keeping his back straight, turning in one movement with the permanent smugness typical of the parade officer on duty.

But those brilliant days when Lieutenant Delmare breathed victory in the air of military camps, those days had gone. The retired senior officer, now forgotten by his ungrateful country, found himself condemned to endure all the consequences of marriage. He was the husband of a pretty young woman, the owner of a comfortable country house and its outbuildings, and in addition a successful industrialist. So the Colonel was in a bad mood, especially that particular evening, for the weather was damp and he was rheumatic.

He strode solemnly up and down his old drawing-room, which was furnished in Louis XV style. At times he would stop in front of a door surmounted by a fresco of naked cupids hanging chains of flowers round the necks of well-behaved does and tame boars; at times he would pause in front of a panel overdecorated with carvings of thin, tormented figures; one would have wearied one's eyes in vain, trying to follow their tortuous antics and endless intertwinings. But these vague, fleeting distractions did not prevent the Colonel, each time he turned in his walk, from casting a clear-sighted, penetrating glance at the two companions of his silent vigil, his attentive eyes going from one to the other, eyes, which for three years had kept watch over a fragile, precious treasure, his wife.

For his wife was nineteen years old, and if you had seen her deep in the chimney-corner beneath the huge, white marble mantelpiece incrusted with burnished copper, if you had seen her, so slender, pale, and sad, her elbow on her knee, so young a girl in this old house, beside her old husband, like a newly-opened flower in an antiquated vase, you would have pitied Colonel Delmare's wife, and perhaps the Colonel even more.

The third occupant of this lonely house was sitting in the same chimney-corner at the other end of the glowing log. He was a man in the full strength and flower of youth, and his glowing cheeks, gleaming, abundant fair hair, and ample sidewhiskers, clashed with the greying hair, faded complexion, and harsh aspect of the master of the house. But the least artistic of men would nevertheless have preferred Delmare's harsh, austere look to the young man's regular, insipid features. The puffy face, engraved in relief on the iron plate at the back of the fireplace, with eyes permanently fixed on the glowing embers, was perhaps less insipid than the pink and white character of this story who was studying the same scene. Nevertheless, his strong, loose-limbed physique, the precision of his brown eyebrows, the smooth whiteness of his brow, his calm, clear eyes, the beauty of his hands, and even the sober elegance of his hunting dress would have let him pass for a very handsome escort in the eyes of any woman who was attached to the so-called philosophic taste of another century. But perhaps M. Delmare's shy, young wife had never yet looked closely at a man; perhaps there was a complete lack of fellow-feeling between the frail, sickly woman and a man who slept soundly and ate well. But there was no doubt that the conjugal Argus* wearied his eagle eye without catching one glance, one whisper, one heart-throb between these two very different people. Absolutely sure then that he had not even a cause for jealousy to occupy his mind, he relapsed into a melancholy even deeper than before and plunged his hands sharply into the depths of his pockets.

The only cheerful, affectionate face in the group was that of a handsome hunting dog, a large pointer, which had stretched its head out on the knees of the seated man. It had a remarkably long body, stout hairy legs, a pointed fox-like nose, and an intelligent face bristling with untidy hairs; behind them like two topazes gleamed two large, tawny eyes. Those hunting-dog's eyes, so bloodthirsty and sinister in the ardour of the hunt, now expressed a feeling of indefinable melancholy and tenderness, and when the master, the object of all that instinctive love which is sometimes so superior to rational affections, stroked the silvery, silky coat of the handsome dog, the animal's eyes gleamed with pleasure and its long tail swept the hearth rhythmically, scattering the ashes on the patterned floor.

This domestic scene, half lit by the flames of the fire, could have been the subject of a picture in the style of Rembrandt. From time to time the room and its inhabitants were bathed in fitful shafts of white light; then, shading into the red hue of the embers, the light gradually faded, the vast room becoming correspondingly dark. Each time M. Delmare turned in his walk as he passed in front of the fire, he appeared like a shadow and then was immediately lost in the mysterious depths of the room. Here and there a few strips of gilt stood out as lines of light on the oval picture frames, heavily ornamented with wreaths, medallions, and imitation ribbons made of wood, on the furniture decorated with ebony and brass, and even on the sharply outlined cornices of the woodwork. But when the gleam of a dying ember gave way to another blaze in the fireplace, the objects which had just been lit up returned to the blackness and other gleaming objects stood out sharply in the dark. In this way all the details of the

scene could be grasped in turn; now it was the table supported
by three large gilded tritons, now the ceiling painted to represent a sky strewn with clouds and stars, now the heavy, long-
fringed, crimson silk hangings shot through with burnished
glints their wide folds seeming to move as they reflected the
changing light.

On seeing the two motionless figures sitting prominently in
front of the fireplace, you would have thought that they were
afraid to disturb the stillness of the scene. They seemed fixed
and turned into stone like the heroes of a fairy-tale, and you
would have thought that the least word, the slightest movement, was going to make the walls of an imaginary city
collapse upon them, while the gloomy master of the house,
whose regular step was the only break in the dark silence, was
rather like a magician who had cast a spell over them.

At last the dog, receiving an affectionate look from its
master, yielded to the magnetic power that the human eye
wields over intelligent animals. It let out a timid, affectionate
bark and thrust its two paws on to its beloved's shoulders
with a matchless supple grace.

'Down, Ophelia! down!'

And the young man solemnly reprimanded the docile animal in English; repentant and ashamed it crawled towards
Madame Delmare as if to ask for her protection. But Madame
Delmare did not emerge from her reverie, and let Ophelia's
head rest on her two white hands which she kept crossed on
her knees without giving the animal one caress.

'Is this bitch then permanently installed in the drawing-
room?' said the Colonel, secretly pleased to find a reason for
being in a bad mood as a distraction. 'To the kennel, Ophelia!
Out, you stupid beast!'

Had anyone then observed Madame Delmare closely, he
might have guessed the painful secret of her whole life in this
trivial, commonplace incident. A barely perceptible shudder
went through her body, and her hands, which unthinkingly
supported the favourite animal's head, gripped its rough,
hairy neck more firmly as if to hold and preserve it.
M. Delmare, pulling his riding crop out of his jacket pocket,
then advanced threateningly on poor Ophelia, who, closing

her eyes and letting out yells of pain and fear in advance, lay down at his feet. Madame Delmare became even paler than usual; her breast heaved convulsively, and turning her big blue eyes towards her husband, she said, with an indefinable look of fear:

'Have mercy, Monsieur, don't kill her.'

These few words made the Colonel start. A feeling of sorrow gave way to his inclination to anger.

'Madame, that's a reproach that I understand very well and that you haven't spared me since the day I killed your spaniel at the hunt in a moment of anger,' he said. 'Is that such a great loss? A dog that always rushed ahead and attacked the game! It would have worn out anyone's patience. Besides, it's only since his death that you've been so fond of him; before that you didn't pay any attention to him, but now that it's an opportunity for you to blame me . . .'

'Have I ever once reproached you?' asked Madame Delmare with the gentleness that out of generosity one uses towards the people one likes, and out of self-respect for those one dislikes.

'I didn't say you had,' continued the Colonel in a tone that was partly a father's and partly a husband's. 'But in some women's tears there are more bitter reproaches than in all the curses of others. Dash it all, Madame! You know very well that I don't like to see tears around me.'

'I don't think you ever see me in tears.'

'But don't I see you continually red-eyed? That's even worse, God knows!'

During this conversation between husband and wife, the young man had got up and very calmly let Ophelia out. Then, after lighting a candle and putting it on the mantelpiece, he came back and sat down opposite Madame Delmare.

This purely chance action had a sudden influence on M. Delmare's mood. As soon as the candle had cast a less flickering and more regular light on his wife than the firelight, he noticed the sickly, depressed appearance which, that evening, affected her whole person, her weary attitude, her long dark hair hanging down her emaciated cheeks, and dark rings under her dulled, inflamed eyes. He took a few turns

round the room and then, coming back to his wife with quite
a sudden change of tone:

'How are you, today, Indiana?' he asked, with the clumsiness of a man whose heart and temperament are rarely in
agreement.

'As usual, thank you,' she replied, without showing any
surprise or resentment.

'As usual, that's not an answer, or rather it's a woman's
answer, a non-committal answer, which doesn't mean yes or
no, well or unwell.'

'Alright, I'm neither well nor unwell.'

'Well,' he continued, with renewed harshness, 'you're
lying. I know you're not well. You told Sir Ralph here. Come
now, have I lied? Speak up, Monsieur Ralph, did she tell you
so?'

'She did tell me,' replied the phlegmatic man whom the
Colonel had addressed, and he paid no attention to the re-
proachful look Indiana gave him.

Just then, a fourth person came in; he was the steward of
the house, a former sergeant in M. Delmare's regiment.

In a few words he explained to M. Delmare that he had
reason to think that, at this time on previous nights, wood
thieves had got into the grounds, and he had come to ask for
a gun so as to make his round before closing the gates.
M. Delmare, who saw a military side to this event, immediately took his hunting gun, gave another one to Lelièvre, and
prepared to leave the room.

'Oh, dear! Would you kill a poor peasant for a few sacks of
wood?' said Madame Delmare, frightened.

'I'll kill like a dog any man that I find prowling round my
land at night,' replied Delmare, irritated by this objection. 'If
you knew the law, Madame, you would know that it authorizes me to do so.'

'It's a terrible law,' continued Indiana, passionately.

Then, immediately suppressing her emotion, she added in a
quieter tone.

'But what about your rheumatism? You forget that it's
raining and you'll be in pain tomorrow if you go out this
evening.'

'You're very much afraid of having to look after your old husband!' replied Delmare, opening the door violently.

And he went out, muttering complaints about his age and his wife.

II

THE two people whom we have just called Indiana Delmare and Sir Ralph, or if you prefer, M. Rodolphe Brown, remained facing each other, as calm and cold as if the husband had been between them. The Englishman did not think at all of justifying himself and Madame Delmare felt that she had nothing serious to reproach him with, for he had spoken only with good intentions. Finally, making an effort to break the silence, she scolded him gently.

'It wasn't right, my dear Ralph,' she said. 'I had forbidden you to repeat that remark which escaped me when I wasn't feeling very well; M. Delmare is the last person I'd have wanted to tell about my illness.'

'I don't understand you, my dear,' replied Sir Ralph. 'You're ill and you don't want to look after yourself. So I had to choose between the risk of losing you and the necessity of informing your husband.'

'Yes,' said Madame Delmare, smiling sadly, 'and you decided *to inform the authorities!*'

'You're wrong, on my word of honour, you're wrong, to let yourself get so irritated with the Colonel in this way. He's a man of honour, a worthy man.'

'But who's saying the opposite, Sir Ralph?'

'Oh, you yourself, without meaning to. Your sadness, your poor health, and, as he himself noticed, your red eyes, tell the whole world, all the time, that you're not happy . . .'

'Say no more, Sir Ralph. You're going too far. I've not allowed you to know so much.'

'I'm making you angry, I see that. I can't help it. I'm not clever. I don't know the subtleties of your language, and then I've a lot in common with your husband. Like him, I've no idea of what to say to women to comfort them in either English or French. Another man, without saying a word, would have made you understand the idea I've just expressed so clumsily. He would have found the art of making great inroads into your confidence without making you aware of his progress, and he might have succeeded in giving a little relief to your heart, which is becoming hard and closed to me. It's not the first time I've noticed how much more power words have than ideas, particularly in France.'

'Oh, you have a profound contempt for women, my dear Ralph. I'm alone here against two; so I must resign myself to never being right.'

'Prove us wrong, my dear cousin, by being well, by regaining your former bloom, cheerfulness, and vivacity. Remember Bourbon Island* and our delightful retreat at Bernica, and our happy childhood and our friendship, which is as old as you . . .'

'I also remember my father . . .' said Indiana, stressing this remark sadly and putting her hand in Sir Ralph's.

They relapsed into a deep silence.

'Indiana,' said Ralph after a pause, 'happiness is always within our grasp. Often one only needs to stretch out one's hand to take hold of it. What do you lack? You are reasonably well-off, and that's better than being very rich; you have an excellent husband who loves you with all his heart, and if I may say so, a sincere and devoted friend . . .'

Madame Delmare pressed Ralph's hand gently, but her demeanour did not change. Her head remained sunk on her chest and her moist eyes fixed on the magical glow of the embers.

'Your sadness, my dear friend, is merely a state of ill-health,' continued Ralph. 'Which of us can escape grief and depression? Look beneath you; you will see there people who rightly envy you. Man is so made; he always longs for what he hasn't got . . .'

I spare you a host of other platitudes uttered by the good Sir Ralph in a monotonous voice as dull as his thoughts. It is not that Sir Ralph was a fool, but in this matter he was quite out of his depth. He lacked neither good sense nor knowledge, but to comfort a woman, as he himself admitted, was something beyond his competence. And he so little understood the sorrows of others that, with the best will in the world to alleviate them, he could only make them worse by alluding to them. He was so well aware of his clumsiness that he rarely risked paying attention to his friends' woes, but this time he made enormous efforts to fulfil what he regarded as the most painful duty of friendship.

When he saw that Madame Delmare had to make an effort to listen to him, he said no more, and the only sounds were the thousand little voices that hum in the burning wood, the plaintive song of the log as it gets hot and swells up, the crackling of the bark as it wrinkles before it explodes, and the phosphorescent eruptions of the sap which give rise to a blue flame. From time to time, the howling of a dog mingled with the faint whistling of the north wind which slipped through the cracks in the door, and with the sound of the rain lashing against the windows. It was one of the saddest evenings that Madame Delmare had yet spent in her little country house in the Brie.

And then, some indefinable vague apprehension weighed on her impressionable heart and delicate nerves. Weak people live in perpetual fear and foreboding. Madame Delmare had all the superstitious feelings of a nervous Creole in poor health. Certain night sounds, certain tricks of moonlight, made her believe in certain events, and for this pensive, sad woman, night told tales of ghosts and mysteries that only she could understand and interpret according to her fears and sufferings.

'You'll say, too, that I'm crazy,' she said, withdrawing her hand which Sir Ralph was still holding, 'but some sort of disaster threatens us. A danger is hanging over someone . . . over me, no doubt . . . but . . . listen, Ralph, I feel moved as if on the eve of a great phase in my destiny . . . I'm afraid,' she added, shivering, 'I feel ill.'

Her lips turned as white as her cheeks. Sir Ralph, alarmed, not by Madame Delmare's forebodings, which he regarded as symptoms of severe depression, but by her mortal pallor, rang the bell hurriedly to summon help. No one came, and as Indiana grew weaker and weaker, Ralph, frightened, lifted her away from the fireside, put her down on a settee, and ran hither and thither, calling the servants, looking for water and smelling salts, not finding anything, breaking all the bells, losing himself in the labyrinth of dark rooms, and wringing his hands in impatience and annoyance with himself.

At last the idea occurred to him of opening the glass door which gave on to the grounds, and of calling in turn Lelièvre and Noun, Madame Delmare's Creole maid.

Some moments later, Noun ran in from one of the darkest paths in the grounds and asked anxiously if Madame Delmare was worse than usual.

'She's very ill,' replied Sir Brown.

They both went back to the drawing-room and attended to Madame Delmare, who had fainted, Sir Ralph with useless, clumsy zeal, Noun with the skill and efficiency of a woman's devotion.

Noun was Madame Delmare's foster sister. The two young people, brought up together, were very fond of each other. Tall, well-built, sparkling with health, lively, brisk, and overflowing with the full-blooded ardour and passion of a Creole, Noun had a resplendent beauty which put Madame Delmare's pale, delicate beauty into the shade, but their good hearts and the strength of their affection stifled any feeling of feminine rivalry between them.

When Madame Delmare recovered consciousness, the first thing she noticed was her maid's distressed face, her wet disordered hair, and the agitation betrayed in all her movements.

'Don't worry, my dear,' she said in a kindly tone; 'you're more upset by my poor health than I am myself. Come, Noun, you must look after yourself. You're getting thin and you're crying as if it weren't up to you to live. My good Noun, the life ahead of you is so happy and beautiful!'

Noun pressed Madame Delmare's hand to her lips effusively and said, almost beside herself as she cast frightened glances around her:

'Oh, my God, Madame, do you know why M. Delmare is in the grounds?'

'Why?' repeated Indiana, immediately losing the faint pink colour that had returned to her cheeks. 'But, wait a minute, I can't think . . . You frighten me! What's the matter, then?'

'M. Delmare asserts there are thieves in the grounds,' replied Noun. 'He's doing the rounds with Lelièvre and they've both got guns . . .'

'Well?' said Indiana who seemed to expect some terrible news.

'Well, Madame,' continued Noun, wringing her hands distraughtly, 'isn't it terrible to think they're going to kill a man? . . .'

'Kill!' cried Madame Delmare, getting up with the terror of a credulous child scared by her nurse's tales.

'Oh yes, they'll kill him,' said Noun, stifling her sobs.

'These two women are crazy,' thought Sir Ralph, who was looking in amazement at the strange scene. 'Still, all women are,' he added to himself.

'But, Noun, what's that you're saying?' continued Madame Delmare. 'Do you think there are thieves?'

'Oh, if it were thieves! But it may be some poor peasant who's come to take a handful of wood for his family.'

'Yes, that would certainly be terrible . . . But it's not likely. No one would put himself at risk in enclosed grounds on the edge of the Fontainebleau forest, where it's so easy to take wood . . . Nonsense! M. Delmare won't find anyone in the grounds; so don't worry . . .'

But Noun was not listening. She was going from the window of the room to her mistress's couch, she was trying to catch the slightest sound, she seemed torn between the desire to run after M. Delmare and that of staying with the sick woman.

Her anxiety seemed so strange and so uncalled for to M. Brown that he departed from his usual gentleness and, gripping her arm, said,

'Are you quite out of your mind? Don't you see that you're frightening your mistress, and that your foolish fears are terribly bad for her?'

Noun had not heard him. She had turned her eyes towards her mistress, who had just started on her couch as if the movement of the air had given her senses an electric shock. At almost the same moment, the sound of a gunshot rattled all the drawing-room windows and Noun fell on her knees.

'What petty feminine fears!' cried Sir Ralph, tired of women's agitation. 'They'll soon triumphantly bring you a rabbit killed in the hunt and you'll laugh at yourselves.'

'No, Ralph,' said Madame Delmare, going towards the door with a steady step, 'I tell you, human blood has been spilt.'

With a piercing shriek, Noun fell on her face.

Then they heard Lelièvre shouting from the grounds:

'There he is! There he is! Good shot, Colonel! The bandit's on the ground ...' Sir Ralph began to be concerned. He followed Madame Delmare. Some moments later, a man, blood-stained and showing no sign of life, was brought on to the verandah.

'Don't make so much noise! Don't shout so much!' the Colonel was saying with a rough cheerfulness to all his frightened servants crowding round the wounded man. 'It's just a farce. My gun was only loaded with salt. I don't think I even hit him. He fell with fright.'

'But this blood, Monsieur,' said Madame Delmare very reproachfully, 'was it fear that made it flow?'

'Why are you here, Madame?' cried M. Delmare. 'What are you doing here?'

'I am here to repair the harm you are doing, as is my duty,' she replied coldly.

And going up to the wounded man with a courage that no one present had yet felt capable of, she brought a light close to his face.

Then instead of the coarse features and clothing they had expected to see, they found a very aristocratic-looking young man, elegantly dressed although he was wearing a riding habit. One of his hands was slightly wounded but his torn clothing and his unconscious state showed he had had a bad fall.

'That's right,' said Lelièvre. 'He fell twenty feet. He was climbing over the top of the wall when the Colonel shot him, and a few little pellets or grains of salt in his right hand will have prevented him from holding on. The fact is, I saw him fall, and once he was on the ground he didn't even think of running away, poor devil.'

'Can you believe that a man who is so well-dressed should want to steal?' asked one of the maids.

'And his pockets are full of money,' said another servant, who had undone the waistcoat of the alleged thief.

'It's strange,' said the Colonel who, not without being deeply moved, was looking at the man stretched out before him. 'If this man is dead, it's not my fault. Look at his hand, Madame, and if you find one little pellet . . .'

'I want to believe you, Monsieur,' replied Madame Delmare, and with a sang-froid and moral strength of which no one would have thought her capable, she was carefully feeling his pulse and the arteries of his neck. 'And indeed,' she added, 'he's not dead but he needs immediate attention. He doesn't look like a thief and perhaps deserves to be looked after, and even if he didn't deserve it, it's our duty, as women, to care for him.'

Then Madame Delmare had the wounded man carried into the nearest room, the billiard room. A mattress was placed on some benches and Indiana helped by her maids, looked after dressing the wounded hand while Sir Ralph, who had some surgical knowledge, bled the wounded man profusely.

Meanwhile, the Colonel, looking embarrassed, was in the situation of a man who has behaved more badly than he had meant to. He felt the need to justify himself in the eyes of the others, or rather for the others to justify him in his own eyes. So he stayed with the servants below the verandah, delivering the heatedly long-winded and completely useless explanations that are always made after the event. Lelièvre had already explained twenty times, with the utmost detail, the gunshot, the fall, and its consequences, while the Colonel, who had become good-humoured again amongst his own staff, as he always did after he had vented his anger, blamed the intentions of a man who gets into private property at night by climbing over the wall. They were all agreeing with their master, when the gardener quietly drew him aside and affirmed that the thief, and a young landowner recently settled in the neighbourhood, were as alike as two peas, and that three days earlier he had seen him speaking to Mademoiselle Noun at the Rubelles* village fête.

This information gave a different direction to M. Delmare's thoughts. A large vein, which with him always swelled up before a storm, stood out on his wide, gleaming, bald forehead.

'My God!' he said to himself, clenching his fists, 'Madame Delmare takes a great interest in this womanizer who steals into my grounds by climbing over the wall!'

Then, pale and trembling with anger, he went into the billiard room.

III

'DON'T worry, Monsieur,' said Indiana. 'The man you killed will be quite well in a few days; at least we hope so, though he can't speak yet.'

'That's not the point, Madame,' said the Colonel sullenly. 'I want you to tell me the name of this interesting invalid and what fit of absent-mindedness made him mistake the wall of my grounds for the driveway to my house.'

'I haven't the slightest idea what it is,' replied Madame Delmare so coldly and proudly that her terrible husband was for a moment quite taken aback.

But returning quickly to his jealous suspicions:

'I'll find out, Madame. You may be sure I'll find out,' he said under his breath.

Then, as Madame Delmare pretended not to notice his rage and continued looking after the wounded man, he left the room so as not to lose his temper in front of the maids, and called back the gardener.

'What's the name of this man who you say looks like our robber?'

'M. de Ramière. He's the man who's just bought M. de Cercy's little English house.'

'What kind of a man is he? A nobleman, a fop, a fine gentleman?'

'A very fine gentleman, a nobleman, I think.'

'He would be,' continued the Colonel pointedly. 'M. de Ramière! Tell me, Louis,' he added in a low voice, 'have you ever seen that fop prowling around here?' ·

'Monsieur . . . last night,' replied Louis hesitantly, 'I certainly saw . . . to say he was a fop, I know nothing about that, but it certainly was a man.'

'And you saw him?'

'Beneath the orangery windows, as clearly as I can see you.'

'And you didn't go after him with your spade handle?'

'Monsieur, I was going to, but I saw a woman in white coming out of the orangery and going up to him. So I said to myself, 'Perhaps it's Monsieur and Madame who have fancied going for a walk before daylight. And I went home to bed. But this morning, I heard Lelièvre talking about a thief whose footprints he saw in the garden, and I said to myself, 'There's something fishy about this.'

'And why didn't you tell me right away, you stupid fellow?'

'Oh well, Monsieur, there are some *delicate situations* in life . . .'

'I understand you. You let yourself doubt. You are a fool. If you ever happen to have an insolent idea of that kind, I'll cut your ears off. I know perfectly well who this robber is and what he was looking for in my garden. I only asked you all these questions to see how you were looking after your orangery. You must realize that I have some rare plants there that Madame values highly and that there are plant-lovers crazy enough to come and rob their neighbours' greenhouses. It was me you saw last night with Madame Delmare.'

And the poor Colonel went away more tortured and angry than before, leaving his gardener not at all convinced that there were horticulturists so fanatical that they would risk being shot so as to gain possession of a sucker or a cutting.

M. Delmare, having returned to the billiard room, paid no attention to the signs of consciousness the wounded man was showing at last, and the Colonel was starting to search the pockets of the intruder's jacket which was lying on a chair, when, stretching out his arm, he said faintly:

'You want to know who I am, Monsieur, but there's no point in searching my pockets. I'll tell you when we're alone together. Till then, spare me the embarrassment of making myself known in the ridiculous and awkward situation in which I am placed.'

'That really is a great pity!' the Colonel replied tartly. 'But I must admit it doesn't bother me much. However, as I hope we'll see each other again alone, I'm willing to defer our acquaintanceship till then. Meanwhile, please tell me where I should have you taken.'

'To the inn of the nearest village, if you'd be so kind.'

'But Monsieur is not in a fit condition to be taken any-where,' Madame Delmare said quickly. 'Isn't that so, Ralph?'

'You're too much affected by Monsieur's condition, Madame,' said the Colonel. 'Leave the room the rest of you,' he said to the maids. 'Monsieur is feeling better and he'll be strong enough now to explain his presence in my house.'

'Yes, Monsieur,' replied the wounded man, 'and I ask all those who were kind enough to look after me to be so good as to listen to the confession of my wrongdoing. I feel that it's very important that there should be no misunderstanding here about my behaviour, and it's important to *me* not to pass for what I am not. I must tell you what underhand scheme led me to your house. By very simple methods, known only to you, you have set up a factory whose work and products are infinitely superior to those of all the factories of that kind in the district. My brother has a very similar establishment in the south of France but its upkeep absorbs enormous amounts of money. His business was heading for disaster, when I heard of the success of yours. So I decided to come and ask your advice, as a generous service which couldn't harm your interests, since my brother deals with products of quite a different kind. But the gate of your English garden was firmly closed to me, and when I asked to speak to you, I was told in reply that you wouldn't even allow me to visit your establishment. Put off by these unkind refusals, I then decided even at the risk of my own life and honour, to save my brother's life and honour. I stole into your grounds at night by climbing over the wall, and I tried to get into the factory to examine the machinery. In short, I had decided to hide in a corner, bribe the workforce, and steal your secret for the benefit of an honest man without hurting you. That was my crime. Now, Monsieur, if you require satisfaction other than what you have just taken, I'm ready to oblige you and even to ask you to take it as soon as I'm strong enough.'

'I think we ought to call it a day, Monsieur,' replied the Colonel, half relieved of a great anxiety. 'The rest of you witnessed the explanation Monsieur has given me. I've been more than satisfied, even if I needed satisfaction. Go now, and leave us to talk about my successful business.'

The servants left the room, but only they were duped by this reconciliation. The wounded man, weakened by his long speech, could not appreciate the tone of the Colonel's last remark. He fell back into the arms of Madame Delmare and lost consciousness a second time. Bending over him, she did not deign to raise her eyes to look at her husband's anger, and M. Delmare and M. Brown, their two faces so different, the one pale and distorted with irritation, the other calm and impassive as usual, questioned each other silently.

M. Delmare did not need to say a word to make himself understood, but he drew Sir Ralph aside and pressing his hands hard, said:

'My good friend, it's a very well planned intrigue. I'm satisfied, perfectly satisfied, with the presence of mind with which this young man was able to preserve my honour in front of my servants. But, by God! He'll pay dearly for the insult which I feel to the depths of my heart. And this woman who is looking after him and pretends not to know him! Oh, how innately cunning these creatures are . . .'

Sir Ralph, appalled, walked steadily three times round the room. After his first round, he concluded, *improbable*, after the second, *impossible*, after the third, *proved*. Then, coming back to the stony-faced Colonel, he pointed to Noun, who stood behind the wounded man, wringing her hands, her eyes haggard and her lips white, petrified with despair, terror, and bewilderment.

There is such an immediate and overwhelming power of conviction in a real discovery that the Colonel was more struck by Sir Ralph's forceful gesture than he would have been by the most eloquent oratory. M. Brown had probably more than one clue to put him on the right track. He had just recalled Noun's presence in the grounds at the very moment when he had been looking for her, her wet hair and damp, muddy shoes which bore witness to her strange whim of taking a walk in the rain, small details which he had not noticed much when Madame Delmare had fainted, but which came back to him now. Then the strange fear and convulsive agitation she had manifested, and the scream she had let out when she heard the gunshot . . .

M. Delmare did not need all these clues. More clear-sighted, perhaps because he was more concerned to be so, he had only to study the girl's face to see that she alone was guilty. But his wife's assiduous attentions to the hero of this amorous adventure were more and more distasteful to him.

'Indiana,' he said, 'go to your room. It's late, and you aren't well. Noun will stay beside Monsieur to look after him tonight, and tomorrow, if he's better, we'll consider how to have him taken home.'

There was no objection to be made to this unexpected arrangement. Madame Delmare, who was so capable of standing up to her husband's violent temper, always gave in when he was gentle. She asked Sir Ralph to stay with the patient a little longer and retired to her room.

It was not unintentionally that the Colonel had made this arrangement. An hour later, when everyone was in bed and the house was quiet, he slipped noiselessly into the room where M. de Ramière was, and concealed behind a curtain, he was able to have his suspicions confirmed by the conversation between the young man and his wife's maid, that it was a matter of an amorous intrigue between them. The young Creole's unusual beauty had created a sensation at the village balls of the neighbourhood. She had not lacked admirers, even amongst the leading people of the district. More than one handsome lancers' officer, garrisoned at Melun, had put himself out to attract her, but Noun was involved in her first love affair and only one admirer's attentions had made an impression on her—M. de Ramière's.

Colonel Delmare had no wish to follow the course of their liaison, so he withdrew as soon as he was quite reassured that his wife had not for a moment been the concern of the Almaviva* of this intrigue. Nevertheless he heard enough to understand the difference between the love felt by poor Noun, who threw herself into it with all the violence of her passionate temperament, and that of the young man of good social position who yielded to a temporary infatuation without giving up the right to return to his senses the next day.

When Madame Delmare woke up she saw Noun at her bedside, sad and embarrassed. But Indiana had naïvely believed M. de Ramière's explanation, all the more so because people interested in the trade had already tried by cunning or deceit to steal the secrets of Delmare's factory. So she attributed her companion's disarray to the emotions and fatigue of the night, and Noun was reassured when she saw the Colonel walk calmly into his wife's room and talk to her about the previous evening's incident as if it were something quite normal.

In the morning, Sir Ralph had checked up on the patient's condition. Although the fall was violent, there had been no serious consequences. The wound had already begun to heal. M. de Ramière, who wanted to be taken to Melun straight away, had distributed the contents of his purse to the servants so as to ensure their keeping quiet about the incident, saying he did not want to frighten his mother, who lived a few miles away. So news of what had happened spread only slowly and in different versions. Some information about the English factory of a M. de Ramière, brother of the intruder, supported the story that he had fortunately made up on the spur of the moment. The Colonel and Sir Brown had the tact to keep Noun's secret without even letting her know they knew it, and the Delmare family soon ceased to be concerned with the incident.

IV

It is perhaps difficult for you to believe that M. Raymon de Ramière, a brilliant young man, intelligent, talented and with many virtues, used to social success and fashionable love-affairs, should have conceived a lasting attachment for the housekeeper of a little industrial establishment in the Brie. But M. de Ramière was neither a fop nor a libertine. We have said he was intelligent, that is to say, he appreciated the advantages of birth at their true value. He was a man of principle who reasoned with himself, but ardent passions would often sweep him away from his theories. At such times he was incapable of reflection, or he would avoid confrontation with his conscience; he would do wrong, as if in spite of himself, and the next day would try to deceive himself about what he had done the night before. Unfortunately the most striking thing about him was not his principles (he shared these with many other white-gloved philosophers and they did not preserve him, any more than them, from inconsistency) but his passions, which principles could not stifle, and which set him apart in that dubious society in which it is so difficult to be different without being ridiculous. Raymon had the art of often being guilty without making himself hated, often unusual without upsetting people; sometimes he even managed to arouse pity in those who had most reason to complain of him. There are men who are spoiled like this by all around them. A cheerful expression and a lively way of speaking are sometimes all that their feelings cost them. We have no intention of judging M. Raymon de Ramière very harshly, nor of sketching his portrait before showing him in action. For the moment we are studying him from a distance, as one of the crowd who see him pass by.

M. de Ramière was in love with the young Creole with big black eyes who had aroused the admiration of the whole county at the Rubelles fête, but in love with her and nothing more. He had perhaps approached her in an idle moment and success had inflamed his desire. He had obtained more than he had asked for, and the day he conquered her easily-won heart he went home, alarmed at his victory, and, striking his forehead, said to himself:

'I only hope she doesn't love me!'

So it was only after he had accepted all the proofs of her love that he began to suspect she loved him. Then he repented, but it was too late; he had to accept the future consequences or make a cowardly retreat. Raymon did not hesitate; he let himself be loved and he himself loved out of gratitude. He scaled the walls of the Delmare estate out of love of danger; he had a nasty fall out of clumsiness and he was so touched by his beautiful young mistress's grief that thereafter he considered himself justified in his own eyes in continuing to dig the abyss into which she was to fall.

As soon as he was well again, there was no icy winter weather, there were no nocturnal dangers, no twinges of remorse which could prevent him from crossing a corner of the forest to meet his Creole and swearing to her that he had never loved anyone but her, that he preferred her to the queens of society, and from uttering the thousand other exaggerations which are always in season with poor, credulous girls. In January Madame Delmare left for Paris with her husband. Sir Ralph Brown, their worthy neighbour, went home to his own estate, and Noun, left in charge of her master's country house, was free to absent herself under different pretexts. It was a misfortune for her, since these easy meetings with her lover greatly shortened the ephemeral happiness she was to enjoy. The forest, its poetic beauty, its garlands of white frost, its transformation in the moonlight, the hidden little gate, the stealthy morning departure when Noun's little feet left their imprint in the snow as she saw him to the gate, all these trimmings of a love-affair had prolonged M. de Ramière's infatuation. Noun, in a white housecoat, with her long black hair, was a noble lady, a queen, a fairy. When he saw her emerge from the red-brick castle, a solid, square, Regency building which had a half-feudal look about it, he could easily take her for a medieval lady of the manor, and in the summer-house full of exotic flowers, where she would intoxicate him with the seductions of youth and passion, he easily forgot everything he was to remember later.

But when, despising precautions and, in her turn braving danger, Noun came to see him in his room with her white apron and her head-scarf attractively arranged in the style of her native country, she was no more than a lady's maid, and a pretty woman's maid, which always makes the serving-girl seem a second best. Yet Noun was very beautiful; that was how she had been dressed when he had seen her for the first time at the village fête, where he had cut through the crowd of interested spectators in order to get near her and had the little triumph of snatching her away from twenty rivals. Noun would remind him tenderly of that day. Poor girl, she did not know that Raymon's love did not go back so far, and that what for her was a day of pride, was for him only a day of vanity. Then the courage with which she was sacrificing her reputation, that courage which ought to have made him love her more, irritated M. de Ramière. The wife of a peer of France who sacrificed herself in that way would be a prized conquest; but a lady's maid! What is heroism in the one becomes impudence in the other. With the one, a host of jealous rivals envies you; with the other, a crowd of scandalized lackeys condemns you. The woman of rank gives up for you the twenty lovers she had; the lady's maid only gives up for you the one husband she might have had.

What do you expect? Raymon was a man with polished manners, an elegant life-style and romantic love-affairs. For him a working-girl was not a woman, and Noun, thanks to her perfect beauty, had taken him by surprise on a day when he was letting himself go with village people. None of that was Raymon's fault. He had been brought up for high society, all his thoughts had been directed towards a lofty goal, all his faculties had been moulded for a princely happiness, and it was in spite of himself that his passionate blood had dragged him into a lower-class love-affair. He had done all he could to be happy in it, but he could be so no longer. What was he to do now? Generously extravagant ideas had certainly crossed his mind. On the days when he had been most in love with his mistress, he had, to be sure, thought of raising her up to him, of legitimizing their union . . . Yes, on my honour, he had thought of it! But love, which legitimizes everything, was dwindling now; it was declining with the dangers of the adventure and the thrill of concealment. A marriage was no longer possible. But, take note, Raymon's reasoning was very sound and entirely in his mistress's interest.

If he had truly loved her, by sacrificing his future, his family, and his reputation, he could still have found happiness with her and consequently have given it to her, for love is a contract as much as marriage is. But now that he felt his love had cooled, what future could he make for a woman of this class? Would he marry her to show her, every day, a sad face, hurt feelings, and a deeply unhappy home? Would he marry her to make her detested by his family, contemptible to his equals, ridiculous to his servants; to risk introducing her into a society where she would feel out of place and humiliation would kill her; to overwhelm her with remorse by making her realize all the evils she had brought on her lover?

No, you will agree with him that it was not possible, that it would not have been generous, that one cannot struggle against society in this way, and such virtuous heroics are like Don Quixote's breaking his lance against a windmill, an iron courage destroyed by a puff of wind, the chivalry of another century which arouses pity in this one.

Having thus considered the whole matter, M. de Ramière realized that it was better to break the unfortunate connection. Noun's visits began to upset him. His mother, who had gone to Paris for the winter, would soon be bound to hear of this little scandal. She was already surprised by his frequent visits to Cercy, their country house, and by his spending whole weeks there. He had, to be sure, claimed to be doing a serious piece of work that he went to complete far from urban noise, but the pretext was beginning to wear thin. Raymon was unhappy at deceiving such a good mother, at depriving her of his attentions for so long. What more is there to say? He left Cercy and did not return.

Noun wept and waited and, in her unhappiness seeing time pass, she risked going so far as to write to him. Poor girl! That was the last straw! A letter from a lady's maid! Yet she had taken the glossy writing paper and perfumed sealing wax from Madame Delmare's writing desk, and the style from her own heart . . . But the spelling! Are you aware what a syllable more or less adds to or detracts from the strength of feelings? Alas! The poor half-civilized girl from Bourbon Island did not even know that language had rules. She thought she wrote and spoke as well as her mistress, and when she saw that Raymon was not coming back she said to herself:

'Yet my letter was certainly written in a style to bring him back.'

But Raymon had not the courage to read that letter to the end. Perhaps it was a masterpiece of naïve, delightful passion; perhaps Virginie wrote no more charming letter to Paul* when she had left her native land . . . But M. de Ramière, afraid of being ashamed of himself, was quick to throw it in the fire. Once again, what do you expect? It is a prejudice inculcated by upbringing, and self-esteem is, in love, what self-interest is in friendship.

M. de Ramière's absence had been noticed in society. That is saying a lot for a man in a society where all the men are alike. One can be an intelligent man and value society, just as one can be a fool and despise it. Raymon liked it and he was right; he was sought after and was popular; for him, the crowd of indifferent or mocking faces had attentive looks and interested smiles. Unhappy people may be misanthropic but people who are liked are rarely surly; at least Raymon thought so. He was grateful for the slightest signs of affection, wanted everyone's good opinion, and was proud of a great number of friendships.

In a society where prejudice reigns supreme, he had been successful in everything; even his failings had been part of his success. And when he looked for the source of the universal affection which had always protected him, he found it in himself, in his desire to gain that affection, in the happiness it inspired in him, and in the hearty goodwill which he lavished inexhaustibly.

He owed this affection also to his mother, whose superior intelligence, friendly conversation, and personal virtues set her apart from other women. It was to her that he owed the excellent principles which always brought him back to what was good and prevented him, despite the ardour of his twenty-five years, from forfeiting public esteem. People were also more indulgent towards him than towards others because his mother had the art of excusing him while blaming him, of advising indulgence while appearing to entreat it. She was one of those women who have lived through such different régimes that their minds have become as adaptable as their fortunes, who have been enriched by the experience of misfortune, who have escaped the scaffolds of '93,* the vices of the Directory,* the vanities of the Empire,* and the grudges of the Restoration.* There are few women of that kind and they are dying out.

It was at a ball at the Spanish Embassy that Raymon made his return to society.

'M. de Ramière, if I'm not mistaken,' said a young woman to her neighbour.

'He's a comet that appears at irregular intervals,' the neighbour replied. 'It's ages since we've heard of that pretty fellow.'

It was a foreign, elderly woman who made this remark and her companion blushed a little.

'He's very good-looking,' she said. 'Isn't he, Madame!'

'Charming, upon my word,' said the old Sicilian lady.

'I bet you're talking of the hero of the eclectic salons,* dark-haired Raymon,' said a handsome Colonel of the Guards.

'He's got a fine head for sketching,' continued the young woman.

'And what you may like still more, a miscreant's head,' said the Colonel.

The young woman was his own wife.

'Why a miscreant's?' asked the foreign lady.

'He has quite southern style passions, Madame, strong as the beautiful sunshine of Palermo.'

Two or three young women bent their pretty flower-adorned heads so that they could hear what the Colonel was saying.

'He really caused havoc in the garrison, this year,' he continued. 'The rest of us will be forced to pick a bad quarrel with him to get rid of him.'

'If he's a Lovelace,* no matter,' said a young girl with a mocking expression. 'I can't stand people whom everyone likes.'

The Sicilian Countess waited till the Colonel was a little further away, then, giving a little rap over Mademoiselle de Nangy's knuckles with her fan, said:

'Don't speak like that. You don't know how we appreciate here a man who wants to be loved.'

'So you think all such men need do is to want?' said the girl with narrow, sardonic eyes.

'Mademoiselle,' said the Colonel, who was coming to ask her to dance, 'take care that the handsome Raymon doesn't hear you.'

Mademoiselle de Nangy began to laugh. But for the whole evening, her attractive group did not dare say another word about M. de Ramière.

V

M. DE RAMIÈRE was neither bored nor displeased as he wandered about in the ebb and flow of the beautifully-dressed crowd.

Yet he was struggling against depression. As he returned to the sphere to which he belonged, he was, as it were, remorseful, ashamed of all the crazy ideas which an unsuitable attachment had put into his head. He looked at these women who sparkled so in the bright lights; he listened to their subtle, sophisticated conversation; he heard people praising their talents, and in the carefully chosen splendours, in the almost regal ball-gowns, in their exquisite courtesy, he felt continually reproached for having demeaned himself below the status he was born to. But in spite of this kind of embarrassment, Raymon suffered from a more genuine remorse, for his intentions were always extremely considerate and a woman's tears broke his heart, however hardened he was.

At this moment, the honours of the evening were awarded to a young woman whose name no one knew, and who, by the novelty of her appearance in society, enjoyed the privilege of arresting everyone's attention. The simplicity of her dress would have been enough to make her stand out in the midst of the diamonds, feathers, and flowers which adorned the other women. Rows of pearls wound into her black hair were her only jewels. The dull white of her necklace, of her crêpe dress, and of her bare shoulders blended together from a distance, and the warmth of the rooms had barely managed to bring to her cheeks a delicate hue like that of a Bengal rose flowering in snow. She was a tiny, dainty, slender little creature; her drawing-room beauty, fairy-like in the bright light of the candles, would have been dimmed by a ray of sunshine. As she danced, she was so light that a puff of wind would have been enough to blow her away, but though light, she had no animation or enjoyment. When she was seated, she stooped as if her body were too pliable, without enough strength to hold her upright, and when she spoke, she smiled sadly. At that

time, tales of the supernatural were at the height of their
popularity, and so connoisseurs of the genre compared the
young woman to a charming spectre, magically evoked, which
would become dim and fade away like a dream when day
began to dawn.

Meanwhile, they crowded round her to ask her to dance.

'Hurry up,' said a romantic dandy to one of his friends.
'The cock is about to crow and your partner's feet already no
longer touch the dance-floor. I bet you can no longer feel her
hand in yours.'

'Do look at M. de Ramière's dark-complexioned face, full
of character,' a woman with artistic pretensions said to her
neighbour. 'Don't you think that, next to that pale, tiny young
creature, his strong colouring sets off admirably the delicate
tones of hers?'

'That young creature,' said a woman who knew everybody
and who at parties fulfilled the function of a directory, 'is the
daughter of that crazy old Carvajal who wanted to set himself
up as a partisan of Joseph Bonaparte* and, a ruined man,
went off to die in Bourbon Island. That beautiful, exotic
flower has made a pretty stupid marriage, I believe, but her
aunt is in favour at court.'

Raymon had come up to the lovely girl from the Indies. A
strange emotion took hold of him each time he looked at her.
He must have seen that pale, sad face in one of his dreams; but
he was sure he had seen her, and he kept on looking at her
with the pleasure experienced at seeing again a caring face
that one feared losing for ever. Raymon's attention upset the
girl who was its object. She was awkward and shy like a
person unused to high society, and her success in it seemed to
embarrass rather than please her. Raymon walked round the
room, finally learned that the lady's name was Madame
Delmare, and went to ask her to dance.

'You don't remember me,' he said when they were alone in
the midst of the crowd, 'but I have not been able to forget you,
Madame. Yet I saw you for only a moment, through a cloud,
but that revealed you to me so kind, so full of pity . . .'

Madame Delmare gave a start.

'Oh yes, Monsieur,' she said eagerly, 'it's you! . . . Yes, I too recognized you.'

Then she blushed and seemed afraid she had behaved improperly. She looked around as if to see whether anyone had heard her. Her shyness added to her natural charm and Raymon felt touched to the heart by the tone of her Creole voice, a little husky and so gentle that it seemed made to pray or bless.

'I was very much afraid I should never have an opportunity to thank you,' he said. 'I couldn't call at your home and I knew you went out very little in society. I was afraid, too, that if I approached you, I would come into contact with M. Delmare and our mutual situation could not make that a pleasant contact. How happy I am to have this moment which allows me to pay the debt my heart owes you.'

'It would be nicer for me if M. Delmare could take his share of the payment,' she said. 'If you knew him better you would know that he is as kind as he is short-tempered. You would pardon him for unintentionally wounding you, for his heart certainly bled more than your wound.'

'Let's not talk of M. Delmare, Madame. I forgive him with all my heart. I had wronged him, he took the law into his own hands; it only remains for me to forget him. But you, Madame, who lavished such generous, tender care on me, I shall remember all my life your behaviour towards me, your pure features, your angelic gentleness, and those hands which poured balm on my wounds and which I could not kiss . . .'

As he spoke, Raymon, ready to take his place in the quadrille with Madame Delmare, was holding her hand. He pressed her hand gently in his own and all the young woman's blood surged back to her heart.

When he brought Madame Delmare back to her place, her aunt, Madame de Carvajal, had left. The crowd at the ball was thinning out. Raymon sat down beside Indiana. He had the ease of manner that comes from some experience in affairs of the heart. It is the strength of our desires, the impetuosity of our love, which makes us stupid in our relations with women.

The man who has worn out his emotions a little is more concerned to please than to love. Yet M. de Ramière felt more deeply moved beside this simple, inexperienced woman than he had been hitherto. Perhaps he owed this fleeting impression to the memory of the night he had spent in her house. What is certain is that, in talking to her eagerly, his heart did not belie his tongue.

But the habit acquired with other women gave his words a power of conviction to which Indiana, in her ignorance, succumbed without realizing that it had not all been invented for her.

Usually, and women are well aware of this, a man who talks well of love is not very much in love. Raymon was an exception. He expressed his passion with skill and he felt it keenly. Only, it was not passion which made him eloquent, it was eloquence which made him passionate. He felt attracted to a woman, became eloquent in order to seduce her, and fell in love with her in the course of the seduction. It was the kind of feeling aroused in lawyers and preachers who weep bitterly as soon as they sweat profusely. He met women who were discriminating enough not to trust these passionate improvisations. But Raymon had committed for love what are called follies. He had eloped with a well-born young woman; he had compromised women in very high positions; he had had three much publicized duels. He had not concealed the disarray and the frenzy of his thoughts from the whole company at a large party, or from the whole audience at a theatre. A man who can do all that without fear of being laughed at or cursed, and who manages to be neither the one nor the other, is unassailable. He can risk everything and hope for everything. So the women who were best able to resist gave in at the thought that when Raymon was involved, he was madly in love. In society, a man capable of folly in love is a fairly scarce prodigy, whom women do not despise.

I do not know how he did it, but as he escorted Madame de Carvajal and Madame Delmare to their carriage, he managed to raise Indiana's little hand to his lips. Never before had a man's furtive, passionate kiss touched her fingers, even though she was born in a burning-hot climate and was nineteen years old; and nineteen years old in Bourbon Island is the equivalent of twenty-five in our country.

Delicate and highly-strung as she was, the kiss almost made her cry out, and she had to be helped into the carriage. Raymon had never before come across such a sensitive temperament. Noun, the Creole, was strong and healthy, and Parisian women do not faint when their hands are kissed.

'If I were to see her twice, I'd lose my head about her,' Raymon said to himself as he went away.

The next day, he had completely forgotten Noun; all that he knew about her was that she belonged to Madame Delmare. Pale Indiana occupied all his thoughts and filled all his dreams. When Raymon began to feel he was in love, he usually sought distractions, not so as to stifle the incipient passion, but on the contrary, to drive out reason which told him to weigh up the consequences. Ardent in the pursuit of pleasure, he worked towards his goal relentlessly. He could not control the violent feelings that arose in his breast, any more than he could rekindle them when he felt them dwindle and expire.

So, the very next day, he managed to find out that M. Delmare had gone on a business trip to Brussels. Before leaving, he had entrusted his wife to Madame de Carvajal, whom he did not like at all but who was Madame Delmare's only relative. He himself, a soldier risen from the ranks, had only a poor, obscure family of which he seemed ashamed for he repeatedly said he was not ashamed of it. But though he perpetually reproached his wife for a contempt which she did not feel at all, he felt he ought not to force her into intimacy with his ill-bred relatives. Moreover, in spite of his aversion to Madame de Carvajal, he could not deny her a great respect for the following reasons.

Madame de Carvajal, who came from a great Spanish family, was one of those women who cannot resign themselves to being a nobody. In the days when Napoleon ruled over Europe, she had sung his praises loudly, and together with her husband and brother-in-law had espoused the cause of Joseph as King of Spain. But when her husband was killed at the fall of the conqueror's ephemeral dynasty, Indiana's father had taken refuge in the French colonies. Madame de Carvajal, who was active and capable, then went to Paris where, by some financial speculation or other, she had created an adequate income for herself out of the remnants of her past splendour. By means of intelligence, scheming, and perseverance, she had, in addition, obtained the favour of the court, and her establishment, though not outstanding, was one of the most respectable amongst the protégés of the civil list.

When, after her father's death, Indiana arrived in France, married to Colonel Delmare, Madame de Carvajal was not particularly flattered by such an obscure connection. However, as M. Delmare's energy and good sense in business were as good as a dowry, she saw his slender capital increase and she bought for Indiana the little country house at Lagny and the factory which belonged to it. In two years, thanks to M. Delmare's expert knowledge and to cash advances from Sir Ralph Brown, his wife's cousin by marriage, the Colonel's business went well; he began to pay his debts, and Madame de Carvajal, in whose eyes money was the first recommendation, showed a great affection for her niece and promised to leave her the rest of her money. Indiana, devoid of ambition, lavished care and attentions on her aunt out of gratitude and not out of self-interest, but there was as much of the latter as of the former in the assiduities of the colonel. His political views were absolutely unshakeable; he would not listen to reason about the unassailable glory of his great Emperor,* and he defended it with the blind obstinacy of a sixty-year-old child. He had, therefore, to make great efforts to be patient so as not to be continually exploding in Madame de Carvajal's salon, where only the Restoration* was applauded. What poor Colonel Delmare suffered at the hands of five or six pious old ladies is beyond estimation. These irritations were partly the cause of his frequent bad temper with his wife.

Now that these matters have been settled, let us return to M. de Ramière. In three days he knew all about these domestic details, so assiduously had he followed up everything which might help him to come closer to the Delmare family. He knew that, by becoming a protégé of Madame Carvajal, he could see Indiana. On the evening of the third day he had himself introduced to her salon.

There were only four or five antediluvian creatures there solemnly playing reversi,* and two or three sons of good families, as insignificant as one can be when one has sixteen quarters of nobility. Indiana was quietly working at a tapestry background on her aunt's loom. She was bending over her work, apparently absorbed in this mechanical occupation, and perhaps pleased to be able to escape in this way from the insipid chatter of her neighbours. I do not know whether, hidden by her long black hair hanging over the flowers in her tapestry, she was reliving, in her heart, the emotions of that fleeting instant which had initiated her into a new life, when the servant's voice announcing several people made her get up. She did so mechanically, for she had not listened to the names, and had barely lifted her eyes from her embroidery when a voice struck her like an electric shock, and she had to lean against her work table so as not to fall.

VI

RAYMON had not expected such a silent drawing-room, with its few subdued figures. It was impossible to pronounce a word which was not heard in every corner of the room. The dowagers who were playing cards seemed to be there only to get in the way of the young people's conversation, and Raymon thought he could read in their stiff features the secret satisfaction of old age which gets its own back by repressing the pleasures of others. He had counted on an easier meeting and a more affectionate conversation than the one he had had at the ball, but the opposite was the case. The unforeseen difficulty made his desire more intense, his looks more ardent, and the indirect remarks he addressed to Madame Delmare more vivacious and animated. This kind of attack was quite new to the poor girl. She had no possible defence, because nothing was asked of her, but she was forced to listen to the offer of a passionate heart, to learn how much she was loved, and to allow herself to be surrounded by all the dangers of seduction without making any resistance. Her embarrassment increased as Raymon grew bolder. Madame de Carvajal, who had valid claims to wit and to whom M. de Ramière's had been praised, left the cards to embark with him on a stylish discussion about love, into which she put a great deal of Spanish passion and German metaphysics. Raymon eagerly accepted the challenge and, under the pretext of replying to the aunt, he said to the niece everything she would have refused to listen to. The poor young woman, with no one to protect her, exposed on all sides to such a sharp and skilful attack, could not summon up the strength to take part in this dangerous conversation. The aunt, eager to make her shine, appealed to her to confirm certain subtle points of sentimental theory. She blushingly admitted that she knew nothing about all that and Raymon, overjoyed at seeing her face change colour and her breast heave, swore that he would teach her.

Indiana slept even less that night than the previous ones. As we have said, she had not yet been in love, but for a long time her heart had been ripe for a feeling that none of the men she had met had been able to inspire in her. Brought up by an eccentric, violent father, she had never known the happiness given by the affection of others. In the colonies M. de Carvajal, inflamed by political passions and tortured by regrets for his ambitions, had become the most brutal of planters and troublesome of neighbours. His daughter had suffered cruelly from his embittered temper. But, through continually seeing the ills of slavery and enduring the vexations of solitude and dependence, she had acquired an unshakeable external patience and an adorable forbearance and kindness to her inferiors; but she had also acquired a will of iron and an incalculable strength of resistance to everything which tended to oppress her. In marrying Delmare she had only changed masters; in coming to live at Lagny she had only changed prisons and places of solitude. She did not love her husband, perhaps only because she was told it was her duty to love him and mental resistance to every kind of moral compulsion had become a kind of second nature to her, a principle of conduct, a law of conscience. No one had tried to teach her any other kind of law than that of blind obedience.

Brought up in the wilds, neglected by her father, and living surrounded by slaves whom she could help and console only with her pity and tears, she had become used to saying, 'A day will come when my life will be completely changed, when I shall do good to others; it will be a day when I shall be loved and I shall give my whole heart to the man who gives me his. Meanwhile I must suffer, say nothing, and keep my love as a reward for my deliverer.' This deliverer, this messiah, had not come. Indiana was still waiting for him. It is true, she no longer dared admit to herself the full implications of her thoughts. She had realized that under the clipped hornbeams at Lagny, even thought must be more restricted than under the wild palm trees of Bourbon Island and, when she surprised herself still saying out of habit, 'A day will come . . . a man will come . . .' she would push this rash wish to the bottom of her heart and say, 'So I must die!'

So she was dying. An unknown sickness was consuming her youth. She had no strength and could not sleep. The doctors looked in vain for some visible illness, but there was none. All her faculties declined, all the organs of her body slowly deteriorated. Her heart was gradually burning away, her eyes were growing dim, her blood circulated only intermittently and feverishly. Before long, the poor captive would die. But however resigned or depressed she might be, her need was unchanged. Without realizing it, her silent broken heart was still seeking a young, generous heart to bring it back to life. The being she had loved most up till then was Noun, the vivacious, courageous companion of her woes, and the man who had shown her the most partiality was her phlegmatic cousin, Sir Ralph. What food for the ravenous activity of her thoughts were a poor girl as ignorant and abandoned as herself, and an Englishman whose only passion was fox-hunting!

Madame Delmare was really unhappy, and the first time she felt the ardent breath of a young, passionate man, the first time a tender, affectionate word enchanted her ears and a quivering mouth left its mark like a red-hot iron on her hand, she did not think of the duties imposed upon her, or of the prudence she had been recommended, or of the future that had been predicted for her. She remembered only the hated past, her long suffering, and her tyrannical masters. Nor did she think that this man might be a liar or a philanderer. She saw him as she wanted him to be and as she had imagined him, and Raymon could have deceived her if he had not been sincere.

But how would he not have been to so beautiful and affectionate a woman? What other woman had ever appeared before him with so much candour and innocence? With whom could he have found so smiling and certain a future? Was she not born to love him, this enslaved woman who was only waiting for a sign in order to break her chain, for a word in order to follow him? Surely the heavens had created for Raymon this sad child of Bourbon Island whom no one had loved and who, but for him, was bound to die.

Nevertheless, in Madame Delmare's heart a feeling of fear followed the feverish happiness which had just overwhelmed her. She thought of her husband who was so touchy, so perceptive, and so vindictive, and she was afraid, not for herself (she was hardened to threats) but for the man who was about to embark on a fight to the death with her tyrant. She was so little acquainted with the ways of society that she turned life into a tragic novel. She was a timid creature, afraid to love for fear of endangering her lover; she did not think at all of the risk of endangering herself.

So that was the secret of her resistance, the motive for her virtue. The next day she made up her mind to avoid M. de Ramière. The same evening one of the leading bankers in Paris was giving a ball. Madame de Carvajal, who loved society life as an old lady without close affections does, wanted to take Indiana, but Raymon was to be there and Indiana resolved not to go. To avoid her aunt's remonstrances, Madame Delmare, who could resist only in deeds, pretended to accept the suggestion. She let her dress be prepared and waited till Madame de Carvajal had dressed. Then she put on a dressing-gown, settled down by the fireside and waited for her, quite determined. When the old Spanish lady, stiff and bejewelled like a Van Dyck* portrait, came for her, Indiana announced that she was ill and did not feel strong enough to go out. In vain her aunt insisted that she should make an effort.

'I'd like to with all my heart,' Indiana replied. 'But you see that I can't stand. I'll only be a nuisance to you this evening. Go to the ball without me, dear aunt. I'll enjoy your pleasure.'

'Go without you!' said Madame Carvajal, who was longing not to have dressed for nothing and who shrank from the horror of an evening on her own. 'But what shall *I* do in a society gathering, an old lady like me, whom people come and talk to only so that they can approach you? What will become of me without my niece's good looks to make me worth anything?'

'Your wit will make up for the lack, dear aunt,' said Indiana.

The Marquise de Carvajal, who only asked to be persuaded, finally left. Indiana then hid her head in her hands and began to cry, for she had made a great sacrifice and thought she had already destroyed the happy castle in the air of the previous day.

But that could not be the way Raymon looked at it. The first thing he saw at the ball were the proud plumes of the old marchioness's headdress. He looked near her in vain for Indiana's white dress and black hair. He went up to Madame de Carvajal and heard her saying in a low voice to another woman:

'My niece is ill, or rather,' she added to justify her presence at the ball, 'it's a young woman's whim. She wanted to stay alone in the drawing-room with a book in her hand, like a beautiful romantic heroine.'

'Would she be avoiding me?' wondered Raymon.

He left the ball immediately, arrived at the marchioness's house, went in without saying a word to the concierge, and asked the first servant he found, half-asleep in the anteroom, for Madame Delmare.

'Madame Delmare is ill.'

'I know. I've come on Madame de Carvajal's behalf to ask how she is.'

'I'll tell Madame . . .'

'You don't need to. Madame Delmare will see me.'

And Raymon went in without being announced. All the other servants had gone to bed. A gloomy silence pervaded the deserted rooms. Only one lamp, with a green taffeta shade, gave a dim light to the big drawing-room. Indiana's back was to the door. Entirely buried in a large armchair she was sadly watching the embers burn, as on the evening Raymon had got into Lagny over the wall. But she was sadder now, for a fleeting joy, a ray of lost happiness, had succeeded a vague suffering and desires without an object.

Raymon came up to her, his dancing slippers making no sound on the thick, soft carpet. He saw her crying, and when she turned her head she found him at her feet, firmly grasping her hands which she strove vainly to withdraw. Then, I must admit, with ineffable joy she saw her plan of resistance fail. She felt that she passionately loved this man, who was not deterred by obstacles and came to bring her happiness in spite of herself. She blessed heaven which rejected her sacrifice, and instead of scolding Raymon she almost thanked him.

As for him, he already knew he was loved. He did not need to see the happiness shining through her tears to understand that he was the master and could be daring. He did not give her time to question him and, assuming her role of interrogator, without explaining his unexpected presence, without trying to make himself less guilty than he was, he said:

'Indiana, you're crying . . . Why are you crying? . . . I want to know!'

She started at hearing herself called by her first name, but there was even more happiness in the surprise aroused by his boldness.

'Why do you ask?' she said. 'I oughtn't to tell you.'

'In fact I know, Indiana. I know the whole story of your life. Nothing that concerns you is unknown to me, because nothing that concerns you is unimportant to me. I wanted to know everything about you and I've learned nothing that one moment spent in your house hadn't told me when your husband got annoyed at seeing you, so beautiful and kind, support me in your soft arms and soothe me with your gentle breath. *He* is jealous. Oh, I well understand that! I would be, Indiana, in his place; or rather, in his place, I would kill myself. For, to be your husband, Madame, to possess you, to hold you in one's arms, and not to deserve you, not to have your heart, is to be the most wretched or the most dastardly of men.'

'Oh for Heaven's sake, say no more!' she exclaimed, closing his mouth with her hands. 'Say no more, for you make me guilty. Why do you talk to me of him? Why do you want to teach me to speak ill of him? If he were to hear you! . . . But I have spoken no ill of him. It's not I who give you authority to commit this crime! *I* do not hate him, I esteem him, I love him! . . .'

'Say that you are horribly afraid of him, for the tyrant has broken your spirit, and fear has become installed at your bedside since you became that man's prey. You, Indiana, sacrificed to that boor, whose iron hand has made you bow your head and blighted your life. Poor girl! So young and so beautiful to have suffered so much already! . . . For it's not I whom you could deceive, Indiana, I, who see you with eyes different from those of the crowd; I know all the secrets of your fate and you can't hope to hide from me. Let those who look at you because you are beautiful say, when they see your pallor and melancholy, "She is ill" . . . Well, so you are. But I, who follow you with my heart, I, whose whole soul surrounds you with solicitude and love, I know very well what your illness is. I know very well that, had heaven been willing and given you to me, unhappy wretch that I am, who ought to have his head broken for arriving so late, you wouldn't be ill. I swear by my life, Indiana, that *I* would have loved you so much that you would have loved me too and would have blessed your chains. I would have carried you in my arms to prevent your feet from being hurt; I would have warmed them with my breath. I would have pressed you against my heart to protect you from suffering. I would have given all my blood to heal yours, and if you had lost sleep with me, I would have spent the night in saying sweet words to you, in smiling at you to restore your courage, while weeping to see you suffer. When at last sleep stole over your silken lashes, I would have touched them lightly with my lips to close them more gently and, kneeling by your bedside, I would have watched over you. I would have compelled the air to caress you lightly, golden dreams to throw you flowers. Silently, I would have kissed the tresses of your hair with delight, I would have counted the heavings of your breast, and on awakening, Indiana, you would have found me, at your feet, guarding you like a jealous master, serving you as a slave, watching for your first smile, seizing on your first thought, your first look, your first kiss . . .'

'Enough, enough!' said Indiana, quite beside herself and her heart beating violently. 'You're hurting me.'

And yet, if one could die of happiness, Indiana would have been dead at that moment.

'Don't speak to me like that, not to *me*,' she said. '*I* am not fated to be happy. Don't show me heaven on earth, not *me*; *I* am marked out to die.'

'To die!' exclaimed Raymon violently, as he grasped her in his arms; 'You, die! Indiana! To die, before you have lived, before you have loved! No, you will not die; I shall not let you die, for my life is now tied to yours. You are the woman I'd dreamed of, the purity I adored; the vision that had always eluded me, the brilliant star which shone before me to tell me, "Keep on going in this life of sorrow, and heaven will send you one of its angels to go with you." From the beginning of time you were destined for me, Indiana, your soul was betrothed to mine! Men and their iron laws have disposed of you. They have snatched from me the companion that God would have chosen for me, if God did not sometimes forget his promises. But what do men and laws matter to us, if I still love you in the arms of another, if you can still love me, accursed and unhappy as I am to have lost you! You see, Indiana, you belong to me, you are the half of my soul which has been seeking for a long time to rejoin the other half. When, in Bourbon Island, you were dreaming of a friend, it was I you were dreaming of. When, at the word "husband", a sweet feeling of fear and hope entered your soul, it was I who was to be your husband. Don't you recognize me! Doesn't it seem to you that we haven't seen each other for twenty years? Didn't I recognize you, my angel, when you staunched my blood with your veil, when you placed your hand on my lifeless heart to restore to it warmth and life? Oh, I remember that well. When I opened my eyes, I said to myself, "There she is! That's how she was in all my dreams, pale, melancholy, and beneficent. She belongs to me; *she* is going to nourish me with unknown felicities." And already the physical life which had just been restored to me was your work. For, you see, it wasn't ordinary circumstances that brought us together; it wasn't chance or a whim, it was fate, it was death, which opened the gates of this new life for me. It was your husband, your master, in obedience to his destiny, who brought me, bleeding, with his own hands, and cast me at your feet, saying "This is for you!" And now, nothing can tear us apart . . .'

'*He*, he can tear us apart!' Madame Delmare interrupted vehemently; succumbing to her lover's effusions she was listening to him, transported with delight. 'Alas! Alas! You don't know him. He's a man who knows no mercy, a man one can't deceive. Raymon, he will kill you! . . .'

Weeping, she hid her face on his breast. Raymon embraced her passionately.

'Let him come,' he cried. 'Let him come and snatch this moment of happiness from me! I defy him! Stay there, Indiana, stay against my heart; there lies your refuge and shelter. Love me and I'll be invulnerable. You know very well he hasn't the power to kill me. I've already been exposed to his blows without any defence. But you, my good angel, you were hovering over me and your wings protected me. Come now, don't be afraid of anything. We'll certainly be able to turn away his anger, and now I'm not even afraid for you, for I'll be there. And when your master wants to oppress you, *I'll* also protect you against him. If necessary, I'll snatch you away from his cruel law. Do you want me to kill him? Tell me you love me and I'll be his murderer, if you condemn him to die . . .'

'You make me shudder. Say no more! If you want to kill anyone, kill me; for I've lived one whole day and I want nothing more . . .'

'Die then, but die of happiness,' cried Raymon, pressing his lips on Indiana's.

But it was too violent a storm for so tender a plant. She turned pale, and putting her hand to her heart, she fainted.

At first, Raymon thought his caresses would bring the blood back to her frozen veins, but in vain he covered her hand with kisses, in vain he called her by the most loving names. It was not an intentional faint, of the kind we see so often. Madame Delmare, who had been seriously ill for a long time, was subject to nervous attacks which lasted for hours. Raymon, in despair, was reduced to calling for help. He rang the bell; a maid appeared, but the bottle she was carrying dropped from her hands and she let out a cry when she recognized Raymon. He, recovering his presence of mind immediately, whispered to her:

'Be quiet, Noun! I knew you were here; I came here for you. I didn't expect to find your mistress, who I thought was at the ball. By making my way in here, I frightened her and she fainted. Be prudent. I'll go.'

Raymon fled, leaving each of these two women with a secret that was to bring despair to the heart of the other.

VII

THE next day, when he woke up Raymon received a second letter from Noun. He did not despise that one and throw it away. On the contrary, he opened it eagerly; it might tell him something about Madame Delmare. It did indeed, but what difficulties this complication of intrigues caused Raymon! It was becoming impossible to hide the girl's secret. Suffering and fear had already made her face thin. Madame Delmare noticed that Noun did not look well, without discovering why. Noun was afraid of the Colonel's harshness, but even more of her mistress's gentleness. She knew quite well that Madame Delmare would forgive her, but she was dying of shame and grief at being forced to confess. What would become of her if Raymon did not shield her from the humiliation which was bound to be heaped upon her? In short, he must look after her or she would throw herself at Madame Delmare's feet and tell her everything.

This fear had a powerful effect on M. de Ramière. His first care was to take Noun away from her mistress.

'Take care not to say anything without my agreement,' he said. 'Try to be at Lagny this evening. I'll be there.'

On the way, he considered how he should behave. Noun had enough good sense not to count on an impossible redress. She had not dared pronounce the word marriage and because she was discreet and generous, Raymon thought himself less guilty. He told himself that he had not deceived her and that Noun must have foreseen her fate more than once. What troubled Raymon was not the thought of offering the poor girl half his fortune; he was prepared to make her rich, to give her all the care and consideration he could think of. What made his situation so painful was being forced to tell her that he no longer loved her, because he was no good at lying. If, at that moment, his behaviour seemed two-faced and treacherous, his heart was sincere, as it had always been. He had loved Noun with his senses, he loved Madame Delmare with all his heart. Till then he had lied neither to the one nor the other. It was a question of not starting to lie, and Raymon felt equally incapable of deceiving poor Noun and of driving her to despair. He had to choose between treachery and cruelty. Raymon was thoroughly unhappy. He reached the gate of the Lagny grounds without having made up his mind.

For her part, Noun, who perhaps did not expect such a prompt rely, had regained a little hope.

'He still loves me,' she said to herself. 'He doesn't want to desert me. He'd forgotten me a little; it's quite natural. In Paris, with lots of parties, the darling of all the women, as he's bound to be, he's allowed himself to be distracted for a short while away from the poor girl from the Indies. Alas! Who am I, that, for me, he should give up so many great ladies, lovelier and richer than me? Who knows?' she said to herself naïvely, 'Perhaps the Queen of France is in love with him.'

Through thinking of the seductive charms with which luxury was bound to influence her lover, Noun thought of a way of making herself more attractive to him. She decked herself out in her mistress's finery, lit a big fire in Madame Delmare's room at Lagny, decorated the mantelpiece with the most beautiful flowers she could find in the hothouse and prepared a snack of fruit and fine wines; in short she arranged all the elegant refinements of the boudoir that she had never thought of before. And when she looked at herself in a large glass panel, she did herself justice in thinking herself prettier than the flowers with which she had tried to enhance her beauty.

'He often told me I didn't need jewellery to be beautiful,' she said to herself, 'and that no lady at court, with all her sparkling diamonds, was worth one of my smiles. Yet those women he used to despise fill his mind now. Now, I must be cheerful, I must look lively and happy. Perhaps tonight I'll regain all the love I used to arouse in him.'

Having left his horse at a little charcoal burner's hut in the forest, Raymon let himself into the grounds to which he had a key. This time, he no longer ran the risk of being taken for a thief. Nearly all the servants had followed their masters; he had taken the gardener into his confidence and he knew all the paths to Lagny as well as those to his own house.

It was a cold night. A thick fog enveloped the trees in the estate and Raymon could scarcely make out their black branches in the white mist which clothed them in diaphanous robes.

He wandered for a while in the winding paths before he could find the door of the summer-house where Noun was waiting for him. She came to him wrapped in a fur-lined cloak with the hood up over her head.

'We can't stay here,' she said. 'It's too cold. Follow me and don't say anything.'

Raymon felt an extreme repugnance to enter Madame Delmare's house as her maid's lover. But he had to agree. Noun walked with a light step ahead of him and this interview would be decisive.

She led him across the courtyard, pacified the dogs, opened the doors without a sound, and, taking his hand, guided him silently through the dark corridors. Finally she took him into a simple, elegant, circular room, where flowering orange-trees were emitting their sweet fragrance and translucent candles were burning in the candelabra.

Noun had scattered Bengal rose petals on the floor; the couch was strewn with violets, a gentle warmth penetrated one's whole body, and the crystal glasses glittered on the table amongst the pieces of fruit which coquettishly showed off their rosy cheeks against the green moss of the baskets.

Dazzled by the sudden transition from darkness to a bright light, Raymon was momentarily blinded, but it did not take him long to realize where he was. All the furnishings were in exquisite taste and of a chaste simplicity; love stories and travel books were scattered on the mahogany bookshelves; on the loom was a pretty tapestry, newly worked in melancholy patience; the harp strings seemed to be still vibrating with songs of sad longing; the engravings depicted the pastoral love of Paul and Virginie, the peaks of Bourbon Island, and the blue coastline of Saint-Paul; the little bed was half-hidden by muslin curtains, the modest little white virginal bed with a palm branch like a sacred emblem at its head, taken perhaps on the day she left from some tree in her native land. It all spoke of Madame Delmare and Raymon was gripped by a

strange shudder at the thought that the cloaked woman who
had led him there was perhaps Indiana herself. This absurd
idea seemed to be confirmed when he saw a white, bejewelled
figure appear in the mirror in front of him, the ghost of a
woman who, on entering a ballroom, casts aside her cloak to
reveal herself, radiant and half-naked in the brilliant lights.
But it was only a momentary error. Indiana would have
uncovered herself less . . . Her modest bosom would have
been glimpsed only under a bodice of three layers of gauze.
She might have decorated her hair with natural camellias, but
they would not have been arranged on her head in such
provocative disorder. She might have encased her feet in satin
slippers, but her chaste dress would not have revealed like this
the secrets of her pretty legs.

Taller and of bigger build than her mistress, Noun was
dressed up rather than dressed in her fine attire. She was
graceful, but graceful without distinction; she had a woman's
beauty but not a fairy's; she suggested pleasure but gave no
promise of ecstasy.

After studying Noun in the mirror without turning his head,
Raymon cast his eyes again on everything which could give a
purer reflection of Indiana, on the musical instruments, the
paintings, and the narrow virginal bed. He became intoxicated by the gentle fragrance left by her presence in this
sanctuary; he trembled with desire as he thought of the day
when Indiana herself would reveal its delights to him. And
Noun, with folded arms, looked at him ecstatically, imagining
that he was lost in happiness at the sight of all the care she had
taken to please him.

But at last he broke the silence, saying:

'Thank you for all the preparations you've made for me.
Thank you above all for bringing me here, but I've enjoyed
this charming surprise enough now. Let's leave this room;
we're out of place, and I ought to respect Madame Delmare,
even in her absence.'

'That's very cruel,' said Noun, who had not understood
him but saw his cold, displeased look. 'It's cruelly disappoint-
ing to have hoped I would please you and to see that you reject
me.'

'No, my dear Noun, I'll never reject you. I came here to talk to you seriously and to show you the affection I owe you. I appreciate your wish to please me, but I loved you more, adorned with your youth and natural charm, than with these borrowed ornaments.'

Noun half-understood and wept.

'I am a wretched girl,' she said. 'I hate myself because you don't love me any more . . . I ought to have foreseen that you wouldn't love me for long, a poor girl like me with no education. I don't blame you for anything. I knew perfectly well that you wouldn't marry me, but if you'd continued to love me, I'd have sacrificed everything with no regrets and no complaints. Alas! I'm ruined, I'm dishonoured! Perhaps I'll be dismissed. I'm going to give life to a being who will be even more unfortunate than me and no one will pity me . . . Everyone will feel entitled to trample on me . . . Well, I'd put up happily with all that, if you still loved me.'

Noun spoke a long time in this vein. Perhaps she did not use the same words, but she said the same things, a hundred times better than I could repeat them to you. Where can one find the secret of the eloquence which a totally ignorant mind suddenly has at its command in the crisis of a true passion and a deep grief? Words then take on a different value from what they have in all other situations in life; trivial words then become sublime because of the feeling which dictates them and the tone in which they are uttered. In giving way uninhibitedly to the full extent of her emotions, a woman of the lowest class then becomes more pathetic and more persuasive than one whose upbringing has taught her moderation and reserve.

Raymon felt flattered at having aroused so warm an attachment, and gratitude, compassion, perhaps a little vanity, momentarily revived his love.

Noun was choked with tears. She had ripped the flowers from her hair, her long tresses fell in strands onto her dazzling, broad shoulders. If, as an aid to her beauty, Madame Delmare had not had her lack of freedom and her suffering, Noun would at that moment have far surpassed her mistress in beauty. She was resplendent with grief and love. Raymon, overcome, took her in his arms, sat her down beside him on the sofa, and pulled up the table laden with decanters to pour a few drops of orange-flower water into a silver cup. Comforted by this sign of concern more than by the soothing drink, Noun dried her tears, threw herself at Raymon's feet, and, passionately clasping his knees, said:

'Love me still; tell me again that you still love me and I'll recover, I'll be saved. Kiss me as you used to and I won't regret ruining myself to give you a few days' pleasure.'

She put her young, brown arms around him, she covered him with her long hair, her large black eyes looked at him with the burning languor, the ardent temperament, and the oriental sensuality which can overcome all efforts of the will, all thoughts of propriety. Raymon forgot everything, his resolutions, his new love, and where he was. He returned Noun's delirious caresses. He dipped his lips in the same cup and the heady wines which were at hand completed the loss of their reason.

Gradually the vague, floating memory of Indiana began to intrude into Raymon's intoxicated mind. The two mirrored panels reflected Noun's image endlessly from one to the other and seemed peopled by a thousand phantoms. In the depths of this double reflection he espied a more slender form, and in the last dim, blurred shadow, which was Noun's reflection in it, he thought he could see the slender, willowy form of Madame Delmare.

Noun, herself dazed by the unfamiliar intoxicating drinks, no longer understood her lover's strange language. If she had not been as drunk as he, she would have realized that at the height of his ecstasy Raymon was thinking of another. She would have seen him kiss the scarf and ribbons that Indiana had worn, breathe in the perfumes that reminded him of her, and crush in his eager hands the material that had covered her breast; but Noun took all these transports for herself, when all that Raymon saw of her was Indiana's dress. When he kissed her black hair, he believed he was kissing Indiana's black hair. It was Indiana he saw in the vapours of the punch that Noun had just set alight. It was she who was summoning him and smiling at him behind the white muslin curtains, and it was again Indiana that he dreamed of on that modest, immaculate bed when, succumbing to love and wine, he led his dishevelled Creole there.

When Raymon woke up, a half-light was filtering through the slits of the shutters and, for a long time, he remained motionless, lost in vague surprise and looking at the place where he was and the bed he had slept in as at a vision in a dream. Everything in Madame Delmare's room had been set to rights. First thing in the morning, Noun, who had fallen asleep queen of the room, had woken up a lady's maid. She had removed the flowers and cleared the remains of the refreshments. The furniture was back in place, nothing betrayed the night's orgy of love, and Indiana's room had recovered its look of innocence and modesty.

Overcome with shame, he got up and wanted to leave the room, but he was locked in. The window was thirty feet above ground and he had to stay stuck in this remorse-filled room, like Ixion* on his wheel.

Then he fell to his knees, his face pressed against the disordered, ravaged bed which made him blush.

'Oh Indiana!' he cried, wringing his hands. 'What an outrage I have committed against you! Could you ever forgive me such an infamy? Even if you were to do so, I would not forgive myself. Resist me now, gentle, trusting Indiana, for you don't know to what a vile brute you are willing to surrender the treasures of your innocence. Reject me, trample me underfoot! I have not respected the abode of your sacred modesty, I got drunk on your wines like a lackey, cheek by jowl with your maid, I sullied your gown with my accursed breath and your modest dress with my infamous kisses on another's breast. I did not fear to poison the rest of your solitary nights and to spill the effusions of seduction and adultery right onto this bed which even your husband respected. What safety will you find henceforth behind these curtains whose mystery I did not fear to profane? What impure dreams, what bitter, consuming thoughts will seep into your mind and harden your heart? What phantoms of vice and shamelessness will creep between the virginal sheets of your resting place? And your sleep, pure as a child's, what chaste divinity will be willing to protect it

now? Have I not opened the door of your alcove to the devil
of lust? Have I not sold it your soul? And the mad ardour
which inflames the limbs of that sensual Creole, will it not
come, like Deianeira's tunic,* and cling to yours and gnaw at
them? Oh guilty wretch, wretch that I am! If only I could wash
away with my blood the shame that I have left on this bed!'

And Raymon bathed it with his tears.

When Noun returned, wearing her scarf and apron, and
saw Raymon on his knees, she thought he was saying his
prayers. She did not know that society people do not say any.
So she stood, waiting silently, till he deigned to notice her
presence.

When he saw her, Raymon felt embarrassed and annoyed,
neither brave enough to scold her nor strong enough to say a
kind word to her.

'Why did you lock me in here?' he said at last. 'Do you
realize that it's broad daylight and that I can't go out without
openly compromising you?'

'So you won't go out,' said Noun affectionately. 'The house
is deserted, no one can find you. The gardener never comes to
this part of the house and I'm the only one with the keys.
You'll stay with me still today; you're my prisoner.'

This arrangement drove Raymon to despair. The only feeling he had now for his mistress was a kind of aversion. But he
had to put up with the situation and, in spite of what he was
suffering in this room, perhaps an unconquerable attraction
still held him there.

When Noun left him to go and get his breakfast, he began
to examine in the daylight all the mute testimony to Indiana's
solitude. He opened her books, leafed through her albums,
then closed them hastily, for he still feared committing
another profanation and violating feminine mysteries. Finally
he began to walk up and down, and he noticed on the wood
panel opposite Madame Delmare's bed a large, richly-framed
picture, covered with a double veil of gauze.

Perhaps it was Indiana's portrait. Raymon, eager to look at
it, forgot his scruples, climbed up onto a chair, undid the
curtain pins, and was surprised to discover the full-length
portrait of a handsome young man.

VIII

'I THINK I know that face,' he said to Noun, trying to look indifferent.

'Fie! Monsieur,' said the girl, putting down on the table the breakfast she was bringing. 'It's not nice to want to pry into my mistress's secrets.'

This idea made Raymon turn pale.

'Secrets!' he said. 'If that's a secret, it's been confided to you, Noun, and you're doubly guilty in bringing me to this room.'

'Oh no, it's not a secret,' Noun said with a smile, 'for it was M. Delmare himself who helped hang Sir Ralph's portrait on that panel. Could Madame have secrets with such a jealous husband?'

'Sir Ralph, you say? Who is Sir Ralph?'

'Sir Rodolphe Brown, Madame's cousin, her childhood friend, I could say mine as well. He's so kind.'

Raymon, surprised, examined the picture anxiously.

We have already said that Sir Ralph, apart from his facial expression, was a very handsome fellow, fair and rosy, with a good physique and abundant hair, always perfectly dressed, and able, if not to turn a romantic head, at least to satisfy the vanity of a materialistic one. The placid baronet was painted in a riding habit, almost as we saw him in the first chapter of this story, and surrounded by his dogs, the beautiful pointer Ophelia at their head, because of her lovely silvery-grey, silky coat and her pure Scottish pedigree. In one hand Sir Ralph held a hunting horn, in the other the bridle of a magnificent dapple-grey, English horse which almost filled the whole of the picture's background. It was an admirably painted portrait, a real family picture with all its perfection of detail, all its trivia of likeness, all its commonplace minutiae. It was a portrait to make a nurse weep, to make dogs bark, and to make a tailor swoon with delight. There was only one thing more insignificant than this portrait, it was the original.

Yet it aroused a feeling of violent anger in Raymon.

'What!' he said to himself. 'That stolid, young Englishman has the privilege of being admitted to Madame Delmare's inner sanctum! The picture of his insipid face is always there looking coldly down on the most intimate actions of her life! He watches over her, he protects her, he follows all her movements, she is his at any time! At night he can see her sleep and surprise the secret of her dreams; in the morning, when, all pale and trembling, she rises from her bed, he can perceive her dainty foot as she steps onto the carpet; and, when she carefully puts on her clothes, when she closes her window-curtains and even forbids the daylight to be too indiscreet in entering her room, when she thinks she's quite alone and well hidden, that insolent face is there feasting on her charms! That man in hunting-boots watches her dress.—Does that gauze usually cover this picture?' he asked the maid.

'Always,' she replied, 'when Madame's away. But don't bother putting it back; Madame's coming back in a few days.'

'In that case, Noun, you should tell her that that face has an impertinent expression . . . If I were M. Delmare, I'd have agreed to leave it here only after putting its eyes out . . . But that's what the crude jealousy of husbands is like! They imagine everything and understand nothing!'

'But what have you got against that kind M. Brown's face?' asked Noun as she made her mistress's bed. 'He's such an excellent master! I used not to like him much before, because I always heard Madame say he was selfish, but since the day he took such great care of you . . .'

'That's right,' interrupted Raymon. 'It was he who looked after me; I recognize him now . . . But I owe his concern only to Madame Delmare's intervention.'

'That's because my mistress is so kind,' said poor Noun. 'Who wouldn't become kind when they're with her?'

Whenever Noun spoke of Madame Delmare, Raymon listened to her with an interest she did not suspect.

So the day went by fairly quietly, without Noun daring to mention the real point of the conversation. At last, towards evening, she made an effort and forced Raymon to declare his intentions.

Raymon's only intention was to get rid of a dangerous accomplice and of a woman he no longer loved. But he wanted to assure her future and, apprehensively, he made her the most liberal offers . . .

This was a bitter blow to the poor girl. She tore her hair and would have battered her head against the wall if Raymon had not forcibly restrained her. Then, using all the resources of language and intelligence which nature had given him, he made her understand that it was not to her, but to the child of which she was going to be the mother, that he wanted to offer help.

'It's my duty,' he said. 'It's as an inheritance for him that I give you my help, and you would be guilty towards him if a false delicacy made you reject it.'

Noun calmed down and wiped her eyes.

'Well,' she said, 'I accept it if you will promise to go on loving me; for in fulfilling your obligations to the child, you won't be doing so for the mother. Your bounty will give *him* enough to live on, but your indifference will kill *me*. Can't you take me as a maid in your house? You see, I'm not demanding; I don't aspire to what another in my place might have had the skill to get. But let me at least be your servant. Find a place for me in your mother's house. She'll be pleased with me, I assure you, and, if you don't love me, at least I'll see you.'

'You're asking the impossible, my dear Noun. In your present condition, you can't think of being anyone's servant. And to deceive my mother, to betray her trust in me, would be something I could never agree to stoop to. Go to Lyons or Bordeaux. I undertake to see that you lack for nothing until you're fit to appear. Then I'll get you a job with someone I know, even in Paris if you like . . . if you're keen to be near me . . . but, under the same roof, that's impossible . . .'

'Impossible!' cried Noun, wringing her hands with grief. 'I see clearly that you despise me; you are ashamed of me . . . Well, I won't go far away; I won't go, humiliated and alone, to die abandoned in some distant town where you'll forget me. What does my reputation matter to me? It's your love I want to keep! . . .'

'Noun, if you're afraid I'm deceiving you, come with me. The same carriage will take us to the place you choose. I'll follow you anywhere, except to Paris, or to my mother's house; I'll follow you, I'll give you all the care I ought . . .'

'Yes, to abandon me the day after you've left me, a useless burden, in a strange country!' she said, with a bitter smile. 'No, Monsieur, no. I'm staying. I don't want to lose everything at once. To follow you, I'd have sacrificed the person I loved best in the world before I knew you. But I'm not so anxious to hide my dishonour as to sacrifice both my love and my friendship. I'll throw myself at Madame Delmare's feet, I'll tell her everything and she'll forgive me, I know; for she's kind and she loves me. We were born almost on the same day, she's my foster sister. We've never separated, she won't want me to leave her. She'll weep with me, she'll take care of me, she'll love my child, my poor child. Who knows? She hasn't the happiness of being a mother, perhaps she'll bring him up as her own . . . Oh, I was crazy to want to leave her, for she's the only person in the world who'll take pity on me.'

This decision put Raymon in a terrible dilemma, when suddenly they heard the sound of a carriage in the courtyard. Noun, terror-stricken, ran to the window.

'It's Madame Delmare!' she cried. 'Go quickly!'

In their disarray, they could not find the key to the secret staircase. Noun took Raymon's arm and hastily pulled him into the corridor, but they had not gone half way when they heard steps in the passage. Madame Delmare's voice could be heard ten steps ahead of them and a candle, carried by an accompanying servant, was already casting its flickering light on their frightened faces. Noun, still pulling Raymon, had time only to retrace her steps and go back to the bedroom with him.

A dressing room with a glass door might offer a refuge for a few moments. But there was no means of locking it and Madame Delmare might go into it as soon as she arrived. So as not to be discovered immediately, Raymon was forced to dash into the bed-recess and hide behind the curtains. It was not likely that Madame Delmare would go to bed right away, and before then, Noun might find a moment in which to contrive his escape.

Indiana came in briskly, threw her hat on the bed, and kissed Noun with the warmth of a sister. There was so little light in the room that she did not notice her companion's agitation.

'Were you expecting me, then?' Indiana asked, going up to the fire. 'How did you know I was coming?'

And, without waiting for a reply, she added,

'Monsieur Delmare will be here tomorrow. I left as soon as I got his letter. I have my reasons for welcoming him here and not in Paris. I'll tell you what they are. But say something; you don't look as pleased to see me as usual.'

'I'm unhappy,' said Noun as she knelt down to take off her mistress's shoes. 'I've got things to tell you too, but later. Now let's go into the sitting-room.'

'Heaven forbid! What an idea! It's mortally cold there.'

'No, there's a good fire.'

'You're dreaming. I've just walked through it.'

'But your supper's waiting for you.'

'I don't want any supper. In any case, there's nothing ready. Go and get my feather-boa; I've left it in the carriage.'

'Presently.'

'Why not right away? Go on!'

As she said this, she gave Noun a playful push and Noun, seeing that she had to be calm and take a risk, went out for a few moments. But she was scarcely out of the room when Madame Delmare bolted the door, took off her fur cloak, and put it on the bed beside her hat. At that moment she was so near Raymon that he tried to draw back, but the bed, evidently on castors which moved easily, gave way with a slight noise. Madame Delmare, surprised but not frightened (for she could think she herself had pushed the bed), nevertheless leaned forward, drew the curtain back a little, and, in the half-light of the fire, discovered a man's head against the wall.

Terrified, she screamed and rushed to the fireplace to ring the bell and call for help. Raymon would rather have been taken again for a thief than be recognized in this situation. But if he did not decide on the latter alternative, Madame Delmare was going to call her servants and compromise herself. He took hope in the love he had inspired in her and, dashing towards her, tried to stop her shrieks and to pull her away from the bell, saying in a low voice for fear of being overheard by Noun who could not have been far away:

'It's me, Indiana. Recognize me and pity an unhappy man who's out of his mind because of you and couldn't accept your return to your husband before seeing you once more.'

But as he was pressing Indiana in his arms, to arouse her feelings as much as to prevent her from ringing the bell, Noun, in great distress, knocked at the door. Madame Delmare, freeing herself from Raymon's arms, ran to open it and collapsed into an armchair.

Pale and half-fainting, Noun threw herself against the passage door to prevent the servants, who were going to and fro, from interrupting this strange scene. Even paler than her mistress, her knees trembling, her back pressed against the door, she awaited her fate.

Raymon felt that with a little skill he might deceive both these women simultaneously.

'Madame,' he said, going down on his knees before Indiana, 'my presence here must seem an outrage to you; I am on my knees before you to beg forgiveness. Grant me a few moments in private, and I'll explain . . .'

'Say no more, Monsieur, and leave my room,' cried Madame Delmare, recovering all the dignity of her position. 'Go openly. Noun, open that door so that all the servants can see him and all the shame of such behaviour fall on him.'

Noun, thinking her situation had been discovered, fell to her knees beside Raymon. Madame Delmare, saying nothing, looked at her with amazement.

Raymon tried to grasp her hand, but she withdrew it indignantly. Red with anger, she got up and, pointing to the door, repeated:

'Go; go, for your conduct is infamous. So that's the means you wanted to use! You, Monsieur, hidden in my room like a thief! So it's your habit to get into families like this. So that's the pure attachment you were swearing to me yesterday evening! That's how you were to protect, respect, and defend me! That's the way you worship me! You see a woman who has helped you with her own hands, who, to bring you back to life, has braved her husband's anger. You deceive her with feigned gratitude, you swear to her a love worthy of her, and as a reward for her care, as a reward for her credulity, you want to surprise her in her sleep and hasten your success by some indescribable infamy. You bribe her maid, you almost sneak into her bed like an already accepted lover. You're not afraid of letting her servants into the secret of an intimacy which doesn't exist ... Go, Monsieur, you've taken care to open my eyes very quickly. Leave, I say, don't stay another moment in my house. And you, miserable girl, who have such little respect for your mistress's honour, you deserve to be dismissed. Get away from that door, I tell you ...'

Noun, half-dead with amazement and despair, had her eyes fixed on Raymon as if to ask him for an explanation of this extraordinary mystery. Then, distraught and trembling, she dragged herself to Indiana and gripping her arm, her face contorted with anger, cried:

'What did you say? This man was in love with you?'

'You were no doubt well aware of that,' said Madame Delmare, pushing her away violently and disdainfully. 'You knew very well what motives a man can have for hiding behind a woman's bed-curtains. Oh Noun,' she added, seeing the girl's despair, 'it was an appalling thing to do and I'd never have thought you capable of it. You were willing to sell the honour of a woman who had such faith in yours! ...'

Madame Delmare was weeping, but from anger as well as from grief. Never had Raymon seen her look so beautiful, but he scarcely dared look at her, for her pride as a woman insulted made him lower his eyes. He stood there, dismayed and petrified by Noun's presence. If he had been alone with Madame Delmare, he might have been capable of softening her. But Noun's expression was terrible; her face was distorted with hate and fury.

A knock at the door startled all three of them. Noun dashed forward again to stop anyone coming in, but Madame Delmare, pushing her back with authority, ordered Raymon with a commanding gesture to withdraw to the side of the room. Then, with the coolness which made her so remarkable in moments of crisis, she wrapped a shawl round herself, half-opened the door, and asked the servant who had knocked what he had to tell her:

'M. Rodolphe Brown has just arrived,' he replied. 'He wants to know if Madame will receive him.'

'Tell M. Rodolphe that I'm delighted with his visit and that I'll join him presently. Light a fire in the drawing-room and get supper ready. Just a moment! Go and fetch me the key to the little garden gate.'

The servant went away. Madame Delmare remained standing, still holding the door half-open, not deigning to listen to Noun and imperiously imposing silence on Raymon.

The servant came back three minutes later. Madame Delmare, still holding the door between herself and M. de Ramière, took the key, told the servant to hurry up the supper, and, as soon as he had gone, turned to Raymon saying:

'My cousin, Sir Brown's arrival, saves you from the scandal to which I was going to expose you. He is a man of honour who would defend me warmly. But as I would be sorry to risk the life of a man like him against the life of a man like you, I am allowing you to go quietly. Noun, who let you in here, will know how to let you out. Go!'

'We shall meet again, Madame,' Raymon replied, making an effort to be self-assured, 'and although I'm very guilty, perhaps you'll regret the severity with which you're treating me now.'

'I hope, Monsieur, that we'll never meet again,' she replied.

And still standing, holding the door open, and without deigning to make a farewell gesture, she saw him out with his trembling, wretched accomplice.

Alone with Noun in the darkness of the grounds, Raymon expected her to reproach him. But she did not say a word. She took him to the gate of the enclosure and, when he wanted to take her hand, she had already gone. He called her quietly, for he wanted to know her decision about him, but she made no reply, and the gardener, appearing just then, said:

'Come, Monsieur, you must go. Madame has arrived and you might be discovered.'

Raymon went, in utter despair, but in his grief at having offended Madame Delmare, he almost forgot Noun and thought only of ways of appeasing her mistress; for it was in his nature to be annoyed by obstacles and to be passionately attached only to what seemed almost unattainable.

In the evening, when, after a silent supper with Sir Ralph, Madame Delmare retired to her room, Noun did not come as usual to help her undress. Indiana rang the bell in vain and, thinking it was deliberate disobedience, she closed her door and went to bed. But she had a terrible night and, as soon as day broke, she went down into the grounds. She was feverish; she needed to feel the penetrating cold and to allay the fire that was consuming her. Only the previous day, at the same time, she was happy, enjoying the novelty of an intoxicating love affair. In twenty-four hours, what awful disappointments! First of all, there was the news of her husband's return several days earlier than she expected. The four or five days she had hoped to spend in Paris were for her a whole lifetime of endless happiness, a whole dream of love from which she would never awake. But the very next morning, she had to give it up, resume her yoke, and come back to meet her master so that he would not meet Raymon at Madame de Carvajal's house; for Indiana thought it would be impossible to deceive her husband if he saw her in Raymon's presence. And then, that Raymon whom she loved like a god, it was *he* who vilely insulted her! Finally, the companion of her life, the young Creole to whom she was deeply attached, was suddenly found unworthy of her trust and esteem!

Madame Delmare had wept all night. She sank down on to the grass, still white with the morning frost, by the bank of the little river which went through the grounds. It was the end of March; nature was beginning to reawaken. Although the morning was cold, it was not without attractions; wisps of fog were still lying on the water like a floating scarf, and the birds were practising their first songs of love and spring.

Indiana felt soothed and a religious feeling filled her heart.

'It's God who willed it so,' she said to herself. 'His providence has given me a rude awakening, but it's a good fortune for me. That man might have dragged me into vice; he would have ruined me, whereas now the baseness of his feelings has been revealed to me and I'll be on my guard against the stormy, fatal passion that was raging in my breast . . . I'll love my husband . . . I'll try to! At least I'll be obedient to him, I'll make him happy by never opposing his wishes. I'll avoid everything which might arouse his jealousy; for now I know what to make of the lying eloquence that men know how to lavish on us. Perhaps I'll be happy, if God takes pity on my sorrows and soon brings me death . . .'

The sound of the mill which provided the power for M. Delmare's factory began to be heard behind the willows on the opposite bank. Ripples were already beginning to appear on the surface of the river rushing through the newly opened lock gates, and as Madame Delmare's melancholy eyes followed the swifter flow of the water, she saw, between the reeds, something like a heap of cloth which the current was trying to pull along. She got up, leaned over the water, and could see clearly a woman's clothes, clothes she knew only too well. Terror deprived her of movement, but the water flowed on, slowly dragging a corpse out of the reeds in which it had become entangled, and bringing it towards Madame Delmare.

A piercing shriek brought the factory workers to the spot. Madame Delmare had fainted on the river bank and Noun's dead body was floating on the water in front of her.

PART 2

IX

Two months have elapsed. Nothing has changed at Lagny in the house I took you into one winter's evening, except that, around its red walls edged with grey stone, and its slate roof yellowed by age-old moss, spring is in bloom. The family, in different parts of the house, is enjoying the mild, fragrant evening; the setting sun gilds the window panes and the sounds of the factory mingle with those of the farm. M. Delmare, sitting on the porch steps, is practising killing swallows in flight. Indiana, seated at her loom by the drawing-room window, leans forward from time to time to look sadly at the Colonel's cruel pastime in the courtyard. Ophelia is leaping, barking, and getting angry at a chase so alien to her habits; and Sir Ralph, astride the stone balustrade, is smoking a cigar and, as usual, looking on impassively at the pleasure or annoyance of others.

'Indiana,' exclaimed the Colonel, putting down his gun. 'Do leave your work; you tire yourself as if you were paid at so much an hour.'

'It's still broad daylight,' Madame Delmare replied.

'Never mind. Come to the window; I've something to tell you.'

Indiana obeyed, and the Colonel, going up to the window which was almost at ground level, said with the playful look typical of an elderly, jealous husband:

'Since you've worked well today and are very good, I'll tell you something that will please you.'

Madame Delmare tried to smile but the smile would have been the despair of a more sensitive man than the Colonel.

'I want to tell you,' he continued, 'that to relieve your boredom, I've invited one of your humble admirers to lunch tomorrow. You're going to ask me which one, for, you little minx, you've quite a nice collection.'

'Perhaps it's our good old parish priest?' asked Madame Delmare, who was always saddened by her husband's gaiety.

'Oh, certainly not!'

'Then it's the Mayor of Chailly or the old lawyer from Fontainebleau.'

'Oh, a woman's cunning! You know quite well that it's not one of them. Come on, Ralph, tell Madame the name that's on the tip of her tongue but that she doesn't want to say herself.'

'You don't need so many preliminaries to announce M. de Ramière,' said Sir Ralph calmly, throwing away his cigar. 'I don't suppose it matters to her.'

Madame Delmare felt the blood rush to her face. She pretended to look for something in the drawing-room and coming back, looking as calm as she could, said, trembling all over:

'I assume you're joking.'

'On the contrary, I'm quite serious. You'll see him here tomorrow at eleven o'clock.'

'What! That man who got into your property to steal your discovery, and that you almost killed like a burglar? . . . You are both very forgiving to forget such grounds for complaint.'

'You set me an example, dearest, by welcoming him so warmly at your aunt's house where he paid you a visit.'

Indiana turned pale. 'That visit wasn't on *my* account,' she said with alacrity, 'and I feel so little flattered by it that if I were you I wouldn't receive him.'

'You're all cunning liars just for the pleasure of it. I'm told you danced with him for the whole evening at a ball.'

'You're not told the truth.'

'But it was your aunt herself who told me! In any case, don't protest so much. I think it's not a bad idea, since your aunt wanted and worked for this reconciliation between us. M. de Ramière has been eager for it for a long time. Without fuss and almost without my knowledge, he's helped me a lot in my business, and as I'm not as fierce as you say, and also don't want to be obliged to a stranger, I thought I'd pay my debt to him.'

'But how?'

'By making a friend of him, by going to Cercy this morning with Sir Ralph. We met there his good old mother, a charming woman, living in a fashionable, comfortable house, but without ostentation and with none of the pride of the old families. After all, he's a good fellow, that Ramière, and I invited him to lunch with us and to visit the factory. I have good reports of his brother and I've made sure he can do me no harm in using the same methods as I do. So I'd rather this family benefit from them than any other. Anyway, secrets aren't kept for long and mine could soon be a farce if industrial progress goes in that direction.'

'You know, my dear Delmare,' said Sir Ralph, 'that it was always *my* view that this secrecy was a mistake. A good citizen's discovery belongs to his country as much as to himself, and if I . . .'

'Oh, my goodness! That's just like you with your practical philanthropy! . . . You'll make me believe your fortune doesn't belong to you and that tomorrow, if the nation takes a fancy to it, you are ready to exchange your income of fifty thousand francs for a beggar's knapsack and staff. It's fitting for a strong chap like you, who's as fond of the comforts of life as a sultan, to preach contempt for wealth!'

'I don't say that to pose as a philanthropist; it's because selfishness, properly understood, leads us to do good to people to prevent them from doing us harm. I'm selfish; that's well known. I've got used to not being ashamed of that any more and, after analysing all the virtues, I've discovered self-interest to be the basis of them all. Love and devotion, which are apparently two generous emotions, are perhaps the most self-interested of all, and patriotism is no less, you may be sure. I've no great love for mankind, but I wouldn't want to make that obvious for anything in the world; for my fear of men is in proportion to the little esteem I have for them. So we're both selfish, but I admit it and *you* deny it.'

An argument arose between them, in which, by giving all the reasons for selfishness, each one tried to prove the selfishness of the other. Madame Delmare took advantage of the situation to go to her room and give herself up to all the reflections that such unexpected news aroused in her.

I ought not only to let you into the secret of her thoughts but also to inform you of how things stood with the different people more or less affected by Noun's death.

It has almost been accepted by the reader and by me that the unfortunate girl threw herself into the river in despair in one of those moments of violent crisis when extreme decisions are easiest. But as she probably did not go back to the house after leaving Raymon, and as nobody saw her or could have an opinion on her intentions, no indication of suicide was available to explain the mystery of her death.

Two people could with certainty attribute it to a voluntary act on her part: M. de Ramière and the Lagny gardener. The former's grief was hidden under cover of illness; fear and remorse made the latter keep silent. The gardener, out of greed, had facilitated the meetings of the two lovers and only he was in a position to notice the young Creole's secret sorrows.

Rightly fearing the reproaches of his superiors and the blame of his equals, he said nothing out of self-interest and when, after discovering the affair, M. Delmare had some suspicions and questioned the gardener about the consequences it might have had during his absence, he boldly denied that it had any.

A few people in the district (it must be said that it was a very isolated region) had certainly seen Noun sometimes take the road to Cercy late in the evening, but there had been no obvious relationship between her and M. de Ramière since the end of January and she had died on the 28 March. According to this information the event could be attributed to chance. As she crossed the grounds at nightfall she might have been misled by the thick fog that had been prevalent for several days, lost her way, and missed the English bridge over the stream which, though narrow, had steep banks and was swollen by rain.

Although Sir Ralph, naturally more observant than you would think from the thoughts he expressed, might in some of his obscure innermost feelings have discovered strong grounds for suspicion against M. de Ramière, he did not mention them to anyone; he thought that any reproach addressed to a man unhappy enough to have such remorse in his life would be useless and cruel. The Colonel had expressed a doubt in this matter to Sir Ralph, who even made him feel that it was important, in Madame Delmare's delicate state of health, to continue concealing from her the possible causes of her childhood companion's suicide. So the unfortunate girl's death was treated in the same way as her love affair. There was an unspoken agreement never to speak about it in front of Indiana, and soon they even never spoke about it at all.

But these precautions were futile, for Madame Delmare, too, had her reasons for suspecting a part of the truth. The bitter reproaches she had addressed to the unhappy girl on that fatal evening seemed to her a sufficient explanation for her maid's sudden decision. So, from the terrible moment when she had been the first to see Noun's dead body floating on the water, her heart, which was already so sad, had received the final blow. Her slow illness now progressed apace, and this young woman, who was perhaps quite strong, refused to get well and hid her suffering from her husband's short-sighted and insensitive affection; she was allowing herself to die under the weight of grief and despair.

'What ill luck for me!' she cried as she went to her room after learning of Raymon's impending arrival at her home. 'A curse on that man, who came in here only to bring death and despair! Oh God! Why do you let him come between you and me, and take control of my fate as he pleases, so that he has only to stretch out his hand and say: "She's mine! I'll drive her out of her mind, I'll make her life a misery and, if she resists me, I'll spread mourning around her, I'll surround her with remorse, regrets, and fears!" Oh God! It's not fair that a poor woman should be persecuted so!'

She began to weep bitterly, for the thought of Raymon brought back to her the more vivid and devastating memory of Noun.

'My poor Noun! My poor childhood playmate! My fellow Creole, my only friend!' she said sorrowfully. 'It's that man who's your murderer. Unhappy child! He was fatal to you as to me! You, who loved me so much, who alone guessed at my sorrows and could relieve them with your innocent gaiety!

What a misfortune for me that I've lost you! Was it for that I brought you from so far away? By what wiles could that man undermine your loyalty and make you commit so base a deed? Oh, I'm sure he utterly deceived you and you understood your fault only when you saw my indignation. I was too severe, Noun. I was so severe that I was cruel. I reduced you to despair, I caused your death! Unhappy girl! Why didn't you wait a few hours till the wind had carried away my resentment against you like a light straw! Why didn't you come and weep on my bosom, saying to me: "I was deceived, I acted without knowing what I was doing but you know very well that I respect and love you"? I would have put my arms round you, we would have wept together, and you wouldn't be dead. Dead! Dead, so young, so beautiful, so full of life! Dead at nineteen years of age and with such a frightful death!'

As she mourned in this way for her companion, Indiana, without realizing it, was also mourning for the illusions of three days, the finest three days of her life, the only ones she had really lived; for during those three days she had loved with a passion that Raymon, even if he had been the most presumptuous of men, could never have imagined. But the more that love had been blind and violent, the more she felt the insult she had received; the first love of a heart like hers is so modest and sensitive!

But Indiana had given way more to a movement of shame and anger than to a well thought out determination. I am sure Raymon would have been granted a pardon if he had had a few more moments in which to beg for it. But fate had thwarted his love and his skill, and Madame Delmare sincerely believed that from now on she hated him.

She began to weep bitterly, for the thought of Raymon brought back to her the more vivid and the vast this memory of Noun.

'My poor colour! My poor childhood playmate! My fellow Creole, my only friend,' she said sorrowfully, 'it was that man who's your murderer. Unhappy child! He was fatal to you as to me! You, who loved me so much, who alone guessed at my sorrows and could relieve them with your innocent gaiety,

I now hates R

X

As for Raymon, it was not out of boastfulness or hurt pride that he aspired more than ever to Madame Delmare's love and forgiveness. He thought they were unattainable, and the love of no other woman, no other happiness on earth, seemed worthwhile. He was made that way. His life was consumed by an insatiable need for exciting events and emotions. He loved society with its rules and its shackles because it offered him opportunities for struggle and resistance, and if he hated disorder and violence, it was because they promised insipid, easy pleasures.

Do not think, however, that he was insensitive to Noun's death. At first he detested himself and loaded his pistols with the very serious intention of blowing his brains out, but a praiseworthy feeling held him back. What would become of his mother . . . his elderly mother, in poor health . . . that poor woman whose whole life had been so troubled and so full of sorrow, who lived only for him, her only asset, her only hope? Must he break her heart, shorten her few remaining days? Definitely not. The best way to atone for his crime was to devote himself henceforth entirely to his mother, and it was with this in mind that he went back to her in Paris and put all his efforts into making her forget the kind of neglect in which he had left her for a great part of the winter.

Raymon had an incredible sway over everyone around him, for, all in all, he was, despite his faults and youthful peccadilloes, a superior man in society. We have not told you on what his reputation for wit and talent was based, because that was unconnected with the events that we had to relate. But the time has come to tell you that this Raymon, whose failings you have just read about, is one of the men who have had the most power and influence over your thoughts, whatever your opinion may be today. You have read his political pamphlets eagerly and, as you read the newspapers of the day, you have often been beguiled by the irresistible charm of his style and the graceful expression of his courteous, sophisticated reasoning.

I am speaking of a time that's already far distant from us, in these days when we no longer count by centuries, nor even by reigns, but by ministries. I am speaking to you of the year when Martignac* was Minister of the Interior, of that period of calm and doubt, thrust right into the middle of our political period, not as a peace treaty, but as an agreed armistice, of those fifteen months of the reign of doctrines which had such a marked influence on principles and behaviour and which perhaps paved the way for the strange outcome of our last revolution.*

It was at this time that one saw the flowering of young talents, unhappy at being born in days of transition and compromise, for they made their contribution to the conciliatory and flexible attitudes of the period. Never, so far as I know, had one seen skill with words and ignorance or concealment of reality taken to such lengths. It was the reign of prohibitions and I do not know what kind of people abused them most, Jesuits in short gowns or lawyers in long ones. Political moderation had entered into behaviour like good manners, and the first kind of courtesy had the same fate as the second: it served to mask hostile groups and taught them to fight without scandal and without fuss. But it must be said in exoneration of the young men of that period, that they were often taken in tow like small boats by big ships, without knowing where they were being led, proud and happy to cut through the waters and fill their new sails.

Placed by his birth and fortune amongst the partisans of absolute monarchy,* Raymon conformed to the prevalent views of his day by adhering religiously to the charter;* at least that is what he thought he was doing and what he tried to prove. But agreements which have lapsed can be interpreted in different ways, and that was already the case with the Charter of Louis XVIII as it was with the Gospel of Jesus Christ; it had become no more than a text that everyone liked to declaim about, with no speech having more effect than a sermon. It was a period of luxury and idleness when, on the edge of a bottomless abyss, civilization was falling asleep, greedy to enjoy its last pleasures.

Raymon, then, had taken up a position on a kind of middle line between the abuse of power and license, a moving territory where upright men were still seeking shelter against the approaching storm, though in vain. To him, as to many other inexperienced minds, the role of conscientious publicist still seemed possible. That was a mistake at a time when there was a pretence of listening to the voice of reason only the better to stifle it on all sides. A man with no political passions, Raymon thought he was not self-interested, and he deceived himself; for society, as it was then organized, was favourable and advantageous to him; it could not be disturbed without the sum of his comfort being diminished, and the perfect stability of a life style, linked to one's way of thinking, is a marvellous lesson in moderation. What man is so ungrateful to Providence as to reproach it with the misfortunes of others, if it has had only smiles and benefits for him? How could one persuade these young supporters of constitutional monarchy that the constitution was already out of date, that it was a burden on the body politic and wearied it, when they found it weighed lightly on them and they reaped only its advantages? Who believes in poverty when he has no experience of it?

Nothing is so easy or so common as self-deception when one does not lack intelligence and is familiar with all the subtleties of language. It is like a queen turned into a prostitute who, demeaning and raising herself, plays all parts, who disguises herself and decks herself in finery, dissembles and conceals herself; it is like a litigant who has an answer to everything, who has always foreseen everything, and has a thousand ways of being right. The most honest of men is the one who thinks and acts best, but the most powerful is the one who writes and speaks best.

Because of his wealth, Raymon did not need to write for money. Raymon wrote because he wanted to and (so he said in all good faith) out of duty. He possessed the rare ability of refuting established facts; this talent had made him a very valuable man to the ministry, which he served much better by his impartial criticism than did its creatures by their blind devotion. He was even more valuable to those elegant young people who were very willing to renounce the absurdities of their old privileges but who also wanted to retain the benefit of their existing advantages.

Indeed they were very talented, those men who still prevented society from collapsing and who themselves, stranded between two rocks, fought calmly and with ease against the harsh truth which was about to engulf them. To succeed thus in convincing oneself against all probability and in making that conviction prevail for a time amongst men who have none, that is the art which is the most puzzling of all, and beyond the comprehension of a rough, blunt mind which has not studied alternative truths.

Raymon had then no sooner returned to this society, the element he was born into, than he felt its vital, stimulating influence. The petty interests of love which had preoccupied him gave way for a moment to wider, more brilliant interests. He brought to them the same boldness and the same enthusiasms, and when he saw himself sought after by the most distinguished people in Paris, he felt that he loved life more than ever. Was he guilty for forgetting a secret remorse so as to reap the reward he deserved for services rendered to his country? In his youthful heart, in his active mind, in all his vigorous, healthy being, he felt life overflowing from all his pores, and destiny making him happy in spite of himself. Then he would ask pardon of an angry spirit which, in his dreams, sometimes came to lament, seeking assistance against the terrors of the grave in the affection of the living.

He had no sooner returned to society life than, as in the past, he felt the need to mingle thoughts of love and plans for love affairs with his political reflections and his intellectual and ambitious dreams. I say ambition, not for honours and money, which did not interest him, but for reputation and aristocratic popularity.

Initially, after the tragic outcome of his double intrigue, he had despaired of ever seeing Madame Delmare again. But as he measured the extent of his loss, his thoughts brooding over the treasure which eluded him, he conceived the hope of recovering it, and at the same time he recovered his determination and his confidence. He calculated the obstacles he would encounter and realized that, to start with, the difficulty to overcome would stem from Indiana herself. So he had to make the husband safeguard the attack. It was not a new idea, but it was a sure one; jealous husbands are particularly suited to this kind of service.

A fortnight after conceiving the idea, Raymon was on his way to Lagny, where he was expected to lunch. You will not insist on my giving you a factual account of the skilfully rendered services by which he had found the means of making himself agreeable to M. Delmare; I prefer, since I am telling you about the characters of the people in this story, to give you a brief outline of the Colonel's.

Do you know what provincial people mean by a *decent man*? It is someone who does not encroach on his neighbour's field, who does not demand from his debtors a penny more than they owe him, who lifts his hat to any person who greets him. It is someone who does not rape girls on the public highway, who does not set fire to anyone's barns, who does not rob anyone in a corner of his estate. Provided he respects religiously the lives and purses of his fellow citizens, nothing else is asked of him. He might beat his wife, ill-treat his servants, ruin his children, that's no one else's business. Society only condemns deeds which are harmful to it; private life is not in its domain.

That was M. Delmare's moral philosophy. He had never studied any social contract other than this one: *Everyone for himself*. He treated all emotional sensitivity as feminine childishness and sentimental hairsplitting. A man without intelligence, tact, or education, he enjoyed a more substantial esteem than that which can be obtained by talents and kindness. He was broad-shouldered and strong-fisted; he could handle a broadsword or a rapier perfectly and, what is more, he was extremely touchy. As he did not always understand a joke, he was obsessed by the idea that he was being laughed at. As he could not give a suitable reply, he only had one way of defending himself; that was to impose silence by threats. His favourite epigrams were always concerned with beatings to be given or affairs of honour to be settled. Because of this, provincial people always coupled his name with the epithet *brave*, because military bravery is evidently to have broad shoulders and a large moustache, to swear loudly and to put one's hand on one's sword for the smallest matter.

May God preserve me from believing that life in military camps turns all men into brutes! But you must let me think that one needs a great reservoir of good breeding to resist those habits of brutal, passive domination. If you have been a serving soldier, you are perfectly familiar with what soldiers call a *Colonel Blimp*, and you will admit that there are a lot of them amongst the remnants of the old Imperial cohorts.* These men who, when gathered together and urged forward by a powerful hand, performed such magical exploits and grew like giants in the smoke of battle, were, however, no longer heroes when they returned to civilian life but merely soldiers, bold, rough fellows who reasoned like machines; one had to be satisfied if they did not behave in society as in a conquered land. It was the fault of the age, not theirs. Naïve souls, they believed the extravagant praise of their glory and allowed themselves to be persuaded that they were great patriots because they were defending their native land, some because they were forced to, others for money and honours. But in any case, how did they defend it, these thousands of men who espoused blindly the mistakes of one single man and who, after saving France, lost it so abjectly? And then, if soldiers' devotion to their captain seems to you great and noble, so be it; it seems so to me too, but I call that fidelity, not patriotism. I congratulate the conquerors of Spain* but I don't thank them. As for the honour of the French name, I don't in the least understand that way of affirming it to our neighbours, and I find it difficult to believe that, at that sad period of our glory, the Emperor's generals were very imbued with it. But I know I am not allowed to talk impartially of these matters. I say no more; posterity will judge.

M. Delmare had all the good qualities and all the failings of such men. Childishly simple about some delicate points of honour, he knew very well how to do the best for his own interests without worrying about the benefit or the harm that might be the consequence for others. His only conscience was the law; his only morality was his right. He had one of those unemotional, unshakably honest temperaments which borrow nothing for fear of not being able to repay, and which lend nothing for fear of not recovering the debt. He was the honest man who takes nothing and gives nothing, who would rather die than take a twig from the King's forest,* but who would kill you there and then for a straw picked up in his own. Useful only to himself, he was harmful to no one. He did not interfere with anything going on around him for fear of being forced to render service to someone. But when he thought his honour required him to do so, no one performed it with greater zeal or more candid chivalry. Trusting as a child and suspicious as a tyrant, he believed a false pledge and was suspicious of a sincere promise. Only formalities mattered to him, as is the case in the military profession. He was so dominated by public opinion that good sense and reason played no part in his decisions, and when he had said 'That's the done thing', he thought he had expressed an argument to which there was no reply.

His temperament was thus as antipathetic as possible to his wife's, his heart the least constituted to understand her, his mind the most incapable of appreciating her. But slavery had undoubtedly made her feel a kind of dumb, virtuous aversion for him which was not always fair. Madame Delmare had too many doubts about her husband's heart; he was only hard and she thought he was cruel. There was more boorishness than anger in his rages, more coarseness than insolence in his manners. He was not naturally nasty; he had moments of pity which made him repentant, and when he repented he was almost sensitive. It was military camp life that had raised brutality to a principle with him. With a less courteous and less gentle wife he would have been timid like a tamed wolf. But Indiana was disheartened by her lot; she made no effort to try to make it better.

XI

As he got out of his tilbury in the courtyard at Lagny, Raymon felt his courage fail him. So he was about to re-enter the house which brought back such terrible memories! His reasoning, in agreement with his passions, might enable him to dominate his emotions but not to stifle them, and just then the feeling of remorse was as keen as that of desire.

The first person who came out to meet him was Sir Ralph Brown and when Raymon saw him in his eternal riding habit, flanked by his dogs and solemn as a Scottish laird, he thought he saw the portrait he had discovered in Madame Delmare's room come to life. A few moments later the Colonel arrived and lunch was served without Indiana's making an appearance. As he crossed the vestibule, passed by the billiard room, and recognized the places that he had seen in such different circumstances, Raymon felt so awful that he barely remembered his purpose in coming now.

'Does Madame Delmare definitely not want to come down to lunch?' the Colonel asked his factotum Lelièvre rather crossly.

'Madame slept badly,' replied Lelièvre, 'and Mademoiselle Noun . . . (oh dear, I can't get that irritating name out of my head) Mademoiselle Fanny, I mean, said that Madame was resting now.'

'Then how is it that I've just seen her at her window? Fanny has made a mistake. Go and tell Madame that lunch is served . . . or rather, Sir Ralph, my dear cousin, be so good as to go upstairs and see for yourself if your cousin is really unwell.'

If the unfortunate name which the servant let slip out of habit made Raymon's nerves tingle painfully, the Colonel's expedient gave them a strange feeling of anger and jealousy.

'Into her room!' he thought. 'He doesn't limit himself to putting Sir Ralph's portrait there; he sends him there in person. That Englishman has rights here which the husband himself seems not to dare to claim.'

As if he had guessed Raymon's thought, M. Delmare said:

'Don't let that surprise you; M. Brown is the family doctor, and then he's our cousin, a good fellow whom we love with all our hearts.'

Ralph was away a good ten minutes. Raymon was absent-minded, ill at ease. He didn't eat; he often looked towards the door. Finally the Englishman reappeared.

'Indiana is really not at all well,' he said. 'I've advised her to go back to bed.'

He sat calmly down to lunch and ate with a hearty appetite. The Colonel did likewise.

'It's definitely a pretext not to see me,' thought Raymon. 'These two men are not taken in and the husband is more displeased than worried about his wife's condition. That's a good sign and things are going more in my favour than I had expected.'

The difficulty strengthened his resolve, and the image of Noun was wiped away from the gloomy wainscoting which at first sight had made him freeze with terror. Soon he had only a vision of the slender form of Madame Delmare wandering along it. In the drawing-room he sat down at her loom, studied the flowers of her tapestry (chatting the while and pretending to be preoccupied), touched all the silk threads, and breathed in the fragrance that her little fingers had left on it. He had seen this work already in Indiana's room; then it had scarcely been begun, now it was covered with flowers which had opened up under her feverish breath and were watered by her daily tears. Raymon felt that he himself was on the verge of tears, and by means of some inexplicable sympathy, as he sadly raised his eyes to the horizon that Indiana habitually studied in her melancholy, he could see in the distance the white walls of Cercy which stood out against a background of brown countryside.

The Colonel's voice aroused him with a start.

'Come, good neighbour,' he said, 'it's time to fulfil my obligations to you and to keep my promises. The factory is going at full blast and the workmen are all on the job. Here are pencil and paper so that you can take notes.'

Raymon followed the Colonel, examined the factory with eager interest, made remarks which showed that he was equally familiar with chemistry and mechanical engineering, listened with unimaginable patience to M. Delmare's endless disquisitions, agreed with some of his ideas, disagreed with others, and in every way behaved so as to show convincingly that he was greatly interested in these matters, while he was barely thinking of them and all his thoughts were directed towards Madame Delmare.

To tell the truth, no science was unfamiliar to him, no discovery indifferent. Besides, he was serving the interests of his brother, who had really put all his capital into a similar, though much larger, enterprise. M. Delmare's precise knowledge, the only kind of superiority he had, provided the best subject to pursue in the conversation at this moment.

Sir Ralph, not much of a businessman, but a very wise politician, added economic considerations of quite a high order to the examination of the factory. The workmen, anxious to show their skills to a connoisseur, surpassed themselves in their understanding and in their activity. Raymon saw everything, understood everything, and replied to everything, but thought only of the love affair which brought him to this place.

When they had exhausted the topic of the mechanism inside the factory, they fell to discussing the volume and strength of the flow of water. They went out and, climbing on to the lockgate, asked the foreman to raise the barriers and ascertain the variations of the water-level.

'Monsieur, if I may say so,' said the foreman, turning to M. Delmare who was fixing the maximum at fifteen feet, 'this year we saw seventeen.'

'And when was that? You're mistaken,' said the Colonel.

'I beg your pardon, Monsieur. It was the evening before your return from Belgium. Yes, it was the night that Mademoiselle Noun was found drowned. You can tell from the fact that the body passed over the dam down there and only stopped here where Monsieur is standing.'

As he was animatedly expressing this opinion, the workman pointed to the spot where Raymon was standing. The unhappy young man became pale as death. He cast a frightened look at the water which was flowing at his feet. It seemed to him that he could see her ghastly pale face reflected in it. He was overcome by giddiness and he would have fallen into the river if M. Brown had not taken him by the arm and dragged him away.

'Agreed,' said the Colonel, who noticed nothing and was thinking so little of Noun that he had no inkling of Raymon's condition. But that's an extraordinary case and the average strength of the flow is . . . But what the devil is wrong with you two?' he asked, stopping suddenly.

'Nothing,' replied Sir Ralph. 'As I turned round I stepped on Monsieur's foot. I'm terribly sorry; I must have hurt him a lot.'

Sir Ralph made this reply so calmly and naturally that Raymon was convinced that the Englishman thought he was telling the truth. A few polite remarks were exchanged and the conversation resumed its course.

Raymon left Lagny a few hours later without seeing Madame Delmare. That was better than he expected. He was afraid he would see her calm and indifferent.

He went back to Lagny, however, without being any more fortunate. This time the Colonel was alone. Raymon employed all his mental resources to propitiate him and skilfully descended to his level in a thousand ways. He lauded Napoleon, whom he did not like, deplored the indifference of the government, which neglected and, in a way, almost poured contempt on the illustrious remnants of the *Grande Armée*; he pushed opposition to the government as far as his opinions would allow and, amongst several of his convictions, he chose those which could flatter M. Delmare's. He even made up a character for himself different from his real one so as to attract the Colonel's trust. He transformed himself into a *bon vivant*, an easy-going companion, a carefree good-for-nothing.

'If that man ever makes a conquest of my wife! . . .' the Colonel said to himself as he saw him going away.

Then he began to chuckle to himself and to think that Raymon was a *charming fellow*.

Madame de Ramière was then at Cercy. Raymon praised Madame Delmare's charms and wit to his mother and, without asking her to visit Indiana, had the skill to make her think of doing so.

'Indeed,' she said, 'she's the only one of my neighbours I don't know, and since I've recently settled in the district, it's for me to begin. We'll go to Lagny next week together.'

The appointed day came.

'She can't avoid me any more,' thought Raymon.

Indeed, Madame Delmare could no longer shrink from the necessity of receiving him. When she saw an elderly lady she did not know getting out of a carriage, she even came to meet her on the steps of the house. At the same time she recognized Raymon in the man who was with her, but she realized that he had deceived his mother to induce her to take this step, and the displeasure this aroused in her gave her the strength to be calm and dignified. She received Madame de Ramière with a mixture of respect and affability, but her coldness towards Raymon was so icy that he felt unable to stand it for long. He was not used to being treated with disdain and his pride was hurt at not being able to conquer with a glance the contempt with which Indiana armed herself against him. So, making up his mind like a man to whom a caprice was of no consequence, he asked if he might join M. Delmare in the grounds and left the two women together.

Gradually Indiana, conquered by the captivating charm which a superior mind combined with a noble and generous heart can deploy in its slightest relationships, became, in her turn, kind, affectionate, and almost light-hearted with Madame de Ramière. She had not known her mother, and Madame de Carvajal, in spite of her gifts and her praise, was far from being one to her, so her heart was in a way fascinated by Raymon's mother.

When Raymon rejoined his mother, just as he was going back into the carriage, he saw Indiana carry to her lips the hand Madame de Ramière held out to her. Poor Indiana felt the need to become attached to somebody. Everything which offered her a hope of interest and affection in her lonely unhappy life was received by her with delight, and, moreover, she told herself that Madame de Ramière was going to keep her from falling into the trap into which Raymon wanted to push her.

'I'll throw myself into the arms of that excellent woman,' she was already thinking, 'and, if necessary, I'll tell her everything. I'll beg her to save me from her son, and her prudence will watch over him and me.'

That was not how Raymon reasoned.

'My good mother!' he said to himself as he returned to Cercy with her. 'Her charm and goodness work miracles. What a lot I owe her already! My education, my success in life, the esteem of society. I only lacked the happiness of owing her the heart of a woman like Indiana.'

As you can see, Raymon loved his mother because of his need for her and of the good things he received from her. That's how all children love their mothers.

Some days later, Raymon received an invitation to go and spend three days at Bellrive, a magnificent, charming house between Cercy and Lagny, belonging to Sir Ralph Brown. With the co-operation of the best huntsmen of the neighbourhood, the owner wanted to destroy some of the game which was consuming his woods and gardens. Raymon did not like Sir Ralph, nor did he care for hunting, but Madame Delmare acted as her cousin's hostess for big parties, and the hope of meeting her made it easy for Raymon to decide to go.

The fact is that, this time, Sir Ralph did not expect Madame Delmare; she had excused herself on the grounds of the bad state of her health. But the Colonel, who got into a bad mood when his wife seemed to be looking for some entertainment, got into an even worse one when she refused the entertainment he was willing to allow her.

'Do you want the whole neighbourhood to think I keep you under lock and key?' he asked. 'You make people think I'm a jealous husband; that's a ridiculous role and I don't want to play it any longer. In any case, what is the meaning of this lack of consideration for your cousin? When we owe him the establishment and prosperity of our business, it is not fitting for you to refuse him such a little service. He needs you and you hesitate! I don't understand your whims. All the people I dislike, you make very welcome, but those I esteem have the misfortune not to please you.'

'It seems to me that's a very ill-deserved reproach,' replied Madame Delmare. 'I love my cousin like a brother and our friendship was already an old one when yours had just begun.'

'Your fine words are all very well, but I know that you don't think the poor devil's sentimental enough. You regard him as selfish because he doesn't like novels and doesn't weep at a dog's death. Anyway, it's not only him I'm talking about. How did you receive M. de Ramière? 'Pon my word, he's a charming young man. When Madame de Carvajal introduces him to you, you receive him splendidly, but when I have the misfortune to want to be nice to him, you find him intolerable, and when he comes to your home, you go to bed. Do you want people to think I'm a man who doesn't know how to behave? It's time for this to stop and for you to begin to live like the rest of the world.'

Raymon judged that it would not help his plans for him to show too much eagerness to come. Threats of indifference succeed with nearly all women who think they are loved. But the hunt had already been under way since early morning when he arrived at Sir Ralph's house, and Madame Delmare was not due to arrive till dinner-time. In the meantime he thought out his course of action.

He realized that he must find a way of vindicating himself, for the decisive moment was drawing near. He had two days in front of him and he divided out his time in the following way: during what remained of the day that was nearly over he must arouse her emotions, on the next day he must persuade her, and on the third day he would be happy. He even looked at his watch and calculated, almost to the hour, the chances of success or failure of his undertaking.

XII

HE had been in the drawing-room for two hours when he heard Madame Delmare's gentle, slightly husky voice in the neighbouring room. Through thinking about his seduction plan, he had become enthusiastic about it like an author for his subject or a lawyer for his case, and his emotion on seeing Indiana could be compared to that of an actor engrossed in his part who, finding himself face to face with the principal character of the play, can no longer distinguish between the artificialities of the stage and reality.

She was so altered that a feeling of genuine concern nevertheless slipped into Raymon's excited mind. Grief and illness had been so strongly imprinted on her face that she was almost not pretty any more, and there was more glory than pleasure in undertaking to conquer her ... But Raymon owed it to himself to give her back happiness and life.

When he saw her so sad and pale, he thought he would not have to fight against a very strong will. So frail an exterior could not conceal a strong moral power of resistance.

He thought he must first arouse her interest in herself, frighten her with her ill-fortune and her wasted condition, so that he could then arouse in her heart the desire and the hope for a better fate.

'Indiana,' he said with a secret self-confidence completely hidden beneath a look of deep sadness, 'so this is how I was to see you again! I didn't know that the moment I've so long awaited and so eagerly sought would bring me such terrible pain!'

Madame Delmare did not at all expect this kind of language. She thought she would find Raymon in the position of an ashamed and guilty man before her, and, instead of accusing himself, of telling her of his repentance and grief, his sorrow and pity was for her alone! So she must look very depressed and very worn, since she aroused pity in the man who ought to have been begging for hers!

A Frenchwoman, someone used to society life, would not have lost her head in such a delicate situation. But Indiana did not know how to behave. She had neither the skill nor the deceitfulness required to retain the advantage of her position. His language brought to her mind the whole range of her suffering, and her eyes glistened with tears.

'I am indeed ill,' she said as, weak and weary, she sat down on the armchair that Raymon brought forward for her! 'I feel very ill, and in your presence, Monsieur, I have the right to complain.'

Raymon had not expected to make such quick progress. He took the bull by the horns, as they say, and grasping a hand that he thought cold and lifeless, he said:

'Indiana, don't say that, don't say that I'm the author of your ills, for you'd make me mad with grief and joy.'

'Joy!' she repeated staring at him, her large blue eyes filled with sadness and amazement.

'I ought to have said hope, for if I'm the cause of your sorrows, Madame, perhaps I can put an end to them. Say one word,' he added, going on his knees beside her on one of the divan cushions which had just fallen down, 'ask me for my blood, my life . . .'

'Oh, say no more!' said Indiana, withdrawing her hand. 'You have made a horribly bad use of promises, so try to repair the harm you have done.'

'I want to, I will!' he exclaimed, trying to regain her hand.

'It's too late,' she said. 'Give me back my companion, my sister; give me back Noun, my only friend.'

A mortal chill coursed through Raymon's veins. This time, he did not need to exaggerate his emotion; there are some, terrible and powerful, which are aroused unaided by art.

'She knows everything,' he thought, 'and she passes judgement on me.'

Nothing was so humiliating for him as to be reproached for his crime by the woman who had been his innocent accomplice, nothing so bitter as to see Noun mourned by her rival.

'Yes,' said Indiana, lifting her head, her face bathed in tears, 'it's your doing . . .'

But she stopped short when she saw Raymon's white face. It must have been terrifying, for he had never before suffered so much.

Then all the goodness of her heart and all the involuntary affection he aroused in Madame Delmare regained their ascendancy over her.

'Forgive me,' she said, frightened. 'I'm hurting you a lot. I've suffered so much. Sit down and let's talk of something else.'

This sudden expression of generous kindness intensified Raymon's emotion. Sobs escaped him; he raised Indiana's hand to his lips and covered it with tears and kisses. This was the first time he had been able to weep since Noun's death and it was Indiana who was relieving his heart from the terrible weight.

'Oh, since you mourn her so,' she said, 'you, who didn't know her, since you so keenly regret the harm you've done me, I daren't reproach you any more. Let us mourn her together, Monsieur, so that from heaven above she can see us and forgive us!'

A cold sweat broke out on Raymon's forehead. If those words: *You who didn't know her* had delivered him from a cruel anxiety, this appeal to his victim's memory, in Indiana's innocent mouth, struck him with superstitious terror. Overcome, he got up; in a state of agitation he went to a window and sat down on the sill to get his breath. When she saw Raymon weeping like a child and turn faint like a woman, she felt a kind of secret joy.

'He's kind,' she said to herself, 'he loves me; his heart is warm and generous. He has done wrong, but his repentance absolves him and I ought to have pardoned him sooner.'

She looked at him affectionately, she regained her trust in him. She mistook the guilty man's remorse for the tenderness of love.

'Don't cry any more,' she said, getting up and going to him. 'It's I who killed her, I alone am guilty. Remorse for this will weigh on me all my life. I gave in to an emotion of angry suspicion. I humiliated her, wounded her to the heart. I vented on her all the anger I felt against you. It was you alone who had insulted me and I punished my poor friend. I was very hard on her.'

'And on me,' said Raymon, suddenly forgetting the past and thinking only of the present.

Madame Delmare blushed.

'Perhaps I ought not to have blamed you for the cruel loss I suffered that night,' she said. 'The insensitivity of such a romantic and guilty plan hurt me greatly . . . I thought you loved me then . . . and you didn't even respect me!'

Raymon regained his strength, his will-power, his love, his hopes; the fatal impression which had made him turn cold vanished like a nightmare. He awoke, young, ardent, full of desire, passion, and hope for the future.

'I am guilty if you hate me,' he said, eagerly throwing himself at her feet. 'But if you love me, I'm not, I never have been. Tell me, Indiana, do you love me?'

'Do you deserve my love?' she said.

'If, to deserve it, I must love you with adoration . . .' said Raymon.

'Listen to me,' she said, letting him take her hands and turning to him her large moist eyes, in which from time to time there shone a melancholy gleam, 'listen to me. Do you know what it means to love a woman like me? No, you don't know. You thought it was just a matter of satisfying a passing whim. You judged my heart in the light of all those blasé hearts over which, till now, you exercised your ephemeral sway. You don't know that I haven't yet been in love, that I won't give all my virgin heart for a heart that is withered and ruined, my enthusiastic love for a love that is lukewarm, my whole life in exchange for one short day!'

'Madame, I love you passionately. My heart is young and ardent, and if it is not worthy of yours, no man's heart will ever be. I know how you must be loved; I didn't wait till today to understand that. Don't I know what your life is like? Didn't I tell you at the ball, the first time I could speak to you? Didn't I read the whole story of your heart in the first glance you let fall on me? And so what do you think I'm in love with? Just with your beauty? Oh, certainly, you're lovely enough to make an older, less passionate man lose his head. But if *I* adore your dainty, charming appearance, it's because beneath it there lies a pure, divine soul, because it is animated by a heavenly fire, because in you I see not only a woman but an angel.'

'I know you possess the gift of praising people, but don't hope to arouse my vanity. It's affection I need, not homage. I must be loved absolutely, eternally, unreservedly. You must be ready to sacrifice everything for me, fortune, reputation, duty, business affairs, principles, family, everything, Monsieur, because I would put the same devotion on the scales and I want yours to equal mine. You must see that you can't give me that sort of love.'

It was not the first time that Raymon saw a woman take love seriously, although, fortunately for society, such cases are rare; but he knew that promises of love are not binding on a man's honour, again fortunately for society. Sometimes, too, the woman who had demanded these solemn pledges from him was the first to break them. So he was not frightened by Madame Delmare's demands, or rather, he did not think of the past or of the future. He was carried away by the irresistible charm of this frail, passionate woman, so weak in body but so strong in heart and mind. She was so beautiful, so animated, so impressive, as she laid down her rules that he stayed, as it were spellbound, at her knees.

'I swear to be yours body and soul,' he said. 'I dedicate my life to you, I devote my blood to you, I abandon my will to you. Take everything, everything is at your disposal, my fortune, my honour, my conscience, my thoughts, my whole being.'

'Be quiet, here's my cousin,' said Indiana agitatedly.

And indeed the phlegmatic Ralph Brown came in quite calmly and said he was very surprised and happy to see his cousin, whom he had not expected. Then he asked to be allowed to kiss her to show his gratitude and, leaning towards her, slowly and methodically, he kissed her on the lips according to the custom of the natives of their country.

Raymon turned pale with anger, and Ralph had barely left the room to give some orders when he went up to Indiana and wanted to wipe out the trace of that impertinent kiss. But Madame Delmare repulsed him calmly, saying:

'Remember you have a long way to go to repair your wrongs towards me if you want me to believe in you.'

Raymon did not appreciate how tactful this refusal was; in it he saw only a refusal and became angry with Sir Ralph. Some moments later, he noticed that when Ralph spoke quietly to Indiana, he said 'tu', and Raymon nearly took the reserve which convention imposed on Ralph at other times for the prudence of a happy lover. But he was soon ashamed of his insulting suspicions as he met the pure look in Indiana's eyes.

In the evening, Raymon deployed his intellectual gifts. There was a large company and they listened to him. He could not escape from the importance his talents bestowed on him. He talked a lot, and if Indiana had been vain she would have had her first taste of happiness in listening to him. But, on the contrary, her straightforward, upright mind took fright at Raymon's superiority. She fought against the magic power he exercised on those around him, a kind of magnetic influence given by heaven or hell to some men, a partial and ephemeral sovereignty, so real that no ordinary person can resist its ascendancy, so fleeting that no trace survives them and after their deaths we are surprised at the reputations they had in their lifetime.

There were many moments when Indiana felt fascinated by so much brilliance, but she immediately told herself sadly that it was not glory but happiness she was thirsting for. She wondered in alarm if this man, for whom life had so many different aspects, would be able to devote all his heart to her, sacrifice to her all his ambitions. And now that, with so much ability and skill, so much ardour and so much coolness, he was defending purely speculative doctrines entirely alien to their love, she took fright at being of so little account in his life while he was everything in hers. Terrified, she told herself that for him she was a three-day whim, but for her he had been the dream of a lifetime.

When he gave her his arm to leave the drawing-room, he slipped a few words of love into her ear, but she replied sadly:

'You're very clever!'

Raymon understood this reproach and spent all the next day at Madame Delmare's feet. The other guests, busy with the hunt, left them in complete liberty.

Raymon was eloquent; Indiana had so great a need to believe him that half his eloquence would have been enough. Women of France, you do not know what a Creole is like. No doubt you would have been convinced less easily, for you are not the one who is being deceived and betrayed!

XIII

WHEN Sir Ralph returned from the hunt and, as usual, took
Madame Delmare's pulse as he greeted her, Raymon, who
was watching him closely, noticed a faint expression of surprise and pleasure on his calm features. And then, obeying
some kind of inner compulsion, the eyes of the two men met
and Sir Ralph's light eyes, fixed like an owl's on Raymon's
dark ones, made the latter lower his involuntarily. For the rest
of the day, in spite of his apparent imperturbability, the baronet's face, when he was with Madame Delmare, had a kind
of attentive look, something that one might have called interest or concern, if his features had been capable of revealing
any specific feeling. But Raymon tried in vain to discover if
there was fear or hope in Sir Ralph's thoughts; they were
impenetrable.

Suddenly, as he was standing a few steps behind Madame
Delmare's chair, he heard Ralph say to her quietly,

'It would be a good idea, cousin, for you to go riding
tomorrow.'

'But you know that, for the moment, I've no horse,' she
replied.

'We'll find one for you. Would you like to follow the hunt
with us?'

Madame Delmare sought different pretexts to excuse herself from going. Raymon realized that she preferred to stay
with him, but he thought he noticed, too, that her cousin was
unusually insistent on preventing her from doing so. Then,
leaving the group he was with, he came up to her and added
his entreaties to Sir Ralph's. He felt annoyed with Madame
Delmare's interfering chaperon, and resolved to disturb his
surveillance.

'If you'll agree to follow the hunt, Madame,' he said to
Indiana, 'you'll encourage me to follow your example. I don't
care much for hunting, but to have the happiness of riding
with you . . .'

'In that case, I'll go,' Indiana replied without thinking.

She exchanged a look of mutual understanding with Raymon but, however fleeting it was, Ralph saw it pass, and during the whole evening Raymon could not look at her or say a word to her without it coming to the eyes or ears of M. Brown. A feeling of dislike, almost of jealousy, then arose in Raymon's heart. By what right was this cousin, this friend of the family, setting himself up as a schoolmaster to the woman he loved? He swore that Sir Ralph would regret it and looked for an opportunity to annoy him without compromising Madame Delmare, but it was impossible. Sir Ralph did the honours of his house with cold, dignified courtesy, which gave no scope for epigrams or contradictions.

The next day, before the hunting horn had been sounded, Raymon saw his host's solemn face come into his room. There was something in his demeanour even stiffer than usual, and Raymon felt his heart beat with the wish and hope for a provocation. But it was simply a question of a saddle-horse that Raymon had brought to Bellerive and that he had expressed the intention of selling. In five minutes, the sale was agreed; Sir Ralph made no difficulties about the price and took out of his pocket a handful of money which he counted out onto the mantelpiece in a peculiarly cold manner, not deigning to pay attention to Raymon's protestations that there was no need to be so punctilious. Then, as Sir Ralph was going away, he came back into the room and said:

'Monsieur, from today, the horse is mine.'

Then Raymon thought he saw that Ralph's purpose was to prevent him from going to the hunt, and he stated rather drily that he was not intending to follow the hunt on foot.

'Monsieur,' Sir Ralph replied with a slight trace of affectation, 'I am too conversant with the laws of hospitality . . .'

And he withdrew.

As he came down the porch steps, Raymon saw Madame Delmare in riding-habit, playing cheerfully with Ophelia, who was tearing her cambric handkerchief. Her cheeks had regained a faint crimson hue, her eyes shone with a long lost brilliance. She had become pretty again already; the curls of her black hair escaped from her little hat; this made her look charming and the cloth habit, buttoned up from top to bottom, outlined her slender, graceful figure. To my mind, the main charm of Creole women is the extreme delicacy of their features and their slight physique, which leave them for a long time with the attractiveness of childhood. Indiana, laughing and playful, now seemed no more than fourteen.

Raymon, struck by her charm, had a feeling of triumph and paid her the least trite compliment he could think of.

'You were anxious about my health,' she said to him quietly; 'don't you see that I want to live?'

He was able to reply only with a happy, grateful look. Sir Ralph himself was bringing his cousin's horse; Raymon recognized the one he had just sold.

Madame Delmare had seen him try it out the previous day in the castle courtyard. 'What! Is M. de Ramière then kind enough to lend me his horse?' she said with surprise.

'Didn't you admire this animal's beauty and docility yesterday?' Sir Ralph asked her. 'It's yours from today. I'm sorry, my dear, that I couldn't give it you sooner.'

'You're becoming facetious, cousin,' said Madame Delmare. 'I don't understand this joke at all. Whom am I to thank? M. de Ramière, who agrees to lend me his horse, or you, who perhaps asked him to do so?'

'You must thank your cousin,' said M. Delmare. 'He bought this horse for you and is making you a present of him.'

'Is that so, my dear Ralph?' asked Madame Delmare, stroking the pretty creature with the happiness of a little girl receiving her first jewellery.

'Didn't we agree that I'd give you a horse in exchange for the chair-cover you're embroidering for me? Go on, mount, don't be afraid. I've observed his character and I tried him out again this morning.'

Indiana threw her arms round Sir Ralph's neck and then leapt on to the horse, boldly making him canter about.

All this family scene took place in a corner of the courtyard under Raymon's eyes. He felt extremely annoyed when he saw this pair's simple trusting affection expressed in front of him, for he loved passionately and perhaps had not even one whole day in which to make Indiana his own.

'How happy I am!' she said, calling him to her side in the avenue. 'It looks as if my kind Ralph has guessed the present which could please me most. And you, Raymon, aren't you happy too to see the horse you used to ride pass into my hands? Oh, I'll love him more than all the others. What name did you give him? Tell me; I don't want to take away from him the name you gave him . . .'

'If there's a happy man here, it's your cousin, who gives you presents and whom you kiss so gladly,' replied Raymon.

'Really, could you be jealous of our friendship and his hearty kisses?' she said, laughing.

'Jealous, perhaps, Indiana; I don't know. But when that young, pink-cheeked cousin places his lips on yours, when he takes you in his arms to lift you on to the horse which he *gives* you and I *sell* you, I confess I suffer. No, Madame, I'm not happy to see you mistress of the horse I loved. I can well appreciate being happy to give it to you, but to play the part of a dealer to provide another with the means of pleasing you, that's a humiliation skilfully arranged by Sir Ralph. If I didn't think he wasn't aware of his own cleverness, I'd like to avenge myself.'

'Oh, for shame! This jealousy is unbecoming! How can you envy our family intimacy, you who, for me, ought to be outside daily life and create an enchanted world inhabited only by you? I'm already not pleased with you, Raymon! I think there's something like wounded pride in this feeling of irritation with my poor cousin. You seem to be more jealous of the slight preference I show him in public than of the exclusive secret affection I might have for another.'

'Forgive me, forgive me, Indiana. I'm in the wrong. I'm not worthy of you, you angel of gentleness and kindness, but I suffered cruelly from the rights which this man seemed to assume.'

'Assume! Him, Raymon! You don't know, then, what secret gratitude binds us to him. You don't know, then, that his mother was my mother's sister, that we were born in the same valley, that as a teenager he protected my earliest years, that he has been my only support, my only teacher, my only companion on Bourbon Island, that he has followed me everywhere, that he left the country I left to come and live in the one I live in, that, in a word, he's the only being who's fond of me and takes an interest in my life!'

'A curse on him! Everything you're telling me, Indiana, adds poison to the wound. So that Englishman's fond of you! Do you know how *I* love you?'

'Oh, let's not make comparisons. If the same kind of affection were to turn you into rivals, I ought to prefer the older one. But don't be afraid, Raymon, that I'll ever ask you to love me the way Ralph does.'

'Well, please do explain him to me; for who could see through his stony mask?'

'Must I pay tribute to my cousin, myself?' she said with a smile. 'I must admit I'm reluctant to paint his picture. I'm so fond of him that I'd like to flatter him. Such as he is, I'm afraid you won't think him handsome enough. So try to help me. Now, what do you think of him?'

'Forgive me if I'm hurting you, but his face suggests a complete nonentity. Yet there's good sense and sound information in what he says when he deigns to speak. But he does so with such difficulty and lack of emotion that nobody profits from his knowledge, his manner of speaking puts you off so much and is so tedious. And then there's something commonplace and laboured about his ideas that is not compensated for by clear, logical expression. I think his mind is imbued with all the ideas that others have given him, and is too apathetic and mediocre to have any of his own. He's just got what it takes to be looked on in society as a serious-minded man. His solemnity constitutes three-quarters of his merit, his carefree attitude does the rest.'

'There is some truth in that portrait,' replied Indiana, 'but there's also prejudice. You boldly hit on doubts that I wouldn't dare acknowledge, I who have known Ralph ever since I was born. It's true his great failing is often to see things through the eyes of others, but that's the fault of his education, not of his intelligence. You think that, but for his education, he'd be a complete nonentity. I think, without it, he would have been less so. I must tell you a detail of his life which will explain his character to you. He had the misfortune to have a brother whom his parents openly preferred to him. This brother had all the brilliant qualities which he lacks. He learned easily; he was talented in all the arts; he had a sparkling wit; though his features were less regular than Ralph's, his face was more expressive. He was affectionate, eager, active; in a word, he was lovable. Ralph, on the contrary, was awkward, melancholy, undemonstrative; he loved solitude, learned with difficulty, and didn't show off what little he knew. When his parents saw he was so different from his older brother, they treated him badly; they did even worse; they humiliated him. Then, though he was but a child, his character became gloomy and withdrawn; an unconquerable shyness paralysed all his faculties. His parents had succeeded in making him hate and despise himself. He became disheartened with life, and from the age of fifteen he was attacked by spleen, a completely physical ailment under the foggy skies of England, a completely moral one under the life-giving skies of Bourbon Island. He has often told me that one day he left home, intending to throw himself into the sea, but as he sat on the shore, gathering his thoughts together on the point of carrying out his plan, he saw me coming towards him in the arms of the negress who had been my wet-nurse. I was then five years old. They say I was pretty and I showed a predilection shared by no one else for my taciturn cousin. It's true he was considerate of me and obliged me in ways I was not used to in my father's house. We were both unhappy and already we understood each other. He taught me his father's language, I lisped my father's to him. This mixture of Spanish and English was perhaps the expression of Ralph's character. When I put my arms round his neck, I noticed he cried and, without understanding why, I began to cry too. Then he pressed me to his heart, and he has told me since, swore to live for me, a neglected if not hated child, to whom at least his friendship would do some good, and his life be of some use. So I was the first and only attachment of his sad life. From that day, we hardly ever left each other. We would spend our days freely and healthily in the mountain solitudes. But perhaps these tales of our childhood bore you and you prefer to gallop and rejoin the hunt.'

'Crazy girl!' exclaimed Raymon, holding back the bridle of the horse Madame Delmare was riding.

'Well, to continue,' she went on. 'Edmond Brown, Ralph's older brother, died at the age of twenty. His mother died herself, of grief, and his father was inconsolable. Ralph would have liked to comfort him in his sorrow, but the coldness with which M. Brown received his first attempts further increased his natural shyness. He spent whole, sad, silent hours with this grief-stricken old man, not daring to say one word or show any sign of affection, for he was so afraid of offering inappropriate or inadequate consolation. His father accused him of lack of feeling and Edmond's death left poor Ralph more unhappy and misunderstood than ever. I was his only consolation.'

'I can't pity him, whatever you say,' Raymon interrupted. 'But there's something in his life and in yours that I don't understand: it's that he didn't marry you.'

'I'll give you a very good reason for that,' she continued. 'When I was of marriageable age, Ralph, who was ten years older than me (which is a huge difference in our climate where women's childhood is so short), Ralph was already married.'

'Is Sir Ralph a widower? I've never heard talk of his wife.'

'Don't ever talk to him about her. She was young, rich, and beautiful, but she had been in love with Edmond; she had been intended for him and when, in obedience to the interests and feelings of her family, she had to marry Ralph, she didn't even try to hide her dislike from him. He had to go with her to England and when, after his wife's death, he came back to Bourbon Island, I was married to M. Delmare and I was going to leave for Europe. Ralph tried to live alone but solitude made his troubles worse. Although he has never spoken to me about Madame Ralph Brown, I've every ground for thinking that he was even more unhappy in his married life than in his family, and that recent, painful memories added to his natural melancholy. He had another attack of spleen, and so he sold his coffee plantations and settled in France. The way he introduced himself to my husband is original and would have made me laugh if I had not been touched by my good Ralph's attachment. "Monsieur," he said to him, "I love your wife. It was I who brought her up. I look on her as my sister and even more as my daughter. She is my only surviving relative and the only affection I have. Allow me to settle near you and permit the three of us to spend our lives together. People say you're a little jealous where your wife is concerned, but they say you're honourable and upright. When I've given you my word that I was never in love with her and that I never will be, you'll be able to look on me with as little anxiety as if I were really your brother-in-law. Isn't that so Monsieur?" M. Delmare, who values highly his reputation for military loyalty, received this frank declaration with a kind of ostentatious trust. But several months of careful observation were necessary for this trust to be as real as he claimed it to be. Now it is unbreakable, like Ralph's calm, faithful heart.'

'Are you quite sure, Indiana, that Sir Ralph isn't deceiving himself a little when he swears he was never in love with you?' asked Raymon.

'I was twelve years old when he left Bourbon Island to follow his wife to England; I was sixteen when he met me again married, and he seemed more pleased than sorry. Now, Ralph is quite old.'

'At twenty-nine?'

'Don't laugh. Ralph's face is young, but his heart is worn out with suffering and he doesn't love anything any more so that he won't suffer any more.'

'Not even you?'

'Not even me. His friendship is now only habit. In the past it was generous, when he undertook to protect and teach me in my childhood, and then I loved him as he loves me today, because I needed him. Today, with all my heart I pay the debt of the past, and I spend my life trying to make his life more pleasant and less burdensome. But when I was a child, I loved instinctively more than with my heart, while he, a grown man, loves me less with his heart than instinctively. He needs me because I am almost the only being who cares for him, and even today, when M. Delmare shows him friendship, Ralph loves my husband almost as much as he does me. The protection, formerly so brave against my father's tyranny, has become lukewarm and prudent against my husband's. He does not reproach himself with seeing me suffer, provided I am with him; he doesn't ask himself if I'm unhappy, he's content to see that I'm alive. He doesn't want to stand up for me in a way that would ameliorate my lot but which, by making him quarrel with M. Delmare, would disturb the calm of his own. Because he was told repeatedly that he was cold-hearted, he has persuaded himself that he is, and his heart has become cold through the passivity in which he has left it dormant. He is a man whom the affection of others might have been able to develop; but it was denied him and he has become withered. Now, he places his happiness in a peaceful life and his pleasure in its comforts. He doesn't enquire about worries that aren't his. I must use the word, Ralph is selfish.'

'Well, so much the better,' said Raymon. 'I'm no longer afraid of him. I'll like him better if you want me to.'

'Yes, like him, Raymon,' she replied. 'He'll appreciate that. And, as for us, let's never worry ourselves about saying precisely why we're loved, but how we're loved. Happy is the person who is loved, for whatever reason.'

'What you're saying is the moan of a sad, lonely heart,' Raymon replied, putting his arm round her graceful, slender waist, 'but for my part, I want you to know why and how, above all why.'

'That's to make me happy, isn't it?' she said, looking at him sadly and ardently.

'It's to give you my life,' said Raymon, lightly touching Indiana's flowing hair with his lips.

A near-by fanfare warned them to be prudent; it was Sir Ralph, who may or may not have seen them.

XIV

WHEN the hounds were let loose, Raymon was surprised at what seemed to take place in Indiana's heart. Her eyes and cheeks sprang to life; her dilated nostrils seemed to reveal an indefinable feeling of terror or pleasure, and suddenly, leaving his side and eagerly pressing her horse's flanks, she dashed forward after Ralph. Raymon did not know that hunting was the only passion that Ralph and Indiana had in common. He did not suspect, either, that this apparently frail, timid woman possessed a more than masculine courage, the kind of mad intrepidity that can sometimes be manifested as a nervous crisis in the weakest of creatures. Women rarely have the physical courage which lies in fighting passively against grief or danger, but they often have the moral courage which is heightened by peril or suffering. Indiana's delicate nerves responded above all to the sounds, the swift movement, and the emotion of the hunt, which is like a war in miniature with its fatigues, its subterfuges, its calculations, its fights, and its luck. Her dreary life, filled with sorrows, needed this stimulus; she seemed then to be aroused from a lethargy and, in one day, expended all the unused energy that had been allowed to seethe in her blood for a year.

Raymon was frightened at seeing her gallop in this way, abandoning herself fearlessly to the fiery mettle of a horse she barely knew, urging it on boldly into the heart of the woods, avoiding with amazing skill the branches which, springing back sharply, struck her face, unhesitatingly crossing ditches, confidently taking risks on slippery clay soil, not worrying about breaking her slender limbs, but anxious to be the first to reach the steaming trail of the boar. He was frightened by such fierce determination and it almost turned him against Madame Delmare. Men, above all when they are in love, want, in their naïve self-satisfaction, to protect women's weakness rather than admire their courage. Shall I make an admission? Raymon felt terrified of the boldness and tenacity which such an intrepid spirit promised in love. Indiana's heart was not like that of poor Noun, who preferred to drown herself rather than fight against her unhappiness.

'If there is as much fire and enthusiasm in her affection as there is in her tastes, if her eager, panting will becomes attached to me as much as her whim does to the flanks of this boar, society will have no shackles for her, laws will have no force,' he thought. 'My destiny will have to give way to her and I shall have to sacrifice my future to her present.'

Shouts of fear and distress, among which could be heard Madame Delmare's voice, roused Raymon from these reflections. He urged his horse on anxiously and was immediately joined by Ralph, who asked him if he had heard the shouts of alarm. The frightened whips soon reached them, shouting in confusion that the boar had stood at bay and knocked Madame Delmare off her horse. Other huntsmen, still more terrified, arrived, calling for Sir Ralph, whose assistance was required for the person hurt.

'It's no use,' said one of the last to arrive. 'There's no hope; your attentions would be too late.'

At this terrible moment Raymon's eyes met M. Brown's pale, gloomy face. He was not screaming, he was not foaming at the mouth, he was not wringing his hands; he simply picked up his hunting-knife and with truly British phlegm, was about to cut his throat, when Raymon snatched his weapon from him and dragged him to the spot where the screams were coming from.

Ralph seemed to emerge from a dream when he saw Madame Delmare dash towards him and help him to rush to the assistance of the Colonel who, apparently lifeless, lay stretched on the ground. He bled him without delay, for he had soon assured himself that M. Delmare was not dead, but he had broken his thigh and was carried to the house.

As for Madame Delmare, it was by mistake that, in the confusion of the moment, she had been named instead of her husband, or rather, Ralph and Raymon had thought they heard the name that most interested them.

Indiana had not had an accident at all, but her fright and dismay almost deprived her of the strength to walk. Raymon supported her in his arms, and became reconciled to her womanly heart when he saw her so deeply affected by her husband's misfortune for she had much to forgive him before pitying him.

Sir Ralph had already recovered his usual calm, but an extraordinary pallor revealed the violent shock he had experienced; he had almost lost one of the only two people he loved.

In that moment of frenzied confusion, Raymon alone had retained enough sanity to understand what he saw; he had been able to judge the degree of Ralph's affection for his cousin and how little it was balanced by his feeling for the Colonel. This observation, which definitely gave the lie to Indiana's opinion, remained in Raymon's memory, though not in the memories of the other witnesses of the scene.

Nevertheless, Raymon never spoke to Madame Delmare of the suicide attempt he had witnessed. There was something selfish and malevolent in this discretion, but perhaps you will forgive it in view of the lover's jealousy which inspired it.

It was with great difficulty that, after six weeks, the Colonel was moved to Lagny, but six months more elapsed before he could walk; the break in the femur was barely mended when the injured limb was affected by acute rheumatism, which condemned M. Delmare to excruciating pain and complete immobility. His wife lavished on him the most tender care. She did not leave his bedside and, without complaint, put up with his bitter, peevish moods, his military rages, and his invalid's injustice.

Despite the troubles of such a dreary life, she became radiant and sparkling with blooming health again, and happiness came to settle in her heart. Raymon loved her, he loved her truly. He came every day; no difficulty deterred him from seeing her; he put up with the husband's infirmities, the cousin's coldness, the constraints of their meetings. A look from him filled Indiana's heart with joy for a whole day. She no longer thought of complaining of life. Her heart was full, her youth had occupation, her moral strength had nourishment.

Gradually, the Colonel came to have friendly feelings for Raymon. He was naïve enough to think that his neighbour's assiduity was proof of the interest that Raymon took in his health. Sometimes Madame de Ramière came too, sanctioning the liaison by her presence, and Indiana became enthusiastically and passionately attached to Raymon's mother. In the end the wife's lover became the husband's friend.

In this constant proximity, Raymon and Ralph were forced into a kind of intimacy. They called each other 'my dear fellow'. They shook hands morning and evening. If they had to ask each other a slight favour, their usual formula was, 'I count on your kind friendship, etc.'

And when they referred to each other, they would say, 'He's a friend of mine.'

But although they were as frank as it is possible for men to be in society, they did not like each other at all. They had totally different opinions about everything, they had no tastes in common, and if they both loved Madame Delmare, it was in such different ways that the feeling divided them instead of bringing them together. They took an unusual pleasure in contradicting each other and in upsetting each other as much as possible by reproaches which, although they were tossed into the conversation as generalities, were no less sharp and bitter.

Their principal and most frequent arguments began about politics and ended about morals. It was in the evening, when they would gather around M. Delmare's chair, that disagreement arose on the slightest pretext. They always maintained the surface courtesy that philosophy imposed on the one and social propriety on the other, but beneath the veil of innuendo they nevertheless said harsh things to each other which amused the Colonel, for he had a bellicose, quarrelsome temperament and, since there were no battles, he loved quarrels.

My own belief is that a man's political opinions are the whole man. Tell me your heart and your head, and I shall tell you your political opinions. In whatever rank or party we happen to be born, sooner or later our character wins the day against the prejudices or beliefs of upbringing. Perhaps you will think I am dogmatic, but how can I bring myself to augur well of a man who espouses certain theories which generosity repels? Show me a man who maintains the utility of the death penalty and, however conscientious and enlightened he may be, I challenge you ever to establish any sympathy between him and me. If such a man wants to instruct me about truths that I do not know, he will not succeed, for it will not be in my power to have faith in him.

Ralph and Raymon differed on every point, and yet, before they knew each other, they did not have firmly held opinions. But from the moment they began to argue, when they each expressed an opinion opposite to the one advanced by the other, they each acquired a total, unshakeable conviction. On every occasion Raymon was the champion of the existing social order, Ralph attacked the system on every point.

That is easily explained: Raymon was happy and very well treated, Ralph had known only the ills and disappointments of life; the one found everything fine, the other was dissatisfied with everything. Men and affairs had treated Ralph badly but heaped favours on Raymon; and like two children, Ralph and Raymon referred everything to themselves, setting themselves up as judges in the last resort of the great problems of the social system, though neither of them was competent.

So Ralph continued to support his dream of a republic from which he wanted to banish all abuses, all prejudices, all injustices, a plan based in its entirety on the hope of a new race of men. Raymon supported his doctrine of hereditary monarchy, preferring, he said, to put up with abuses, prejudices, and injustices rather than to see scaffolds built again and innocent blood flow.

The Colonel was nearly always on Ralph's side at the beginning of the discussion. He hated the Bourbons* and in his opinions he expressed all the animosity he felt. But Raymon soon brought him over skilfully to his side by proving that, as a principle, the monarchy was much closer to the Empire* than to the Republic.* Ralph had so little talent for persuasion, the poor baronet was so direct and awkward, his frankness was so clumsy, his logic so dreary, his principles so uncompromising! He spared no one, he toned down no truth.

'What the deuce!' he would say to the Colonel when the latter cursed England's intervention.* 'So what has a whole nation, which fought fairly against you, done to you, who are, I assume, a sensible, reasonable man?'

'Fairly?' Delmare would repeat, clenching his teeth and brandishing his crutch.

'Let the powers settle diplomatic questions between them', Sir Ralph would continue, 'since we've adopted a form of government which forbids us to discuss our interests ourselves. If a nation is responsible for its legislature's mistakes, which will you find more guilty than yours?'

'So, Monsieur, shame on France, which deserted Napoleon and put up with a king proclaimed by foreign bayonets!'* the Colonel would cry.

'*I* don't say shame on France,' Ralph would continue. 'I say misfortune for France. I pity her for having been so weak and so sick on the day she was purged of her tyrant that she was forced to accept your rag of a Constitutional Charter,* a shred of liberty that you're beginning to respect today, when you should be throwing it away and reconquering your liberty completely.'

Then Raymon would pick up the gauntlet thrown down by Sir Ralph. A knight of the Charter, he wanted to be the knight of liberty as well, and he proved skilfully to Ralph that the one was the expression of the other, that if he tore up the Charter he would be overturning his idol himself. In vain the baronet would flounder in the faulty arguments in which M. de Ramière ensnared him. Raymon proved admirably that a more broadly based franchise would infallibly lead to the excesses of 1793,* and that the nation was not yet mature enough for liberty, which was not the same as license. When Sir Ralph claimed that it was absurd to want to imprison a constitution in a given number of articles, that what was initially adequate, later became inadequate, supported his argument with the example of the convalescent whose needs increase daily. Raymon would then reply, to all the commonplaces clumsily regurgitated by M. Brown, that the Charter was not an inflexible circle, that it would come to terms with France's needs, and he gave it an elasticity which he said would make it adaptable later to national needs, but which in fact was only adapted to the crown's.

As for Delmare, he had not taken one step forward since 1815.* He was a stick-in-the-mud, as prejudiced and obsti-

nate as the Coblenz émigrés,* the perpetual victims of his
hate-filled irony. He was like a grown-up child who had never
understood anything about the great drama of Napoleon's
fall. He had seen only the fortune of war when it was the
power of public opinion that had triumphed. He kept on
talking of treason and the sale of the fatherland, as if a whole
nation could betray one man, as if France would have let itself
be sold by a few generals. He would accuse the Bourbons of
tyranny and regret the great days of the Empire, when there
was not enough labour to till the land and families lacked
bread. He would rail against Franchet's* police and extol
Fouché's.* He was still at the day after Waterloo.

It was a really strange experience to listen to the sentimental
stupidities of Delmare and M. de Ramière, both of them
philanthropic dreamers, the one under Napoleon's sword, the
other under St Louis' sceptre,* M. Delmare standing firmly at
the foot of the Pyramids,* Raymon seated in the regal shade
of the oak of Vincennes.* Their Utopias, which conflicted at
first, became compatible in the end. Raymon ensnared the
Colonel with his chivalrous speeches; for one concession he
demanded ten and imperceptibly he accustomed M. Delmare
to seeing twenty-five years of victories spiral upwards under
the folds of the white flag.* If Ralph had not continually
interrupted Raymon's flowery rhetoric with his abrupt, blunt
remarks, he would have been bound to win Delmare over to
the throne of 1815,* but Ralph hurt the Colonel's self-esteem
and the clumsy directness that he used to shake his opinion
only served to anchor him more firmly to his imperial convictions. Then all M. de Ramière's efforts were wasted. Ralph
trampled heavily on the flowers of his eloquence and the
Colonel returned determinedly to his tricolour.* He would
swear *to shake the dust off it one fine day*, he would spit on
the lilies, he would bring back the Duc de Reichstadt* to the
throne of *his father*; he would start again on the conquest of
the world and would always conclude by complaining of the
shame which burdened France, of the rheumatism that nailed
him to his chair, and of the ingratitude of the Bourbons
towards the old moustachioed soldiers who had been burned
by the desert sun* and stuck in the ice floes of the Moskva.*

'My poor friend,' Ralph would say, 'do be fair: you think it's bad that the Restoration has not rewarded services rendered to the Empire and that it pays the émigrés. Tell me, if Napoleon could come back to life tomorrow with all his power, would you think it right that he should withdraw his favour from you and bestow it on the partisans of the legal sovereign? Everyone for himself and for his own side. These are discussions of business matters, arguments about personal interest, which are of very little interest to France now that you are almost as disabled as the infantrymen of the emigration and that gouty, married, or disgruntled, you are all equally useless to her. Yet France must feed the lot of you and you vie with each other in complaining about her. When the Republic's day* dawns, it will liberate itself from all your demands and justice will be done.'

These obvious commonplaces offended the Colonel like so many personal insults, and Ralph, who with all his good sense did not understand that the petty-mindedness of a man whom he esteemed could go so far, became used to upsetting him unsparingly.

Before Raymon's arrival there was a tacit agreement between these two men to avoid any subject of controversy in which delicate susceptibilities might have been mutually hurt. But Raymon brought into their quiet household all the subtleties of language, all the petty treacheries of civilized society. He taught them that people can say anything to each other, reproach each other with anything, and always retract under the pretext of having a discussion. He introduced into their home the habit of argument which was then tolerated in fashionable drawing-rooms because the passionate hatreds of the Hundred Days* had finally soothed down and been absorbed into various different feelings. But the Colonel had retained his in all their strength, and Ralph made a great mistake in thinking that M. Delmare might listen to the language of reason. He turned daily more bitter against Ralph and came closer to Raymon, who, without giving way too much, knew how to express himself elegantly so as to spare the Colonel's *amour-propre*.

It is very unwise to introduce politics into families as a pastime. If peaceful, happy families still exist today, I advise them not to subscribe to any newspaper, not to read the smallest item of the budget, to retreat to the depths of their country estates as if to an oasis, and to erect an impassable barrier between themselves and the rest of society; for, if they let the clamour of our disputes reach them, that's an end to their peace and unity. You cannot imagine what bitterness and gall divisions of opinion bring between near relatives. Most of the time it is only an opportunity to reproach each other for character failings, intellectual weaknesses, and evil emotions.

They would not have dared to treat each other as rascals, fools, ambitious schemers, or cowards. They clothe the same ideas with the names of *Jesuit*, *royalist*, *revolutionary*, and *happy man*. The words are different but the insults are the same, and they are all the more biting in that the family members have allowed themselves to pursue and attack each other ceaselessly, without indulgence and without restraint. Then they have no more tolerance for each other's faults, no more charitable attitudes, no more generous, sensitive reserve; nothing is overlooked any more, everything is linked to a political opinion, and beneath this mask they breathe out hatred and vengeance. Happy country-dwellers (if there is still country in France), flee, flee from politics, and read *Peau d'Ane** in your family circle! . . . But the contagion is such that there is no retreat hidden enough, no solitude absolute enough, to conceal and protect the man who wants to spare his easy-going temperament the storms of our civil discords.

The little manor-house at Brie had in vain defended itself for a few years against this fatal invasion; it had finally lost its carefree attitude, its busy domestic life, its long evenings of silence and meditation. Noisy arguments aroused its dormant echoes; bitter, threatening words frightened the faded cherubs who had been smiling for a hundred years in the dusty wainscoting. The emotions of the present day had made their way into that ancient dwelling; all those old-fashioned decorations, all those remnants of a pleasure-loving, frivolous age,* saw with terror the entry of our age of scepticism and ranting oratory, represented by three people who shut themselves up together every day to quarrel from morning to night.

XV

In spite of these perpetual quarrels, Madame Delmare, with the confidence of youth, gave herself up to the hope of a happy future. It was her first taste of happiness and her lively imagination, her full young heart, were able to embellish it with everything it had lacked. She was ingenious in creating keen, pure joys for herself, in completing for herself the favours which destiny might have in store for her. Raymon loved her. Indeed, he was not lying when he told her that she was the only love of his life; he had never before loved so purely nor for such a long time. In her presence he would forget everything that was not her. Society and politics were erased from his memory. He was happy with this domestic life, with the family routine which she created for him. He admired her patience and her strength. He was amazed at the contrast between her intelligence and her character. Above all, he was surprised that after the solemnity of their initial agreement, she should prove so undemanding, happy with such furtive and infrequent joys, and trusting with such blind abandon. This was because love was a new, generous passion in her heart, and a thousand sensitive, noble feelings were linked to it which gave her a strength that Raymon could not understand.

As for him, to start with he was distressed by the constant presence of her husband and her cousin. He had thought he would handle this love affair like all the others he had experienced, but soon Indiana compelled him to rise to her level. The resignation with which she put up with being watched, the look of happiness with which she secretly gazed at him, her eyes which spoke to him in eloquent but silent language, her heavenly smile when a sudden allusion in conversation brought their hearts close to each other, these were soon subtle, exquisite pleasures that Raymon appreciated, thanks to the refinement of his mind and to the culture he had acquired by education.

What a difference between this chaste being who seemed not to contemplate the possibility of a consummation of their love and all those women concerned only to hasten it while pretending to flee from it! When, by chance, Raymon found himself alone with her, Indiana's cheeks were not animated by a warmer red, she did not turn away her eyes in embarrassment. No, her clear, calm eyes still gazed at him with ecstatic delight, an angelic smile was still on her lips, which were as rosy as those of a little girl who has not yet known any kisses but her mother's. When he saw her so trusting, so much in love, so pure, living only the life of the heart and not realizing that there was torment in her lover's when he was at her feet, Raymon no longer dared be a man, fearing to seem inferior to her dreams of him, and through pride he became virtuous like her.

Madame Delmare, ignorant as real Creoles are, had never till then thought of considering the serious matters that were now discussed in her presence every day. She had been brought up by Sir Ralph, who had a poor opinion of the intelligence and reasoning power of women and had confined himself to giving her some practical knowledge of immediate use. So she scarcely knew an outline of world history and any serious discourse bored her to tears. But when she heard Raymon apply all the charm of his wit, all the poetry of his language, to these dry subjects, she listened and tried to understand; then she timidly ventured to ask naïve questions which a ten year old girl, brought up in a wider world, would have answered capably. Raymon enjoyed enlightening her untutored intelligence, which seemed bound to be receptive to his principles. But despite his sway over her young, unsophisticated mind, his sophistry sometimes met with resistance.

To the interests of civilization set up as principles, Indiana opposed the honest ideas and the simple laws of good sense and humanity. Her counter-arguments were characterized by a straightforward frankness which sometimes embarrassed Raymon but whose childlike simplicity always charmed him. He applied himself as he would to a serious undertaking; he made it an important task for himself to bring her gradually to an acceptance of his beliefs and principles. He would have

been proud to overrule her conscientious and naturally enlightened convictions, but he had some difficulty in attaining
his objective. Ralph's generous theories, his implacable hatred
of society's vices, his keen impatience at seeing the dominance
of other laws and other ways, these were indeed sympathetic
feelings to which Indiana's unhappy memories responded. But
suddenly Raymon would annihilate his opponent by pointing
out to him that his dislike of the present stemmed from
selfishness. He would warmly describe his own affections, his
devotion to the royal family, whom he knew how to make
attractive by giving them all the heroism of loyalty in dangerous situations, his respect for the persecuted religion of his
fathers, his religious feelings, which he did not subject to
reasoning and which, he would say, he retained by instinct
and from necessity. And then the happiness of loving his
fellow man, of being bound to the present generation by all
the bonds of honour and philanthropy; the pleasure of render-
ing service to his country by rejecting dangerous innovations,
by maintaining internal peace, by giving, if necessary, all his
blood to spare the least of his compatriots one drop of theirs!
He depicted all these benevolent utopias with so much art and
charm that Indiana let herself be carried away by the need to
love and respect everything that Raymon loved and respected.
In fact, it was proved that Ralph was an egoist. When he
supported a generous idea, they smiled; it was established that
his mind and his heart were then in contradiction. Was it
not better to believe Raymon, who had such a warm, large,
expansive heart?

Nevertheless, there were many moments when Raymon
almost forgot his love and thought only of his antipathy. In
Madame Delmare's presence, he could see only Sir Ralph
who, with his rough, cold, good sense, dared to attack him, a
man of superior talents, who had wiped the floor with powerful opponents. He was humiliated at seeing himself fighting
against such a poor adversary and then he would overwhelm
him with the weight of his eloquence. He would bring all the
resources of his talent into play, and Ralph, bewildered, slow
to collect his thoughts, slower still to express them, suffered
from the consciousness of his weakness.

In those moments it seemed to Indiana that Raymon's thoughts were completely detached from her. She had fits of anxiety and terror, thinking that perhaps all these grand, noble sentiments, so well expressed, were only a pompous display of words, the ironic fluency of a lawyer, listening to his own words and practising the sentimental play-acting designed to captivate the good feelings of the audience. Above all, she would be apprehensive when, her eye meeting his, she thought she saw in it not the pleasure of being understood by her, but triumphant pride at having delivered a good speech. Then she would be afraid and think of Ralph, the egoist; perhaps they were being unfair to him, but Ralph did not know what to say to prolong this uncertainty and Raymon was skilful at removing it.

So there was only one person whose life was really disturbed, only one happiness in the household really ruined; it was the life and happiness of Ralph, a man unfortunate from birth, for whom life had never had its bright side, its complete, all-pervasive joys. His was a great but obscure misfortune pitied by no one and of which he complained to no one, a truly accursed destiny but one devoid of poetry or adventure, an ordinary, commonplace, sad destiny softened by no friendship, charmed by no love, one which wasted away in silence with the heroism that comes from the love of life and the need for hope. He was a solitary being who, like everyone else, had had a father and a mother, a brother, a wife, a son, and a sweetheart, but who had not profited nor retained anything from all these affections. He was a stranger in life who went on his way, melancholy and indifferent, not even having the exaggerated sense of his misfortune which makes some people find a certain glamour in sorrow.

In spite of his strength of character, Ralph sometimes felt weary of virtue. He hated Raymon and, by saying one word, he could drive him out of Lagny. But he did not say it, because Ralph had one belief, only one that was stronger than Raymon's thousands of beliefs. It was not the Church, nor the monarchy, nor society, nor reputation, nor the law, that dictated his sacrifices and his courage; it was his conscience.

He had lived alone so much that he had never been able to count on others. But in his isolation he had also learned to know himself. He had made a friend of his own heart. By dint of falling back on his own thoughts, of asking himself why others inflicted injustices upon him, he had assured himself that he had no vice for which he deserved them. He was no longer annoyed by them because he had little esteem for himself, knowing that he was uninteresting and ordinary. He understood why people took no account of him and he was resigned to the fact. But his heart told him he was capable of all the feelings he did not inspire, and if he was ready to forgive others everything, he had decided to tolerate nothing in himself. This wholly introverted life, these wholly private feelings, gave him all the appearance of being selfish, and perhaps nothing resembles selfishness more closely than self-respect.

As it often happens, however, that when trying too hard to do good we do less good, it happened that Sir Ralph made a great mistake by being so sensitively scrupulous, and he did Madame Delmare irreparable harm in the fear of burdening his conscience with a reproach. His mistake was not to inform her of the real cause of Noun's death. Had he done so, she would no doubt have reflected on the dangers of her love for Raymon. But we shall see later why M. Brown dared not enlighten his cousin and what painful scruples made him keep silent on such an important matter. When he decided to break his silence, it was too late; Raymon had had time to establish his sway.

An unexpected event had just shattered the future prospects of the Colonel and his wife. A Belgian trading establishment, on which all the prosperity of Delmare's business depended, had suddenly gone bankrupt, and the Colonel, barely well again, had just set off in great haste for Antwerp.

Aware that he was still weak and unfit, his wife had wanted to go with him, but M. Delmare, threatened with complete ruin and resolved to honour all his obligations, was afraid that his journey would look like a flight, and so he wanted to leave his wife at Lagny as a guarantee of his return. Similarly, he refused Sir Ralph's company and begged him to remain to be a support to Madame Delmare, in case there was trouble from anxious or zealous creditors.

In these distressing circumstances, Indiana's only fear was of the possibility of leaving Lagny and of being separated from Raymon, but he reassured her by pointing out that the Colonel was bound to go to Paris. Moreover, he swore that he would follow her wherever she might go and under whatever pretext, and the credulous woman thought herself almost happy through a misfortune which allowed her to put Raymon's love to the test. As for him, a vague hope, a persistent nagging thought, filled his mind since he had heard of these events. At last he was going to be alone with Indiana; it would be the first time in six months. She had never seemed to try to avoid him, and though in no hurry to triumph over a love whose naïve chastity had the charm of the unusual for him, he was beginning to feel that his honour was involved in bringing it to a favourable outcome. He honourably repelled any malicious insinuation about his relationship with Madame Delmare. He very modestly asserted that there was only a pleasant, calm friendship between her and him. But, for nothing in the world would he have been willing to confess, even to his best friend, that he had been loved passionately for six months but had so far obtained nothing from that love.

He was a little put out in his expectations when he saw that Sir Ralph seemed determined to replace M. Delmare as far as surveillance was concerned, that Indiana's cousin settled in at Lagny first thing in the morning and only returned to Belleville in the evening; and as they had to follow the same road for part of the way to reach their respective homes, Ralph even behaved with an intolerable show of politeness in timing his departure to coincide with Raymon's. M. de Ramière soon came to detest this constraint and at the same time Madame Delmare thought it contained a suspicion that was insulting to her, and the intention of assuming a despotic power over her behaviour.

Raymon dared not request a secret interview. Whenever he had attempted to do so, Madame Delmare had reminded him of certain conditions agreed between them. However, a week had already elapsed since the Colonel's departure. He might soon be home again. Raymon must make the most of the opportunity. To allow victory to Sir Ralph was dishonour for Raymon. One morning he slipped the following letter into Madame Delmare's hand:

'Indiana, don't you love me then as I love you? My darling, I am unhappy and you don't notice it. I am sad, and anxious about your future, not about mine, for wherever you may be, I shall go to live and die. But I'm afraid of poverty for you. Delicate and frail as you are, my poor dear, how will you put up with privations? You have a rich, open-handed cousin; perhaps your husband will accept from his hands what he will refuse from mine. Ralph will ameliorate your lot, but *I* shall do nothing for you!

'Don't you see clearly, my dear, that I have reason to be depressed and sad? *You* are heroic, you are cheerful whatever happens, you don't want me to be distressed. Oh, how I need your gentle words, your gentle looks to sustain my courage! But by an unimaginable trick of fate, these days that I had hoped to pass freely at your feet have brought me an even more bitter constraint.

'Just say one word, Indiana, so that we may be alone for at least an hour, so that I can weep over your white hands and tell you all I suffer, so that words from you may comfort and reassure me.

'And then, Indiana, I have a childish whim, a real lover's whim; I should like to go into your room. Oh, don't be alarmed, my gentle Creole! I appreciate not only that I must respect you, but that I must fear you. It's precisely for that reason that I should like to go into your room, kneel down in the very place where I saw you so angry with me and where, in spite of my presumption, I did not dare to look at you. I'd like to prostrate myself there, to spend a happy hour of meditation there. The only favour I ask of you, Indiana, is to place your hand on my heart, to purify it from its crime, to calm it if it beats too fast and to give it back all your trust if, at last, you think me worthy of you. Oh, yes, I'd like to prove to you that I am worthy of you now, that I know you really well, that I worship you with a more pure and holy devotion than ever a young girl rendered to her Madonna. I'd like to be sure that you're no longer afraid of me, that you esteem me as much as I revere you. Resting on your heart, I should like the life of the angels for an hour. Tell me, Indiana, will you allow me! One hour, the first, perhaps the last!

'It's time to pardon me, Indiana, to give me back your trust that was so cruelly snatched away, so dearly redeemed. Are you not satisfied with me? Tell me, haven't I spent six months behind your chair, limiting all my pleasures to looking at your snow-white neck through the ringlets of your black hair as you leaned over your work, to breathing in the perfume which emanates from you and which is wafted faintly towards me by the air from the window where you sit? Does such submission not then deserve the reward of a kiss? A sisterly kiss, if you like, a kiss on the brow. I shall remain faithful to our agreements, I swear it. I shall ask for nothing . . . But, oh cruel one, are you not willing to grant me anything? Then is it of yourself that you're afraid?'

Madame Delmare went up to her room to read this letter. She answered it immediately and slipped the reply into Raymon's hand together with a garden key that he knew only too well.

'I, afraid of you, Raymon? Oh, not now! I know the nature of your love too well; I am too blissfully happy in my belief in it. Come then, I'm not afraid of myself either. If I loved you less, perhaps I'd be less calm. But I love you in a way you don't even realize. Leave here early, so that Ralph won't have the slightest suspicion. Come back at midnight. You know the grounds and the house. Here is the key to the little door; lock it again behind you.'

This ingenuous, generous trust made Raymon blush. He had tried to inspire it with the intention of abusing it. He had counted on the night hour, the opportunity, the danger. If Indiana had shown any fear, she would have been lost, but she was untroubled, she entrusted herself to his good faith. He swore not to make her regret her trust. In any case, the important thing was to spend a night in her room, so as not to appear foolish in his own eyes, so as to make Ralph's prudence ineffectual and to be able to laugh at him inwardly. It was a personal satisfaction he required.

XVI

But that evening Ralph was really intolerable; he was duller, more dreary, more tiresome than ever. He could say nothing to the point and, to crown all his clumsiness, it was already late in the evening and he had not yet shown any sign of going. Madame Delmare began to be uneasy. She looked in turn at the clock which showed eleven o'clock, at the door which was creaking in the wind, and at the expressionless face of her cousin who, settled opposite her in the chimney-corner, was placidly looking at the embers without seeming to suspect that his presence was unwelcome.

Yet, at that moment, Sir Ralph's mask of indifference, his immobile features, hid deep, painful concern. He was a man whom nothing escaped, because he observed everything without emotion. He was not duped by Raymon's pretended departure; he was well aware at that moment of Madame Delmare's anxiety. He suffered from it more than she did herself and he hesitated irresolutely between the desire to give her useful warning and the fear of giving way to feelings he disapproved of. Finally, his cousin's welfare carried the day and he summoned up all his spiritual strength to break the silence.

'That reminds me that a year ago today you and I were sitting at this fireside as we are now,' he said suddenly, following the train of thought that occupied his mind. 'The clock showed almost the same time, the weather was bleak and cold like this evening . . . you weren't well and you had melancholy thoughts; it's enough almost to make me believe in the truth of presentiments.'

'What's he getting at?' thought Madame Delmare, looking at her cousin with mingled surprise and anxiety.

'Do you remember, Indiana, that then you felt worse than usual?' he continued. '*I* remember your words as if they were still ringing in my ears. "You'll think I'm mad", you said, "but a danger is approaching us and threatening someone; probably me," you added. "I feel on edge as if a great phase of my destiny was imminent; I am afraid . . ." Those were your own words, Indiana.'

'I'm no longer ill,' replied Indiana, who had suddenly again turned as pale as she was at the time Ralph was speaking of. 'I don't believe any more in those empty fears.'

'I *do* believe in them,' he continued, 'for, that evening, you were a prophet. A great danger was threatening us, a disastrous influence was surrounding this peaceful dwelling . . .'

'Oh, my goodness, I don't understand you!'

'You will understand me, my poor dear. It was that evening that Raymon de Ramière came in here . . . You remember the state he was in . . .'

Ralph waited a few moments without daring to raise his eyes and look at his cousin. As she did not reply, he continued:

'I was given the task of bringing him back to life and I did so, as much to please you as in accordance with feelings of humanity. But, to tell the truth, Indiana, it was my misfortune to save that man's life. It was really I who did all the harm.'

'I don't know what harm you're talking about,' Indiana replied curtly.

She was deeply hurt by the explanation that she knew was coming.

'I'm talking about that unfortunate girl's death,' said Ralph. 'But for him, she would still be alive. That beautiful, honest girl, who loved you so, would still be at your side.'

Up to this point, Madame Delmare did not understand. She was angered to the depths of her heart by the strange, cruel words her cousin used to reproach her for her attachment to M. de Ramière.

'That's enough,' she said, getting up.

But Ralph did not appear to pay any attention to her remark.

'What's always surprised me,' he said, 'is that you didn't guess the real motive that led M. de Ramière to come here by climbing over the wall.'

A suspicion flashed through Indiana's mind. Her legs trembled beneath her and she sat down again.

Ralph had just plunged the knife in and had made a ghastly wound. He no sooner saw the effect of his work than he was horrified at what he had done. He thought only of the pain he had just caused to the person he loved best in the world. He felt his heart was breaking. He would have wept bitterly if he had been able to weep. But the unfortunate man had not the gift of tears; he had no facility for giving eloquent expression to the language of the heart. The external coldness with which he carried out this cruel operation made him seem like an executioner in Indiana's eyes.

'It's the first time I see your antipathy for M. de Ramière expressed in a way that is unworthy of you,' she said bitterly, 'but I don't see how your vengeance requires you to tarnish the memory of one who was dear to me and whose misfortune ought to have made her sacred to us. I haven't asked you questions, Sir Ralph. I don't know what you're talking about. Please allow me not to continue this conversation any further.'

She got up and left M. Brown bewildered and shattered.

He had indeed foreseen that he would enlighten Madame Delmare only at his own expense. His conscience had told him that he had to speak, whatever the outcome, and he had just done so with all the abruptness and clumsiness of which he was capable. What he had not properly appreciated was the violent reaction to so belated a remedy.

He left Lagny in despair and began to wander about in the forest almost out of his mind.

It was midnight; Raymon was at the park gate. He opened it, but as he went in he began to have cold feet. What was he going to do at this rendezvous? He had made good resolutions; would he be rewarded then by a chaste interview, by a fraternal kiss, for the suffering he was imposing on himself at this moment? For, if you remember under what circumstances he had previously walked along those paths and crossed that garden, stealthily, at night, you will appreciate that a certain degree of moral courage was required to go in search of pleasure by such a road and despite such memories.

At the end of October, the weather in the regions around Paris becomes foggy and damp, especially in the evening near the rivers. By chance, that night was blanketed with white fog, as the corresponding nights of the preceding spring had been. Raymon was not sure of his way as he walked under the trees

shrouded in mist. He passed in front of the door of a green-
house which, in the winter, contained a very fine collection of
geraniums. He cast a glance at the door and, in spite of
himself, his heart beat faster at the absurd idea that perhaps it
was going to open and a woman, wrapped in a cloak, was
going to emerge from it . . . Raymon smiled at this superstitious weakness and continued on his way. Nevertheless, a
cold fear had gripped him and his heart grew tense as he
approached the river.

He had to cross it to enter the flower garden but the only
crossing at this spot was a little wooden bridge thrown up
from one bank to the other. The fog became thicker still on
the river-bed and Raymon clung to the handrail so as not to
lose his way in the reeds which were growing along the banks.
The moon was rising then and, trying to shine through the
mist, cast an uncertain light on the plants which were swaying
in the wind and in the currents of the water. Wailing sounds
like broken human speech seemed carried by the breeze,
which lightly touched the leaves and hovered over the ripples
of the water. Raymon heard a faint sob beside him and a
sudden movement shook the reeds; it was a curlew flying
away as he approached. That river-bird's cry is exactly like the
wail of an abandoned child, and when it flies out from among
the reeds it seems like the last effort of a drowning man.
Perhaps you will think Raymon was very weak and cowardly;
his teeth chattered and he nearly fell. But he soon realized how
ridiculous his terror was and he crossed the bridge.

He was halfway over when a barely discernible human form
rose up in front of him at the end of the handrail as if it had
been waiting for him to cross. Raymon's thoughts became
confused, his bewildered mind had not the strength to reason.
He retraced his steps and hid under the trees, gazing with a
fixed, terrified stare at that indistinct apparition which remained there, elusive and vague like the mist from the river
and the quivering moonbeams. He was beginning to think,
however, that his preoccupied mind had deceived him and
that what he took for a human form was only the shadow of
a tree or the branch of a shrub, when he distinctly saw it
move, walk, and come towards him.

If his legs had not at that moment refused entirely to be of any use, he would have fled as quickly and cravenly as a child who passes by a cemetery at night and thinks he hears light footsteps running behind him, skimming over the grass. But he felt paralysed and, to support himself, put his arms round the trunk of a willow tree to which he had retreated. Then Sir Ralph, wrapped in a light-coloured cloak, which from three paces away made him look like a ghost, passed close by him and disappeared into the path by which Raymon had just come.

'You clumsy spy!' thought Raymon as he saw Ralph looking for his footprints. 'I'll escape from your despicable surveillance, and while you mount guard here I'll be happy over there.'

He crossed the bridge as lightly as a bird and with the confidence of an accepted lover. His terrors had completely gone; Noun had never existed. He was coming back to real life; Indiana was waiting for him in the house; Ralph was at the other end of the grounds on sentry duty to prevent him from going any further.

'Be on the look-out,' said Raymon cheerfully, seeing Ralph from a distance, looking for him in the wrong direction. 'Be on the look-out for me, good Rodolphe Brown; officious friend, protect my happiness. And if the dogs are aroused, if the servants are worried, calm them down, quieten them by telling them, "*I* am watching, sleep in peace."'

After that, Raymon felt no more remorse, had no more scruples, no more virtue; he had paid dearly enough for the hour that was striking. The blood which had been frozen in his veins now flowed back to his brain with frenzied violence. A short while ago the pale terrors of death, the funereal visions of the grave; now the passionate realities of love, the keen joys of life. Raymon felt young and daring as one is when, after being wrapped in the shrouds of a doom-laden dream, one is awakened and revived by a cheerful ray of sunlight.

'Poor Ralph!' he thought as, with a bold, light step, he went up the secret stairs. 'It's your own doing!'

PART 3

XVII

AFTER leaving Sir Ralph, Madame Delmare had shut herself in her room and a thousand disturbing thoughts had crossed her mind. It was not the first time that a vague suspicion had cast its ominous light on the frail edifice of her happiness. M. Delmare had already in conversation let slip some of those crude jokes which pass for compliments. He had congratulated Raymon on his chivalrous conquests in such a way as almost to put ears that knew nothing of the incident on to the right track. Every time Madame Delmare had a word with the gardener, Noun's name had come up, like a fatal necessity, in connection with the most trivial details; and then M. de Ramière's had slipped in, too, by some kind of linkage of ideas which seemed to have taken hold of the man's mind and obsessed him in spite of himself. Madame Delmare had been struck by his strange, clumsy questions. His language became confused when talking of the most unimportant matter. He seemed to be weighed down by a remorse which he betrayed in trying to conceal it. At other times, it was in Raymon's own embarrassment that Indiana found indications that she did not seek but which haunted her. One circumstance in particular would have enlightened her if she had not shut her heart to all mistrust. On Noun's finger they had found a very valuable ring which Madame Delmare had seen the girl wearing for some time before her death, and which she claimed to have found. Since then, Madame Delmare had always worn this token of grief and she had often seen Raymon turn pale when he grasped her hand to carry it to his lips. Once he had begged her never to talk to him of Noun, because he regarded himself as guilty of her death; and as she tried to rid him of that painful thought by taking all the wrongdoing on herself, he had replied:

'No, poor Indiana, don't accuse yourself. You don't know how guilty I am.'

These words, uttered gloomily and bitterly, had frightened Madame Delmare. She had not dared insist, and now that she was beginning to find an explanation for all these fragments of discoveries she still had not the courage to apply her mind to them and to piece them together.

She opened her window and, seeing the calm night and the beautiful, pale moon behind the silvery mist on the horizon, remembering that Raymon was about to come, that perhaps he was in the grounds, and thinking of all the happiness she had been looking forward to for that mysterious hour of love, she cursed Ralph, who, with a word, had just poisoned her hopes and destroyed her peace for ever. She even felt that she hated him, the unhappy man who had been a father to her and who had just sacrificed his future for her. For his future was Indiana's friendship; that was the only possession he valued and he resigned himself to losing it in order to save her.

Indiana could not read in the depths of his heart, nor had she been able to see to the bottom of Raymon's. She was unjust, not through ingratitude but through ignorance. Under the influence of a strong passion, she could not but feel deeply the blow she had just received. For one moment she blamed Ralph for the whole crime, preferring to accuse him rather than to suspect Raymon.

And then she had little time to collect her thoughts, to make a decision; Raymon was about to come. Perhaps it was even him she had seen in the last few minutes walking about near the little bridge. What aversion Ralph would have inspired in her at that moment if she had guessed that he was the shadowy figure who kept appearing and disappearing in the fog and who, placed like a spirit at the entrance to the Elysian fields,* tried to prohibit access to the guilty man!

Suddenly there occurred to her one of those bizarre, half-formed ideas that are conceived only by anxious and unhappy creatures. She risked her whole fate on a strange, subtle test that Raymon could not be on his guard against. She had scarcely finished preparing this mysterious device when she heard Raymon's steps on the secret staircase. She ran to open the door to him, then returned to her seat, so agitated that she felt she was going to fall. But, as in all the crises in her life, she retained a great clarity of judgement, a great strength of mind.

Raymon was still pale and out of breath when he opened the door; he was impatient to see the light and regain his grip on reality. Indiana had her back turned to him. She was wrapped in a fur-lined cloak; by a strange chance, it was the same one that Noun had chosen at the time of their last rendezvous to go to meet him in the grounds. I don't know if you remember that Raymon had had then, for a moment, the improbable idea that the woman wrapped up and concealed in the cloak was Madame Delmare. Now, when in the faint, vacillating lamplight he saw the same apparition slumped sadly on a chair, in the same place where so many memories lay in wait for him, in this room, pervaded by his remorse, which he had not entered since the most ill-fated hour of his life, he drew back involuntarily. He stayed at the door, fixing his frightened gaze on the motionless figure and trembling like a coward in case, when it turned round, it would reveal the livid features of a drowned woman.

Madame Delmare did not in the least suspect the effect she was having on Raymon. She had tied a scarf of Indian silk loosely round her head in the Creole manner. It was Noun's usual head-covering. Raymon, overcome by fear, nearly fell backwards, thinking he saw the realization of his superstitious thoughts. But as he recognized the woman he had come to seduce, he forgot the one he had seduced, and approached Indiana. She looked grave and thoughtful; she gazed at him steadily, but with more close attention than affection, and did not make a single movement to bring him to her side more quickly.

Raymon, surprised at this reception, attributed it to some chaste scruple, to a young woman's sensitive reserve. He went down on his knees saying:

'My beloved, are you afraid of me?'

But then he noticed that Madame Delmare was holding something which she seemed to be showing him with a playful affectation of gravity. He bent over to look and saw a mass of black hair of irregular length, which looked as if it had been cut hurriedly and which Indiana was holding together and smoothing in her hands.

'Do you recognize it?' she asked, fixing on him her limpid eyes, from which flashed a strange, penetrating gleam.

Raymon hesitated, looked again at the scarf round her head, and thought he understood.

'Naughty girl!' he said, taking the hair in his hand. 'But why did you cut it off? It was so beautiful and I loved it so dearly.'

'You were asking me yesterday,' she said with a kind of smile, 'if I would sacrifice it to you.'

'Oh, Indiana,' cried Raymon, 'you know very well that henceforth you will be still more beautiful for me. Do give it me. I don't want to be sorry that your head is without the hair I used to admire every day. Now I'll be able to kiss it freely every day. Give it to me so that it will never leave me.'

But as he took hold of it, as he gathered up in his hands the rich bundle of hair with some locks reaching right to the ground, Raymon thought he felt something dry and rough in it that his fingers had never felt in the tresses round Indiana's brow. He experienced, too, an indefinable nervous shudder when he felt it was cold and heavy, as if it had already been cut a long time, and when he noticed that it had lost its fragrant moisture and vital warmth. And then he examined it closely and sought in vain for the blue sheen which made it look like a crow's blue-tinged wing. This hair was completely black, like Indian hair, heavy and lifeless.

Indiana's bright, piercing eyes still followed Raymon's. His turned involuntarily to a half-open ebony box, from which some locks of the same hair were still protruding.

'It's not yours!' he said, removing the Indian kerchief, which was hiding Madame Delmare's.

Her hair was quite intact and fell abundantly around her shoulders. But she motioned him away and, still pointing to the cut hair said:

'Don't you recognize that hair, then? Have you never admired it, never caressed it? Has the damp night air made it lose all its fragrance? Haven't you one thought, one tear, for the girl who used to wear this ring?'

Raymon collapsed onto a chair. Noun's hair fell from his trembling hands. So many painful emotions had exhausted him. He was a man of irascible temperament, with rapidly circulating blood and deeply irritable nerves. He shuddered from head to foot and fell to the floor in a faint.

When he regained consciousness, Madame Delmare, kneeling beside him, was shedding tears over him and begging his pardon. But Raymon no longer loved her.

'You have given me excruciating pain,' he said, 'a pain which it is not in your power to remedy. You will never give me back, I feel, the trust that I had in your heart. You have just shown me how much vengeance and cruelty it contains. Poor Noun! Poor unlucky girl! It was her I wronged, and not you. It was she who had the right to avenge herself, but she didn't do so. She killed herself so as to leave the future to me. She sacrificed her life to avert trouble for me. *You*, Madame, would not have done so much! Give me that hair, it's mine, it belongs to me. It's all I have left of the only woman who truly loved me. Unhappy Noun! You deserved a better love! And it's you, Madame, who reproach me with her death, you whom I loved so much that I forgot her, that I confronted the frightful tortures of remorse; you who, on the faith of a kiss, made me cross that river and go over the bridge, alone, with terror at my side, pursued by the infernal illusions of my crime! And when you discover with what intoxicating passion I love you, you dig your woman's nails into my heart so as to find a last drop of blood which can still flow for you! Oh, when I spurned such a devoted love to pursue one that is so ferocious, I was as crazy as I was guilty.'

Madame Delmare made no reply. Pale and motionless with dishevelled hair and staring eyes, she moved Raymon to pity. He took her hand.

'And yet,' he said, 'the love I have for you is so blind that, in spite of myself, I feel I can still forget both the past and the present, the crime which has blighted my life and the one you have just committed. Love me still and I forgive you.'

Madame Delmare's despair rekindled desire as well as pride in her lover's heart. On seeing her so afraid of losing his love, so humble before him, so resigned to accepting his edicts for the future as vindication of the past, he remembered what his intentions had been when he had eluded Ralph's vigilance and he realized all the advantages of his position. For a few moments he pretended to be in a state of profound sadness, of gloomy meditation. He barely responded to Indiana's tears and caresses. He waited till her broken heart had burst into sobs, till she had appreciated all the horror of being deserted, till she had worn out her strength in agonizing fears. And then, when he saw her at his knees, half-dead, exhausted, awaiting death at a word from him, he grasped her in his arms with passionate frenzy and drew her to his breast. She yielded like a weak child; she abandoned her lips to him without resistance. She was almost lifeless.

But suddenly, as if waking from her dream, she snatched herself away from his burning caresses, fled to the end of the room, to the spot where Sir Ralph occupied the wall-panel, and as if she had put herself under the protection of that solemn personage with his pure brow and tranquil mouth, she pressed herself against the portrait, panting, distraught, and gripped by a strange fear. This made Raymon think that her emotions had been aroused in his arms, that she was afraid of herself, that she was his. He ran to her, pulled her forcibly from her retreat, and declared that he had come with the intention of keeping his promises but that her cruelty to him had freed him from his vows.

'I am no longer now your slave or your ally,' he said. 'I am only the man who loves you to distraction and holds you in his arms, you unkind, capricious, cruel woman, but one who is beautiful, mad, and adored. With gentle, trusting words, you would have calmed my blood; had you been serene and generous like yesterday, you would have made me mild and submissive as usual. But you made me in turn unhappy, cowardly, ill, furious, desperate. Now you must make me happy or I feel I can no longer believe in you, that I can no longer love and bless you. Forgive me, Indiana, forgive me! If I frighten you, it's your own fault. You have made me suffer so much that I have lost my reason.'

Indiana trembled from head to foot. She was so ignorant of life that she thought resistance was impossible. She was ready to grant from fear what she wanted to refuse from love. But as she struggled weakly in Raymon's arms, she said despairingly:

'So you'd be capable of using force with me!'

Raymon paused, struck by this moral resistance which outlasted her physical resistance. He quickly pushed her away.

'Never!' he cried. 'I'd rather die than have you against your will.'

He fell to his knees, and everything with which the mind can replace the heart, the poetry that the imagination can supply to the ardour of the blood, he put into a fervent and dangerous entreaty. But when he saw that she was not surrendering, he yielded to necessity and reproached her with not loving him, a despicable commonplace which made him laugh and feel almost ashamed of having an affair with a woman who was so naïve as not to laugh at it herself.

This reproach went to Indiana's heart more quickly than all the protestations with which Raymon had embellished his speeches.

But suddenly she remembered.

'Raymon,' she said, 'the girl you loved so dearly, the one we were talking about a few moments ago . . . Presumably she refused you nothing?'

'Nothing,' said Raymon, losing patience at this inopportune reminder. 'You keep on reminding me of her; you should instead be making me forget how much she loved me!'

'Tell me,' continued Indiana, gravely and thoughtfully. 'Be brave; I must say something more. Perhaps you were not as guilty towards me as I thought. It would be nice if I could pardon what I looked on as a mortal insult . . . Tell me then . . . when I surprised you there . . . whom did you come for? Her or me?'

Raymon hesitated. Then, as he thought that Madame Delmare would soon know the truth, that perhaps she knew it already, he replied:

'For her.'

'Well, I prefer it that way,' she said sadly. 'I prefer an infidelity to an insult. Be honest right to the end, Raymon. How long had you been in my room when I came in? Remem-

ber that Ralph knows everything and that if I want to question
him . . .'

'There is no need of Sir Ralph as an informer, Madame. I
had been here since the night before.'

'And you spent the night in this room? . . . Your silence tells
me all I need to know.'

They both remained silent for a few moments. Indiana got
up and was about to say something, when a sharp knock on
her door froze the blood in her veins. She and Raymon stood
quite still, not daring to breathe.

A piece of paper was slipped under the door. It was a leaf
from a notebook; on it were written in pencil, almost illegibly,
the words:

'Your husband is here.

                    RALPH.'

XVIII

'It's a wretchedly fabricated lie,' said Raymon, as soon as the faint sound of Sir Ralph's steps had died away. 'Sir Ralph needs a lesson and I'll give him one such as . . .'

'I forbid you,' said Indiana coldly and decisively. 'My husband is here. Ralph never lies. We are lost, you and I. There was a time when I would have frozen with terror at the thought. Today I don't care!'

'Well,' said Raymon, enthusiastically grasping her in his arms, 'since death is at hand, be mine! Forgive me everything, and in this supreme moment let your last word be one of love, my last breath one of happiness.'

'This moment of terror and courage might have been the most wonderful of my life,' she said, 'but you have spoiled it for me.'

The sound of wheels could be heard in the farmyard and the entrance bell was rung roughly and impatiently.

'I know that ring,' said Indiana tersely and coolly. 'Ralph didn't tell a lie, but you have time to escape. Run!'

'No, I don't want to,' cried Raymon. 'I suspect some foul betrayal, and you won't be its only victim. I shall remain and my body will protect you.'

'There is no betrayal . . . Don't you see that the servants are aroused and the gate is about to be opened . . . Run, the trees in the garden will hide you, and then the moon isn't up yet. Not another word. Go!'

Raymon was forced to obey, but she went with him to the foot of the staircase and cast a searching look at the tree-clumps in the flower-garden. All was silent and calm. She stayed a long time on the last step, listening in terror to the sound of his steps on the gravel path and not thinking any more of her husband's arrival. What did his suspicions and anger matter, provided that Raymon was out of danger!

As for him, he crossed the river and grounds with a quick, light step. He reached the little gate but had some difficulty opening it. He had only just gone through it when Sir Ralph appeared before him and, as calmly as if he had gone up to him at a large party, said:

'Do me the favour of handing me that key. If anyone looks for it, there won't be any trouble if it's found in my hands.'

Raymon would have preferred the most mortal insult to this ironic generosity.

'I wouldn't be the man to forget a genuine service,' he said, 'but I would be the man to avenge an insult and punish a treachery.'

Sir Ralph did not change the tone of his voice or the expression of his face.

'I don't want your gratitude,' he replied, 'and I await your vengeance unconcernedly. But now is not the moment to talk to each other. That's your path; think of Madame Delmare's honour.'

And he disappeared.

This night of violent emotions had had such a shattering effect on Raymon's mind that, for the moment, he would have been prepared to believe in magic. He arrived at Cercy at daybreak and went to bed with a fever.

As for Madame Delmare, she did the honours of the breakfast table for her husband and cousin with great calm and dignity. She had not yet reflected on her situation. She was completely dominated by instinct, which imposed calmness and presence of mind on her. The Colonel was gloomy and worried, but his business alone occupied his mind and there were no jealous suspicions in his thoughts.

Towards evening, Raymon felt strong enough to turn his mind to his love-affair, but his love had greatly diminished. He liked obstacles, but he recoiled from troubles and he foresaw a great many now that Indiana had the right to reproach him. Finally, he remembered that his honour required him to ask for news of her, so he sent his servant to Lagny to find out what was happening there. The messenger brought back the following letter which Madame Delmare had handed to him:

'Last night I hoped I would lose my reason or my life. To my misfortune, I have retained both, but I shall not complain; I have deserved the pain I am feeling. I wanted to live that passionate life; it would be cowardly to draw back today. I don't know if you're guilty and I don't want to know. We'll never return to that subject, will we? It hurts us both too much; so I'll mention it now for the last time.

'You made one remark to me which gave me a cruel pleasure. Poor Noun! From heaven above, forgive me. You suffer no longer, you love no longer, perhaps you pity me! ... You told me, Raymon, that you sacrificed that unhappy girl to me, that you loved me more than her ... Oh, don't take back what you said, you said it. I need so much to believe it, that I do believe it. And yet your behaviour last night, your entreaties, your wild declarations, ought to have made me doubt it. I forgave you because of the agitated state you were in. Now you have been able to reflect, to return to your right mind. Tell me, are you willing to give up loving me in that way? I love you with the heart, and I have thought until now that I would be able to inspire in you a love as pure as my own. And then I hadn't thought too much about the future. I hadn't looked very far ahead and I wasn't frightened by the idea that one day, conquered by your devotion, I would sacrifice my scruples and my reluctance to you. But today, that can no longer be the case. In such a future I can only see a frightening equality with Noun. Oh, to be loved no more than she was loved! If I believed that ... And yet she was more beautiful than me, far more beautiful. Why did you prefer me? You must have loved me differently and better ... That's what I wanted to tell you. Will you give up being my lover in the way you were hers? In that case, I can still esteem you, believe in your remorse, in your sincerity, in your love; if not, think no more about me, you'll never see me again. Perhaps I shall die as a result, but I prefer to die than to descend to being merely your mistress.'

Raymon was in some embarrassment as to how to reply. Her pride offended him. Till then he had never believed that a woman who had thrown herself into his arms would have been able to resist him openly and give reasons for her resistance.

'She doesn't love me,' he said to himself. 'She is cold-hearted and arrogant.'

From that moment, he no longer loved her. She had wounded his self-esteem; she had disappointed the hope of one of his conquests, ruined the expectation of one of his pleasures. As far as he was concerned, she was no longer even what Noun had been. Poor Indiana! She who had wanted to be more! Her passionate love was misunderstood, her blind trust had been despised. Raymon had never understood her; how could he have loved her for long?

Then, in his annoyance, he vowed he would triumph over her. He no longer vowed this out of pride, but in a spirit of vengeance. For him it was no longer a question of attaining happiness, but of punishing an insult, not of possessing a woman but of humiliating her. He vowed he would be her master and then he would abandon her so as to have the pleasure of seeing her at his feet.

In his first reaction, he wrote the following letter:

'You want me to promise you . . . You crazy girl, can you think of such a thing? I promise everything you want, because I can only obey you . . . But if I don't keep my promises, I shan't be guilty before God or you. If you loved me, Indiana, you wouldn't inflict these cruel tortures on me, you wouldn't expose me to being false to my word, you wouldn't be ashamed to be my mistress . . . But you think you would demean yourself in my arms . . .'

Raymon felt that his bitterness was becoming apparent in spite of himself. He tore up this beginning and, having given himself time for reflection, he began again:

'You admit that you nearly went out of your mind last night. I went out of mine completely. I was guilty . . . but no, I was crazy. Forget those painful, intoxicating hours. I'm calm now; I've thought things over; I'm still worthy of you. Bless you, angel from heaven, for having saved me from myself, for having reminded me how I ought to love you. Command me, now, Indiana! I am your slave, you know that very well. I would give my life for one hour in your arms, but I am capable of suffering a whole lifetime to get one of your smiles. I shall be your friend, your brother, nothing more. If I suffer, you will be unaware of it. If, at your side, my blood is kindled, if my heart is inflamed, if a cloud passes over my eyes when I touch your hand, if a gentle kiss from your lips, a sisterly kiss, burns my brow, I shall command my blood to calm down, my head to become cool again, my mouth to respect you. I shall be gentle, I shall be submissive, I shall be unhappy and enjoy my tortures if you are to be happier that way, provided I still hear you say you love me. Oh, say that to me; give me back your trust and my happiness; tell me when we shall see each other again. I don't know what the outcome of last night's events may have been. How is it that you don't tell me anything about it, that you have been leaving me in agony since this morning? Carle saw the three of you walking in the grounds. The Colonel looked ill and sad, but not angry. So that Ralph won't have betrayed us! What a strange man! But what reliance can we place on his discretion, and how shall I dare show myself again at Lagny, now that our fate is in his hands? Yet I shall dare. Even if I have to stoop so low as to implore him, I shall humble my pride, I shall conquer my aversion, I shall do everything rather than lose you. One word from you and I shall burden my life with as much remorse as I can take. For you I would even desert my mother; for you I would commit any crime. Oh! if you realized the extent of my love, Indiana! . . .'

The pen fell from Raymon's hands. He was horribly tired, he was falling asleep. Nevertheless he read over the letter to assure himself that his ideas had not been influenced by his sleepiness. But he found it impossible to understand what he meant, so much was his mind affected by the exhaustion of his physical strength. He rang for his servant, ordered him to set off for Lagny before daybreak, and slept the deep, precious sleep whose soothing delights are known only to people who are satisfied with themselves. Madame Delmare did not go to bed. She was not conscious of fatigue. She spent the night writing, and when she received Raymon's letter she replied to it without delay:

'Thank you, Raymon, thank you! You give me strength and life. Now I can face everything bravely, endure everything, for you love me and the hardest tests don't frighten you. Yes, we'll see each other again, we'll face everything. Ralph can do as he likes with our secret. I'm not worrying about anything any more, since you love me. I'm no longer even afraid of my husband.

'You want to know the state of our affairs? . . . I forgot to tell you about them yesterday though they have taken quite an important turn as regards my financial situation. We are ruined. There is talk of selling Lagny; there is even a suggestion that we might go and live in the colonies . . . But what does all that matter? I can't bring myself to bother about that. I know definitely we'll never be parted. You have sworn that to me, Raymon. I count on your promise; count on my courage. Nothing will frighten me, nothing will deter me. My place is designated at your side, and death alone will be able to tear me from it.'

'What extravagant feminine emotionalism!' said Raymon, crumpling the letter. 'Romantic plans, dangerous enterprises, appeal to their weak imaginations just as bitter food stimulates sick people's appetites. I've succeeded, I've regained my power, and as for those imprudent follies she threatens me with, we'll see! That's just like those false, frivolous creatures, always ready to undertake the impossible and turning generosity into a show of virtue requiring scandal. To see that letter, who would believe that she rations her kisses and is stingy with her caresses?'

The same day, he went to Lagny. Ralph was not there. The Colonel received Raymon in a friendly manner and spoke to him in confidence. He took him into the grounds so as to be able to speak more freely, and there he told him that he was completely ruined and that the factory would be up for sale the next day. Raymon offered his help, but Delmare declined it.

'No, my friend,' he said, 'I've suffered too much from the thought that I owed my lot to Ralph's kindness; I have been anxious to pay my debt to him. The sale of this property will put me in a position to pay all my debts at once. It's true I'll have nothing left. But I have courage, vigour, and business experience; the future is before us. I've built up my little fortune once, I can do it again. I must do so for my wife; she is young and I don't want to leave her in poverty. She still owns a modest dwelling in Bourbon Island. I want to take refuge there and start in business again. In a few years' time, in ten years at most, I hope we'll meet again.'

Raymon pressed the Colonel's hand, smiling inwardly at seeing his confidence in the future, at hearing him speak of ten years as if it were one day, when his bald head and enfeebled body indicated failing health and a spent life. Nevertheless, he pretended to share his hopes.

'I'm delighted to see that you don't let yourself be discouraged by these reversals of fortune,' he said. 'In that, I recognize your manly heart, your fearless character. But does Madame Delmare show the same courage? Don't you fear some resistance to your plans for leaving the country?'

'I'm sorry about it,' the Colonel replied, 'but women are made to obey and not to give advice. I haven't yet definitely told Indiana of my decision. Apart from you, my friend, I don't see that she has much to regret here. And yet, if it's only from a spirit of contradiction, I foresee tears, nervous attacks ... The devil take women! Anyway, it doesn't matter. I count on you, my dear Raymon, to make my wife listen to reason. She trusts you. Use your influence to stop her crying. I loathe tears.'

Raymon promised to return the next day to tell Madame Delmare her husband's decision.

'You're doing me a real service,' said the Colonel. 'I'll take Ralph to the farm so that you'll be free to talk to her.

'Well, what luck!' thought Raymon, as he departed.

XIX

M. DELMARE'S plans were quite in accord with what Raymon wanted. He foresaw that this love-affair, which, as far as he was concerned, was nearing its end, would soon lead to his being pestered and harassed. He was quite pleased to see events turning out in such a way as to preserve him from the irksome, inevitable consequences of a played-out affair. All that remained for him now was to take advantage of the last moments of Madame Delmare's emotional excitement and then to leave to his benevolent fate the care of ridding him of her tears and reproaches.

So he went to Lagny the next day with the intention of bringing the unhappy woman's enthusiasm to its climax.

'Do you know, Indiana, the task your husband has laid on me with regard to you?' he said when he arrived. 'A strange commission, to be sure! I have to beg you to go to Bourbon Island, to plead with you to leave me, to tear out my heart and my life. Do you think he's made a good choice of advocate?'

Madame Delmare's melancholy gravity imposed a kind of respect on Raymon's wiles.

'Why do you come and talk to me about all this?' she asked. 'Are you afraid that I'll let myself be persuaded? Do you fear that I'll obey? Be reassured, Raymon, I've made up my mind. I've spent two nights considering the matter from all angles. I know what I'm laying myself open to. I know what I must face, what I must sacrifice, what I must despise. I am ready to cross this stormy patch of my fate. Will you not be my support and my guide?'

Raymon was tempted to be afraid of her calmness and to take her crazy threats literally. But then he entrenched himself in his opinion that Indiana did not love him and that she was now applying to her situation the exaggerated feelings she had acquired from books. He made strenuous efforts to be passionately eloquent, to improvise dramatically, so as to remain at his romantic mistress's level, and he succeeded in prolonging her error. But for a calm, impartial spectator, this love scene would have been the fiction of the theatre in conflict with reality. Raymon's exaggerated feelings, his poetic ideas, would have seemed a cold, cruel parody of the genuine feelings that Indiana expressed so simply: the one was cerebral, the other spoke from the heart.

Raymon, who, nevertheless, was a little afraid that she would fulfil her promises if he did not skilfully undermine the resistance plan she had formed, persuaded her to feign submission or indifference until the moment when she could declare open rebellion. He said she must not announce her intention before leaving Lagny, so as to avoid scandal in front of the servants and Ralph's dangerous intervention in the matter.

But Ralph did not leave his unfortunate friends. In vain he offered all his fortune, his house at Belleville, his income from England, and the sale of his colonial plantations. The Colonel was inflexible. His friendship for Ralph had diminished. He did not want to be in debt to him any more. Ralph, gifted with Raymon's skill and wit, might perhaps have been able to persuade him. But when he had clearly set out his ideas and declared his feelings, the poor baronet thought he had said all there was to say and he never expected a refusal to be retracted. He left Bellerive and followed M. and Madame Delmare to Paris, where they awaited their departure for Bourbon Island.

The house at Lagny was put up for sale with the factory and outbuildings. For Madame Delmare it was a sad, gloomy winter. To be sure, Raymon was in Paris and saw her every day; he was attentive and affectionate but he would stay barely an hour with her. You know that society was Raymon's element, his life; he needed the noise, the activity, the crowd, in order to breathe, to gain full mastery of his wit, his ease of manner, all his superiority. In a small, intimate group he could make himself agreeable, but at a society gathering he would become brilliant again; then, no longer the member of a particular coterie, the friend of this one or that one, he would be the man of superior intellect who belongs to everybody and for whom society is a natural element.

And then Raymon had principles; we have already told you that. When he saw the Colonel show him so much trust and friendship, look on him as a model of honour and sincerity, and appoint him as a mediator between his wife and himself, he resolved to justify the trust, to deserve the friendship, to reconcile M. and Madame Delmare and to rebuff any preference on the part of the wife which might have disturbed the peace of the husband. He became once again a moral, virtuous, reasonable person. You will see for how long.

Indiana, who did not understand this conversion, suffered acutely at seeing herself neglected. She still had the happiness, however, of not admitting to herself the complete ruin of her hopes. She was easy to deceive; she asked for nothing more; her real life was so bitter and dreary. Her husband was becoming almost impossible. In public he made a show of the courage and indifference of a man of spirit; in the privacy of his own home he was no better than an irritable, obstinate, ridiculous child. Indiana was the victim of his troubles and, we must admit, it was largely her own fault. If she had raised her voice, if she had complained affectionately but forcibly, Delmare, who was merely rough, would have blushed to be thought of as unkind. Nothing was easier than to soften his heart and dominate his mind, if one was willing to descend to his level and enter into the range of ideas that were within the grasp of his mind. But Indiana's submission was stiff and haughty. She always obeyed in silence. But it was the silence and the submission of a slave who has made a virtue of hatred and a merit of misfortune. Her resignation was like the dignity of a king who accepts fetters and a dungeon rather than abdicate and renounce an empty title. A commonplace woman would have dominated that unrefined man. She would have spoken in his way but would have reserved the right to think differently. She would have pretended to respect his prejudices but, in private, she would have trampled them underfoot. She would have been affectionate but she would have deceived him. Indiana saw many women who behaved in this way, but she felt so much above them that she would have blushed to imitate them. As she was virtuous and chaste, she thought she was not obliged to flatter her master in her words

so long as she respected him in her deeds. She wanted none of
his affection because she could not respond to it. She would
have considered herself much more guilty in making a show
of love for her husband whom she did not love, than in
granting it to the lover who inspired love in her. Deception,
that was the crime in her eyes, and twenty times a day she
felt ready to declare that she loved Raymon; only the fear of
losing Raymon held her back. Her cold obedience irritated the
Colonel much more than a skilful rebellion would have done.
If his pride would have suffered from not being the absolute
master in his house, he suffered much more from being so in
a hateful or ridiculous way. He would have liked to convince,
but he merely commanded; to reign, but he merely governed.
Sometimes, in his own home, he gave a badly explained order
or thoughtlessly issued orders harmful to his own interests.
Madame Delmare had them carried out without scrutiny or
question, with the indifference of a horse that draws the
plough in one direction or another.

When he saw the consequence of his ill-comprehended
ideas, of his misunderstood wishes, Delmare would fly into a
rage, but when, calmly and coldly, she proved to him that she
had only strictly obeyed his orders, he was reduced to turning
his anger against himself. To such a man, with his petty *amour
propre* but violent sensations, it caused cruel pain and was a
biting insult.

He would then have killed his wife if he had been in Smyrna
or Cairo. And yet, in the depths of his heart he loved the weak
woman who lived under his sway and kept the secret of her ill
usage with a religious prudence. He loved her or he pitied her,
I don't know which. He would have liked her to love him, for
he was proud of her superior breeding. He would have been
elevated in his own eyes if she had deigned to stoop so far as
to come to terms with his ideas and principles. When he went
into her room in the morning, intending to pick a quarrel with
her, sometimes he would find her asleep and he would not
dare to wake her up. He would gaze at her in silence; he would
be alarmed at the delicacy of her constitution, at the pallor of
her cheeks, at the air of calm melancholy, of resigned unhappiness, expressed in her still, silent face. In her features he

would find a thousand subjects for reproach, remorse, anger, and fear. He would blush at feeling the influence that so frail a creature had exercised over his destiny, over him, a man of iron, used to commanding others, to seeing heavily armed squadrons, fiery horses, and men of war march at a word from him.

So a woman who was still a child had made him unhappy! She forced him to look within himself, to examine his decisions, to modify many of them, to retract several, and all that without deigning to say 'You are wrong; please do it this way.' She had never pleaded with him; she had never deigned to show she was his equal or to admit she was his partner. This woman, whom he could have crushed in his hand if he had so wished, there she lay, a puny creature, perhaps dreaming of another under his eyes, and defying him even in her sleep. He was tempted to strangle her, to drag her by her hair, to trample her underfoot, to force her to cry for mercy, to beg for his pardon. But she was so pretty, so fair and dainty, that he would take pity on her, like a child who is moved to compassion when looking at the bird he was intending to kill. And that man of steel would weep like a woman and leave the room so that she would not have the triumph of seeing him weep. To tell the truth, I do not know which of them was more unhappy, he or she. She was cruel out of virtue as he was kind out of weakness; she had too much patience, he did not have enough; she had the failings of her virtues but he had the virtues of his failings.

Around these two ill-assorted beings jostled a crowd of friends who tried to bring them closer together, some for lack of anything else to do, others from self-importance, others still from ill-advised affection. Some took the wife's side, others took the husband's. These people quarrelled with each other about M. and Madame Delmare, but the two did not quarrel at all; for with Indiana's systematic submission, whatever he did, the Colonel could never manage to start a quarrel. And then people who knew nothing about the matter came along and wanted to make themselves necessary. They advised submission to Madame Delmare, not seeing that she was already too submissive; others advised the husband to be inflexible and not to let his authority go to the distaff side. These latter, thick-headed people, who feel so insignificant that they are always afraid of being trodden on and always support each other, constitute a species you will find everywhere; they always get under other people's feet and make a lot of noise so as to be noticed.

M. and Madame Delmare had in particular got to know people at Melun and Fontainebleau. In Paris the couple resumed acquaintance with them and they were the keenest to pursue the scandal which was brewing around the Colonel and his wife. The mentality of small towns is the most spiteful in the world, as you no doubt know. There, worthwhile people are always misunderstood and superior minds are born public enemies. If a fool or a boor has to be defended, you will see them come running up. If you have a quarrel with someone, they come to watch as if at a play; they make bets; they crowd round you right up to the soles of your shoes, so eager are they to see and hear. They cover the loser with mud and curses; the one who is always in the wrong is the weaker one. If you are up in arms against prejudice, pettiness, and vice, you are insulting them personally; you attack them in what they hold most dear; you are a dangerous traitor. You will be summoned before the courts to make reparation by people whose names you do not know, but you will be convicted of having referred to them in your dishonest allusions. What more can I say? If you meet one of these people, take care not to step on his shadow, even at sunset when a man's shadow stretches for thirty feet. All that territory belongs to the small town inhabitant; you have no right to set foot in it. If you breathe the air he breathes, you wrong him, you ruin his health; if you drink at his fountain, you dry it up; if you increase trade in his region, you increase the price of the commodities he has to buy; if you offer him snuff, you poison it; if you praise his wife's domestic virtues, you are being coldly ironic, for in your heart you despise her ignorance; if you have the bad luck to think of a compliment to pay him in his house, he will not appreciate it and he will go about everywhere saying that you have insulted him. Take your household gods and convey them to the heart of the woods or far into the desolate moors. Only there, and at best, the small-town inhabitant will leave you in peace.

Even within the many walls enclosing Paris, the small town returned to the attack on the unhappy household. Well-off families from Fontainebleau and Melun came to settle in the capital for the winter and brought with them the benefits of their provincial ways. Coteries grew up around Delmare and his wife, and everything humanly possible was attempted to make their respective positions worse. Their unhappiness was increased and their mutual obstinacy did not diminish.

Ralph had the good sense not to interfere in their differences. Madame Delmare had suspected him of embittering her husband against her, or at least of wanting to expel Raymon from her intimacy, but she soon recognized the injustice of her accusations. The Colonel's complete peace of mind with respect to M. de Ramière was irrefutable evidence of her cousin's silence. She then felt she wanted to thank him, but he carefully avoided all discussion of the matter. Whenever she was alone with him, he eluded her attempted explanations and pretended not to understand them. It was such a delicate subject that Madame Delmare was not bold enough to force Ralph to embark on it; she just tried by her loving concern and her delicate, affectionate attentions to make him understand how grateful she was. But Ralph seemed not to notice them and Indiana's pride suffered from the proud generosity he showed her. She was afraid of playing the part of a guilty woman who begs for the indulgence of a strict witness. She again became cold and stiff with poor Ralph. It seemed to her that, in this matter, his behaviour accorded with his selfishness, that he was still fond of her although he no longer esteemed her, that he needed her company only as a pastime, that he did not want to give up habits that she had formed for him in her home or the attentions which she unwearingly lavished on him. Moreover, she thought he was disinclined to accuse her of wronging her husband or herself.

'That's just like his contempt for women,' she thought. 'In his eyes they are merely domestic animals, fit to keep a house in order, prepare meals, and serve tea. He doesn't do them the honour of discussing things with them. Their faults can't affect him, provided they're not relevant to him personally and in no way disturb the material habits of his life. Ralph doesn't need my heart. Provided my hands retain the skill of preparing his pudding and plucking the strings of my harp for him, what does it matter to him that I love another, that I suffer in silence, that I cannot patiently endure the yoke which is crushing me? I am his servant; he asks nothing more of me.'

XX

INDIANA no longer reproached Raymon. He defended himself so badly that she was afraid of finding him too guilty. There was one thing she feared much more than being deceived and that was being deserted. She could no longer do without believing in him, without hope of the future he had promised her; for the life she lived with M. Delmare and M. Ralph had become hateful to her and if she had not expected to be delivered soon from the domination of these two men, she too would have drowned herself. She often thought of it. She told herself that if Raymon treated her like Noun, her only remaining resource against escaping an unbearable future was to rejoin Noun. This grim thought followed her everywhere and she took pleasure in it.

Meanwhile the date fixed for their departure was drawing near. The Colonel did not seem to have any suspicion of the resistance his wife was contemplating. Every day he put some of his affairs in order; every day he freed himself from one of his debts; these preparations were looked at calmly by Madame Delmare, so sure was she of her own courage. She too, on her side, was preparing for the struggle against difficulties. She tried to gain support in advance from Madame de Carvajal. She told her of her dislike of the journey, and the old marchioness who, in all good faith, based great hopes of attracting *clientèle* to her salon on her niece's beauty, declared that it was the Colonel's duty to leave his wife in France. She said it would be barbaric to expose Madame Delmare to the fatigue and danger of an ocean crossing when, for a little while now, she had been in better health; in a word, it was for him to go and work at rebuilding his fortune, but Indiana should stay with her old aunt and look after her. At first M. Delmare thought these insinuations were the senseless ramblings of an old woman, but he was obliged to pay more attention when Madame de Carvajal made him understand clearly that that was the price of her inheritance. Although Delmare loved money like a man who had worked strenuously all his life to amass it, there was pride in his character. He pronounced his decision firmly and declared that his wife would accompany him whatever the risk. The Marchioness, who could not believe that money was not the absolute ruler of every sensible man, did not regard this reply as M. Delmare's last word. She continued to encourage her niece's resistance, proposing to cover it in the eyes of the world under the cloak of her responsibility. All the insensitivity of a mind corrupted by intrigue and ambition, all the hypocrisy of a heart warped by a show of piety, were needed for Madame de Carvajal to be able to close her eyes to the real reasons for Indiana's rebellion. Her passion for M. de Ramière was a secret now only for her husband; but as Indiana had not yet given any scope for scandal, the secret was only passed around in whispers, and Madame de Carvajal had been confidentially told of it by more than twenty people. The silly old woman was flattered by it; all she wanted was that her niece should be in the forefront of society and Raymond's love was an excellent start. Yet Madame de Carvajal's character was not of the Regency type.* The Restoration had given minds of that sort an impetus towards virtue, and as decorous behaviour was required at court, the Marchioness hated nothing so much as scandal which ruins and destroys. Under Madame du Barry,* her principles would have been less rigid; under the Dauphin's wife,* she became strait-laced. But all this was for outside show, for appearances. She kept her disapproval and her contempt for glaring misdemeanours, and before condemning an affair she always awaited its outcome. She was indulgent to infidelities committed in privacy indoors. She became Spanish again when passing judgement on passions obvious outside the shutters; in her eyes, guilt lay only with those which were displayed in the street in view of the passers-by. Indiana, passionate but chaste, in love but restrained, was a valuable object to show off and exploit. A woman like her could captivate the topmost brains of this hypocritical society and withstand the dangers of the most delicate missions. Excellent speculations could be attempted on the responsibility of so pure a soul and so ardent a temperament. Poor Indiana! Fortunately her fatal destiny surpassed all her expectations and dragged her into a path to wretchedness where the terrible protection of her aunt did not go in search of her.

Raymon did not worry about what was to become of her. This love-affair had already reached the ultimate degree of distaste and boredom. To be boring is to descend as far down as possible in the heart of one's beloved. Fortunately for the last days of her illusion, Indiana did not yet suspect it.

One morning, on returning from a ball, he found Madame Delmare in his room. She had gone there at midnight; for five long hours she had been waiting for him. It was at the coldest time of the year. She had been there, without a fire, suffering from cold and anxiety with the melancholy patience that the course of her life had taught her. She looked up when she saw him come in and Raymon, stunned with amazement, could see no expression of annoyance or reproach on her pale face.

'I was waiting for you,' she said gently. 'Since you hadn't come to see me for three days and meanwhile things have happened that you ought to be informed of without delay, I left home last night to come and tell you about them.'

'You've been unbelievably imprudent!' said Raymon, carefully closing the door behind him. 'And my servants know you're here! They've just told me.'

'I made no secret of my presence,' she replied coldly, 'and, as for the word you use, I think it ill-chosen.'

'I said imprudent; I ought to have said insane.'

'*I* would have said *courageous*. But it doesn't matter. Listen to me. M. Delmare intends to leave for Bordeaux in three days, and from there for the colonies. It was agreed between us that you would save me from violence if he used any. There's no doubt that he will, for I told him my decision yesterday evening and I was locked in my room. I escaped by a window. Look, my hands are bloodstained. At this moment they may be looking for me. But Ralph is at Bellerive and he won't be able to say where I am. I've decided to stay in hiding till M. Delmare has made up his mind to leave me behind. Have you thought of securing a refuge for me, of making preparations for my escape? It's such a long time since I've been able to see you alone that I don't know what stage your preparations have reached. But one day, when I expressed doubts about your resolution, you told me you couldn't conceive of love without trust. You pointed out that you had never doubted me; you showed me I was unjust, and then I was afraid of being below your level if I didn't abandon these childish suspicions and the innumerable feminine demands that degrade commonplace love-affairs. I bore with resignation the shortness of your visits, the constraint of our interviews, the eagerness with which you seemed to avoid any open expression of feeling between us; I kept my trust in you. Heaven is my witness that anxiety and terror gnawed at my heart. I repulsed them as criminal thoughts. Today I have come to seek the reward for my faith. The moment has come. Tell me, do you accept my sacrifices?'

The crisis was so urgent that Raymon no longer had the courage to pretend. Desperate, furious at seeing himself caught in his own snares, he lost his head and let himself go in brutal, coarse language.

'You're mad,' he cried, throwing himself into a chair. 'Where have you dreamed about love? In what novel written for ladies' maids have you studied society, I ask you?'

Then he stopped, realizing he had been far too rough and trying to think how to tell her these things in other words and send her away without insulting her.

But she was calm like someone prepared to hear anything.

'Go on,' she said crossing her arms over her heart which gradually ceased to throb so violently. 'I'm listening to you. No doubt you've more than that to tell me.'

'Yet another effort of the imagination, yet another love scene,' thought Raymon.

And springing to his feet, he cried:

'Never, never will I accept such sacrifices. When I told you I'd have the strength, I boasted, Indiana, or rather I maligned myself, for only a coward can agree to dishonour the woman he loves. In your ignorance of life, you didn't understand the seriousness of such a plan, and I, in my despair at the thought of losing you, I didn't want to give it careful thought . . .'

'Careful thought is coming back to you pretty quickly!' she said, withdrawing her hand which he wanted to take.

'Indiana,' he went on, 'don't you see that you impose dishonour on me while reserving heroism for yourself, and that you are condemning me because I want to remain worthy of your love? Could you still love me, ignorant and naïve woman that you are, if I sacrificed your life to my pleasures, your reputation to my own interests?'

'You're saying very contradictory things,' said Indiana. 'If, by staying at your side, I make you happy, what do you fear from public opinion? Do you care about it more than you do for me?'

'Oh, it's not for my own sake that I care about it, Indiana! . . .'

'So it's for mine? I've foreseen your scruples and, to rid you of all remorse, I've taken the initiative. I haven't waited for you to come and snatch me away from my home; I haven't even consulted you before stepping outside the threshold of my house for ever. That decisive step has been taken and your conscience can't reproach you with it. At this moment, Raymon, I am dishonoured. In your absence, I counted by this clock the hours that consummated my shame. And now, although daybreak finds my brow as pure as it was yesterday, I'm a lost woman in public opinion. Yesterday, there was still compassion for me in women's hearts; today there will be nothing but contempt. I weighed all that up before taking action.'

'Abominable woman's foresight!' thought Raymon.

And then, struggling against her as against a bailiff who had come to seize his furniture, he said in a caressing, fatherly tone:

'You're exaggerating to yourself the importance of the step you've taken. No, my dear, all is not lost because of one blunder. I'll order my servants to say nothing . . .'

'Will you order mine to say nothing? They're probably looking for me anxiously at this very moment. And my husband, do you think he'll quietly keep the secret? Do you think he'll be willing to have me back tomorrow when I've spent a whole night under your roof? Do you advise me to go back to throw myself at his feet and ask him, as a token of his mercy, to be so good as to put back on my neck the chain that has destroyed my life and blighted my youth? Would you consent, without regret, to the woman you loved so much being returned to the sway of another, when you are master of her fate, when you can keep her in your arms for the rest of your life, when she is there in your power, offering to stay there for ever? Would you have no reluctance, would you not be afraid to give her back straight away to that implacable master who is waiting for her, perhaps only to kill her?'

A sudden thought crossed Raymon's mind. The moment had arrived to conquer her feminine pride or it never would. She had come to offer him all the sacrifices he did not want and she stood there in front of him haughtily confident that she ran the risk of no other dangers than those she had foreseen. Raymon thought of a way of getting rid of her unwelcome devotion and of gaining something from it. He was too good a friend of Delmare's, he owed too much consideration to the Colonel's trust in him, to rob him of his wife; he must content himself with seducing her.

'You are right, my Indiana,' he exclaimed eagerly. 'You bring me back to myself. You revive my ardour which had been frozen by the thought of your dangers and the fear of hurting you. Forgive my childish concern and try to understand all the affection and genuine love contained in it. But your sweet voice makes all my blood tingle, your passionate words pour fire into my veins; forgive me, forgive me for being able to think of anything other than the ineffable moment when I shall possess you. Let me forget all the dangers that beset us and thank you on my knees for the happiness you bring me. Let me live completely in this blissful hour that I am spending at your feet and which all my blood would not pay for. Let him come then to snatch you from my ardent embrace, that stupid husband who locks you up and falls asleep in his coarse brutality. Let him come and drag you from my arms, you, my beloved, my life! Henceforth you no longer belong to him; you are my lover, my companion, my mistress . . .'

While speaking in this way, Raymon grew more and more excited, as he usually did when pleading the cause of his passions. The situation was heady, romantic; it was filled with dangers. Raymon, like a true descendant of a race of valiant knights, loved risk. Every sound he heard in the street seemed to him to be the arrival of the husband coming to claim his wife and his rival's blood. To seek the raptures of love in the exciting emotions of such a situation was a pleasure worthy of Raymon. For a quarter of an hour he loved Madame Delmare passionately; he lavished on her the seductions of a burning eloquence. His language was powerful, his behaviour sincere —this man whose ardent spirit treated love as an agreeable accomplishment. He enacted passion so well that he deceived himself. Shame on that foolish woman! With delight she let herself be taken in by these deceptive protestations. She felt happy; she was radiant with hope and joy. She forgave everything, she nearly accorded everything.

But Raymon lost his own cause by being in too much of a hurry. If he had used his skill to prolong for another twenty-four hours the situation in which Indiana had ventured to put herself at risk, she might have been his. But the day was breaking bright and crimson; it was casting floods of light into the room and the sounds from outside were increasing every moment. Raymon cast a glance at the clock, which showed seven o'clock.

'It's time to make an end of the matter,' he thought. 'Delmare might arrive at any moment, and before that I must make her decide to go home voluntarily.'

He became more pressing and less affectionate. His pale lips betrayed the torment of an impatience more domineering than tactful. There was a certain abruptness, almost anger, in his kisses. Indiana took fright. A good angel spread its wings over that wavering, troubled heart. She recovered herself and repulsed the cold selfish attacks of vice.

'Leave me,' she said. 'I don't want to give out of weakness what I want to be able to grant out of love or gratitude. You don't need proofs of my affection; my presence here is proof enough and I bring the future with me. But let me keep all the strength of my conscience to fight against the powerful obstacles that still separate us. I need stoicism and calm.'

'What are you talking about?' asked Raymon angrily. He was not listening to her and was furious at her resistance.

And, completely losing his head, hurt and annoyed, he pushed her away roughly, walked up and down the room, his heart heavy and his head on fire. He took up a water jug and gulped down a large glass of water, which suddenly calmed his agitation and cooled his love. Then, looking at her ironically, he said:

'Come, Madame, it's time for you to leave.'

At last a ray of light enlightened Indiana and laid Raymon's heart bare before her.

'You're right,' she said.

And she made her way to the door.

'But take your cloak and your boa,' he said, stopping her.

'Yes, of course, these traces of my presence might compromise you,' she replied.

'You are a child,' he said coaxingly as he put her cloak around her as if she were a baby. 'You know very well that I love you. But, really, you delight in torturing me and you drive me mad. Wait while I call a cab for you. If I could, I would take you all the way home but that would ruin you.'

'And do you think then that I'm not ruined already?' she said bitterly.

'No, my dear,' replied Raymon, who wanted only to persuade her to leave him in peace. 'Your absence hasn't been noticed, since no one has yet come here to enquire for you. Although I would have been the last person to be suspected, it would be natural to make enquiries at the houses of your acquaintances. And then you can go and place yourself under your aunt's protection; in fact that's the course I advise you to take. She will arrange everything. People will assume you spent the night at her house.'

Madame Delmare was not listening. She was gazing stupidly at the huge, red sun as it rose above the horizon of sparkling roofs. Raymon tried to rouse her from her daze. She turned to look at him but did not seem to recognize him. Her cheeks had a greenish pallor and her dry lips seemed paralysed.

Raymon took fright. He recalled the other girl's suicide and in his dread, not knowing what to do, afraid of being twice a criminal in his own eyes but feeling too mentally exhausted to manage to deceive her further, he sat her down gently on a chair, locked her in, and went up to his mother's room.

XXI

He found her awake. She was used to rising early, as a result of the habits of hard-working activity contracted during the emigration* and lost when prosperity* returned.

When she saw Raymon, pale and agitated, come into her room so late, in evening dress, she realized that he was struggling with one of the crises of his stormy life.

She had always been his last resort and his saviour in these turbulent situations, which left a lasting, painful impression only in her maternal heart. Her life had been blighted and worn out by all that Raymon's had gained and retrieved. Her son's character, impetuous yet cold, calculating but passionate, was a consequence of her inexhaustible love and generous affection for him. He would have been better with a less kind mother, but she had made him used to taking advantage of all the sacrifices she agreed to make for him; she had taught him to strive for and to ensure his own well-being as keenly and strongly as she strove for it. Because she thought she was made to preserve him from all sorrow and to sacrifice all her interests to him, he had become used to thinking the whole world was made for him and must be placed in his hand at a word from his mother. By dint of generosity she had succeeded only in making a selfish heart.

She turned pale, that poor mother, and sitting up in bed looked at him anxiously. Already her look was saying, 'What can I do for you? Where must I go?'

'Mother,' he said, grasping the withered, transparent hand she held out to him, 'I'm terribly unhappy; I need your help. Deliver me from the troubles which beset me. I love Madame Delmare; you know that . . .'

'I didn't know,' said Madame de Ramière in a tone of affectionate reproach.

'Don't try to deny it, mother dear,' said Raymon, who had no time to lose. 'You know but your admirable tact prevented you from being the first to mention it. Well, she is driving me to despair, and I am losing my reason.'

'Well, tell me all about it,' said Madame de Ramière with the youthful eagerness inspired by the ardour of her maternal love.

'I don't want to hide anything from you, especially as, this time, I'm not guilty. For some months I've been trying to calm her romantic imagination and bring her back to a sense of her duties. But all my care only manages to arouse that thirst for danger, that craving for adventure which abounds in the minds of the women of her country. This very moment, as I'm talking to you, she is here, in my room, against my will, and I don't know how to get her to leave.'

'Poor child!' said Madame de Ramière, dressing hurriedly. 'She's so shy and gentle. I'll go and see her, I'll talk to her. That's what you've come to ask me to do isn't it?'

'Yes, yes,' said Raymon, softened by his mother's affectionate reply. 'Go and make her listen to the language of reason and kindness. I'm sure that when you tell her what's right, she'll want to do it. Perhaps she'll yield to your loving manner; she'll regain control of herself, the unfortunate girl! She is suffering so much.'

Raymon threw himself into a chair and began to cry, the morning's different emotions had so shattered his nerves. His mother wept with him and only decided to go downstairs after forcing him to take a few drops of ether.

Indiana was not crying and she got up calmly and with dignity when she recognized Madame de Ramière. Raymon's mother so little expected this noble, controlled bearing that she felt embarrassed in front of the young woman as if she lacked consideration for her in surprising her in her son's room.

Then she gave way to her heart's genuine, deep feeling and opened her arms in a rush of affection. Madame Delmare threw herself into them; her despair broke out into bitter sobs and the two women wept together for a long time in each other's arms.

But when Madame de Ramière wanted to speak, Indiana stopped her.

'Don't say anything to me, Madame,' she said, wiping away her tears. 'You won't find any words which don't cause me pain. Your interest and your embrace are enough to prove to me your generous affection. My heart is relieved as much as it can be. I'll go now. I don't need your entreaties to understand what I have to do.'

'That's why I didn't come to send you away, but to comfort you,' said Madame de Ramière.

'I can't be comforted,' replied Indiana, kissing her. 'Love me, that will help me a little. But don't speak to me. Good-bye, Madame. You believe in God; pray to Him for me.'

'You shan't go away alone,' cried Madame de Ramière. 'I intend to take you back to your husband's house myself, to justify you, to defend and protect you.'

'Generous woman!' said Indiana, clasping her to her heart. 'You cannot do it. You are the only one not to know Raymon's secret. All Paris will be talking of it this evening and you have no place in such a story. Let me endure the scandal alone. I'll not suffer for long.'

'What do you mean? Would you commit the crime of making an attempt on your life? My dear child, you, too, believe in God.'

'Yes, Madame, so I leave for Bourbon Island in three days.'

'Come to my arms, my darling child, come, let me bless you. God will reward your courage . . .'

'I hope so,' said Indiana, looking up to heaven.

Madame de Ramière wanted at least to send for a cab, but Indiana objected. She wanted to go home alone without fuss. In vain did Madame de Ramière express alarm at seeing her, weak and distraught, set out on such a long walk.

'I have the strength,' she replied. 'A word from Raymon was enough to give it me.'

She wrapped her cloak around her, lowered her black lace veil, and left the house by a secret exit to which Madame de Ramière led her. As soon as she began to walk in the street, she felt that her trembling legs almost refused to carry her. At every moment she seemed to feel her furious husband's rough hand grasp hold of her, throw her down, and drag her in the gutter. Soon the street noises, the indifferent faces of the passers-by, and the penetrating morning cold restored her strength and composure; but it was a painful strength and a gloomy composure, like the calm that settles over the waters of the sea and alarms the far-sighted sailor more than the upheavals of the storm. She walked along by the Seine from the Institut as far as the Corps Législatif,* but she forgot to cross the bridge and continued to walk along by the river, lost in a dazed reverie, in a mindless meditation and continuing to walk on aimlessly.

Little by little she reached the water's edge. The river was washing lumps of ice up to her feet and making them break with a sharp chilling sound on the stones of the river bank. The greenish water exerted a powerful attraction on Indiana's senses. One gets used to terrible ideas; by dint of accepting them, one comes to like them. The example of Noun's suicide had soothed Indiana's hours of despair for so long now that she had turned suicide into a kind of enticing pleasure. One thought alone, a religious thought, had prevented her from deciding on it definitely, but at that moment coherent thought was no longer in control of her exhausted brain. She barely remembered that God existed, that Raymon had ever existed, and she walked on, getting nearer and nearer to the river-bank, in obedience to the instinct of unhappiness and the magnetic power of suffering.

When she felt the biting cold of the water washing over her shoes, she awoke as if from sleepwalking. On looking around to see where she was, she saw Paris behind her and the Seine rushing by beneath her feet, carrying along in its oily mass of water the white reflection of the houses and the greyish blue of the sky. The ceaseless flow of the water and the immobility of the ground became confused in her disturbed perceptions and it seemed to her that the water was still and the ground moving. In this moment of dizziness, she leaned against a wall and bent over, fascinated, towards what she took for solid ground ... But the barking of a dog that was leaping around her distracted her attention and delayed for a few moments the accomplishment of her purpose. Then a man, who, guided by the dog's voice, was running up to her, grasped her round the waist, pulled her away, and set her down on the remains of an abandoned boat by the river-bank. She looked straight at him but did not recognize him. He knelt at her feet, took off his cloak, and wrapped it round her, took her hands in his to warm them and called her by name. But her brain was too weak to make any effort; for forty-eight hours she had forgotten to eat.

But when warmth had returned a little to her numbed limbs, she saw Ralph on his knees before her, holding her hands and watching for the return of her reason.

'Did you meet Noun?' she asked.

Then she added, distraught in her obsession:

'I saw her go by on this path,' (and she pointed to the river). 'I wanted to follow her but she was walking too quickly and I'm not strong enough to walk. It was like a nightmare.'

Ralph looked at her in distress. He too felt as if his head was splitting and his brain giving way.

'Let's go,' he said.

'Let's go,' she replied, 'but first look for my feet; I've lost them there on those pebbles.'

Ralph realized that her feet were wet and numbed by the cold. He carried her in his arms to a house where they found refuge and where a kind woman's care restored her reason. Meanwhile Ralph sent a message to M. Delmare that his wife was found, but the Colonel had not yet come home when the news arrived. He was continuing his search in a frenzy of anxiety and anger. Ralph, more perceptive, had already gone to M. de Ramière's house but he had found Raymon, who had just gone to bed, coldly ironic. Then he had thought of Noun and he had followed the river in one direction while his servant explored it in the other. Ophelia had immediately hit upon his mistress's track and had quickly guided Sir Ralph to the place where he had found her.

When Indiana recovered her memory of what had happened on that wretched night, she tried in vain to recall the period of her delirium. So she could not explain to her cousin what thoughts had motivated her during the previous hour. But he guessed them and understood the state of her heart without questioning her. He simply took her hand and said, gently and gravely:

'Cousin, I insist on your making me one promise. That's the last proof of friendship I'll trouble you with.'

'Tell me what it is,' she replied. 'To oblige you is the last pleasure left to me.'

'Well, swear to me that you will never have recourse to suicide again without giving me warning,' continued Ralph. 'I swear to you on my honour not to oppose it in any way. I only want to be told about it in advance. As for other considerations, I care about them as little as you do, and you know that I've often had the same idea . . .'

'Why are you talking to me about suicide?' asked Madame Delmare. 'I've never intended to make an attempt on my life. I fear God; but for that! . . .'

'A little while ago, Indiana, when I grasped you in my arms, when that poor beast' (and he stroked Ophelia) 'tugged at your dress, you had forgotten God and the whole universe, your cousin Ralph like all the rest . . .'

A tear welled up in Indiana's eye. She pressed Ralph's hand. 'Why did you stop me?' she said sadly. 'I would be in God's bosom now, for I wasn't guilty. I wasn't conscious of what I was doing.'

'I was well aware of that and I thought it was better to kill oneself intentionally. We'll talk about it again some time if you like.'

Indiana shuddered. The carriage in which they were being driven stopped in front of the house where she was to be reunited with her husband. She had not the strength to go upstairs. Ralph carried her right up to her room. All their domestic staff was reduced to one maid-servant, who had gone to talk about Madame Delmare's flight with the neighbours, and Lelièvre, who, giving up the search in despair, had gone to the mortuary to inquire about the corpses brought in that morning. So Ralph stayed with Madame Delmare to look after her. She was suffering intensely, when the loudly rung doorbell announced the Colonel's return. A shudder of terror and hatred ran through her whole being. She suddenly caught hold of her cousin's arm.

'Listen Ralph,' she said, 'if you have any affection for me, you'll spare me the sight of that man in my present state. I don't want to make him sorry for me; I'd rather have his anger

than his pity . . . Don't open the door, or send him away. Tell
him I haven't been found . . .'

Her lips quivered, her arms tightened round Ralph with
convulsive strength to hold him back. Divided between two
conflicting feelings, the poor baronet did not know what he
should do. Delmare was pulling the bell hard enough to break
it and his wife was half-dead in her chair.

'You're thinking only of his anger,' Ralph said at last. 'You
don't think of the torments he has suffered, of his anxiety.
You always imagine he hates you . . . If you had seen his
distress this morning! . . .'

Indiana, exhausted, let go her arms and Ralph went to open
the door.

'Is she here?' shouted the Colonel as he came in. 'A thousand devils! I've run about enough looking for her. I'm very
much obliged to her for the pleasant task she's forced on me!
May heaven confound her. I don't want to see her, for I'd
kill her.'

'You forget that she can hear you,' replied Ralph quietly.
'She's in no state to bear any painful emotions. Restrain
yourself.'

'Twenty-five thousand curses!' roared the Colonel. '*I've*
borne plenty myself since this morning. It's as well for me that
my nerves are like cables. Who, if you please, is the more
injured, the more tired, has the more right to be ill—she or I?
And where did you find her? What was she doing? It's because
of her that I treated that silly old Carvajal woman outrage-
ously; she gave me ambiguous replies and blamed me for
this fine escapade . . . What a mess! I'm at the end of my
tether!'

As he was saying these things in his harsh, rough voice,
Delmare flung himself into a chair. He wiped his brow which
was dripping with sweat despite the fierce seasonal cold. With
many oaths he told of his fatigues, his anxieties, his sufferings.
He asked a thousand questions but fortunately he did not
listen to the answers, for poor Ralph could not tell a lie and
he saw nothing in what he had to tell which could pacify the
Colonel. Ralph sat on a table, impassive and dumb as if he

had absolutely no connection with these two people, and yet more unhappy because of their woes than they were themselves.

When Madame Delmare heard her husband's curses, she felt stronger than she expected to. She preferred his anger, which reconciled her with herself, to a generosity which would have aroused her remorse. She wiped away the last trace of her tears and summoned up what remained of her strength; she did not worry about using it all up in one day, so heavily did life weigh upon her. When her husband came up to her looking harsh and commanding, his manner and tone of voice suddenly changed, and in front of her he was embarrassed, tamed by the superiority of her character. Then he tried to be cold and dignified like her, but he could not manage to.

'Will you deign to tell me, Madame, where you spent the morning and perhaps the night?' he asked.

The word *perhaps* told Madame Delmare that it was quite late before her absence had been noticed. This increased her courage.

'No, Monsieur,' she replied. 'I don't intend to tell you.'

Delmare turned green with anger and astonishment.

'Do you really expect to conceal the information from me?' he asked in a quavering voice.

'I don't much care,' she replied icily. 'If I refuse to answer you, it's entirely for form's sake. I want to convince you that you have no right to ask me that question.'

'I haven't the right, a thousand demons! Then who is master here, you or me? Then who wears a skirt and ought to be working a distaff? Do you claim the right to take the beard off my chin? It would look well on you, a silly weak woman!'

'I know I'm the slave and you're the lord. The law of the land has made you my master. You can tie up my body, bind my hands, control my actions. You have the right of the stronger, and society confirms you in it. But over my will, Monsieur, you have no power. God alone can bend and subdue it. So look for a law, a dungeon, an instrument of torture that gives you a hold over me! It's as if you wanted to touch the air and grasp space.'

'Be quiet, you foolish, impertinent creature. Your novelistic language annoys us.'

'You can impose silence on me, but you can't stop me thinking.'

'Silly pride, arrogance of a worm! You take advantage of our pity for you. But you'll see that your strong character can be subdued without too much difficulty.'

'I don't advise you to try. It would disturb your peace and would do nothing for your dignity.'

'Do you think so?' he said, bruising her hand as he pressed it between his first finger and thumb.

'I think so,' she said with no change of expression.

Ralph stepped forward, gripped the Colonel's arm in his iron hand, and bent it like a reed, saying in a pacifying tone:

'I request you not to touch a hair of that woman's head.'

Delmare wanted to go at him, but he felt he was in the wrong and he feared nothing in the world so much as being ashamed of himself. He merely pushed Ralph away, saying:

'Mind your own business.'

Then, turning back to his wife and keeping his arms close to his chest so as to resist the temptation to hit her, he said:

'So, Madame, you're starting open revolt against me. You refuse to follow me to Bourbon Island. You want a separation. Well, by God, so do I!'

'I don't want it any more,' she replied. 'Yesterday I wanted it. That was what I wanted. This morning it's not so any more. You used violence in locking me in my room. I left by the window to prove to you that if you don't control a woman's will, your power over her is a mockery. I spent several hours beyond your power. I went to breathe the air of liberty, to show you that morally you're not my master and that I depend only on myself on the earth. As I walked along, I reflected that I owed it to my duty and my conscience to return and place myself under your protection; I did it of my own free will. My cousin *accompanied* me here, and did not *bring me back*. If I hadn't been willing to follow him, he wouldn't have been able to force me, as you can imagine. So, Monsieur, don't waste your time arguing against my conviction. You will never have any influence on it; you lost the right from the moment you claimed to do so by force. I am prepared to help you and follow you, not because that is what you want but because that is what I intend. You can condemn me but I shall never obey anyone but myself.'

'I'm sorry for you; you're out of your mind,' said the Colonel shrugging his shoulders.

And he retreated to his own room to put his papers in order, very pleased in his innermost heart with Madame Delmare's decision and fearing no more obstacles. For he respected his wife's word as much as he despised her ideas.

XXII

GIVING in to fatigue, Raymon had fallen into a deep sleep after a curt reception of Sir Ralph, who had to come to his house to make enquiries. When he woke up, a feeling of relief pervaded his heart; he believed that the most serious crisis of this affair was at last over. For a long time he had foreseen that a time would come when he would be in conflict with this feminine love, when he would have to defend his liberty against the demands of a romantic passion, and he had prepared himself in advance to fight against its demands. So he had at last taken that difficult step: he had said no, he would not need to take it again, for everything had happened for the best. Indiana had not wept too much, she had not been too insistent. She had proved to be reasonable. She had understood at the first word and had made up her mind quickly and proudly.

Raymon was very pleased with his providence, for he had one of his own in which he believed like a good son and on which he relied to arrange everything to the detriment of others rather than to his own. He had been so well treated up till then that he did not want to have doubts. To see the consequences of his errors and be worried about them would have been, in his eyes, to commit the crime of ingratitude against the good God who watched over him.

Raymon got up, still very weary from the efforts of imagination which the circumstances of that painful scene had forced upon him. His mother came home; she had just been to ask Madame de Carvajal about Madame Delmare's health and frame of mind. The Marchioness had not been worried about Indiana; she was nevertheless in great distress when Madame de Ramière questioned her closely, but the only thing that touched her about Madame Delmare's disappearance was the scandal that would result. She complained bitterly about her niece, whom, the day before, she was praising to the skies, and Madame de Ramière realized that by taking this step the unhappy Indiana had alienated her aunt for ever and lost her sole remaining support.

For anyone who knew the Marchioness's innermost feelings, it would not have been a great loss. But Madame de Carvajal passed for being irreproachably virtuous, even in Madame de Ramière's eyes. Her youth had been wrapped in the mysteries of prudence or lost in the whirlwind of revolutions. Raymon's mother wept over Indiana's lot and tried to find excuses for her. Madame de Carvajal told her sharply that she was perhaps not disinterested enough in this matter to judge.

'But what will become of that unhappy young woman?' said Madame de Ramière. 'If her husband ill-treats her, who will protect her?'

'She'll become what God wills,' replied the Marchioness. 'For my part, I'll have nothing more to do with her and I never want to see her again.'

Madame de Ramière, anxious and kind-hearted, was determined to have news of Madame Delmare at any price. She had herself driven to the end of the street where Indiana lived, and sent a servant to question the porter, telling him to try to see Sir Ralph if he were in the house. She awaited the result of this enquiry in her carriage and presently Ralph himself came out to her.

Perhaps the only person who made a correct judgement about Ralph was Madame de Ramière. A few words between them were enough to make them realize the sincere disinterestedness of both in the matter.

Ralph related what had happened in the course of the morning, and as he only had suspicions about the night's events he did not try to confirm them. But Madame de Ramière thought she ought to tell him what she knew, making him a party to her desire to end this disastrous and impossible liaison. Ralph, who felt more at his ease with her than with anyone else, let his face betray deep emotion when he received this confidence.

'You say, Madame, that she spent the night in your house,' he murmured, repressing a sort of nervous shudder which ran through his veins.

'A solitary, unhappy night, no doubt. Raymon, who was certainly not guilty of complicity, didn't come home till six o'clock and at seven he came to my room to beg me to calm the unhappy girl's mind.'

'She wanted to leave her husband! She wanted to be dishonoured!' replied Ralph, with an intense look and his heart strangely perturbed. 'So she is deeply in love with this man who is unworthy of her! . . .'

Ralph forgot he was talking to Raymon's mother.

'I've suspected so for a long time,' he continued. 'Why did I not foresee the day when she would complete her ruin? I would have killed her first.'

This language in Ralph's mouth came as a strange surprise to Madame de Ramière. She thought she was speaking to a calm, indulgent man and she regretted having believed in appearances.

'Good God!' she said, frightened. 'Then do you, too, judge her without pity? Will you desert her like her aunt? Then are you all pitiless and merciless? Won't she have one friend left after an error from which she has already suffered so much?'

'Don't be afraid of anything of that kind as far as I'm concerned, Madame,' replied Ralph. 'I've known all about it for six months and I've said nothing. I surprised their first kiss and I didn't throw M. de Ramière off his horse. I've often come across their love messages in the woods and I didn't tear them up with my whip. I've met M. de Ramière on the bridge he used to cross to go and meet her. It was at night; we were alone, and I'm four times as strong as he is, yet I didn't throw him into the river. And when, having let him go, I discovered that he had eluded my vigilance and got into her house, instead of breaking down the doors and throwing him out of the window I quietly warned them of her husband's approach and saved his life in order to save her honour. So you see, Madame, that I have pity and am merciful. This morning I had him in my power. I knew very well that he was the cause of all our woes and if I had no right to accuse him without proofs, I was at least entitled to pick a quarrel with him for his arrogant, mocking attitude. Well, I put up with his insulting contempt because I knew that his death would kill Indiana. I let him turn over and fall asleep again while Indiana, half-dead and out of her mind, was on the bank of the Seine, about to rejoin his other victim... You see, Madame, that I am patient with people I hate and indulgent to those I love.'

Madame de Ramière, sitting in her carriage facing Ralph, gazed at him with a mixture of surprise and fear. He was so different from how she had always seen him that she almost thought it possible that he had suddenly gone out of his mind. The allusion he had just made to Noun's death confirmed her in this idea, for she knew absolutely nothing about that story and took the words Ralph let slip in his indignation for a stray thought unrelated to his subject. He was, in fact, in one of those violent moods which occur at least once in the lives of the most reasonable men and are so close to madness that one degree more would put them in a towering rage. His anger was pale and intense, however, as it is with cool-tempered people, but it was deep as it is with noble hearts. This unusual frame of mind, quite extraordinary in his case, made him terrible to look upon.

Madame de Ramière took his hand and said gently:

'You are suffering greatly, my dear Monsieur Ralph, for you hurt me without pity. You forget that the man you are speaking of is my son and that his wrongdoing, if there is any, must rend my heart even more than yours.'

Ralph immediately regained his self-control and, kissing Madame de Ramière's hand in a demonstration of friendship almost as unusual as his outburst of anger, said:

'Forgive me, Madame. You're right. I suffer greatly and forget what I ought to respect. Forget yourself the bitterness I've allowed to surface. I'll be able to lock it up again in my heart.'

Although reassured by this reply, Madame de Ramière retained a hidden anxiety when she saw the deep hatred Ralph harboured for her son. She tried to make excuses for Raymon in his enemy's eyes. Ralph stopped her.

'I can guess your thoughts, Madame,' he said, 'but rest assured. M. de Ramière and I are not going to see each other again in the near future. As for my cousin, don't regret having enlightened me. If everyone deserts her, I swear that she will have at least one friend left.'

When, towards evening, Madame de Ramière came home, she found Raymon in front of the fire, luxuriously warming his cashmere slippered feet and drinking tea to banish the last traces of the morning's upset to his nerves. He was still depressed by his bogus emotions, but sweet thoughts of the future were reviving his spirits. He felt he had become free again, and he gave himself up entirely to complacent meditations on that priceless state which he usually looked after so badly.

'Why am I destined to tire so quickly of that ineffable mental freedom which I always have to pay such a high price to recover?' he asked himself. 'When I'm caught in a woman's toils, I can't wait to break them in order to recover my tranquillity and peace of mind. May I be cursed if I sacrifice them so soon again! The troubles those two Creoles have caused me will serve as a warning, and in future I'm only going to have affairs with frivolous, light-hearted Parisians . . . with real society women. Perhaps it would be a good idea for me to get married and put an end to it all, as they say . . .'

He was deep in these comfortable, conventional thoughts, when his mother came in, tired and distressed.

'She's better,' she said. 'Everything went well. I hope she'll calm down . . .'

'Who?' asked Raymon, suddenly aroused out of his castle in the air.

But the next day, he thought he had still one task to fulfil. That was to regain Indiana's esteem, if not her love. He did not want her to be able to boast that she had left him. He wanted her to persuade herself that she had yielded to the influence of his good sense and generosity. He still wanted to dominate her after rejecting her. So he wrote her the following letter:

'I'm not writing to ask your forgiveness, my dear, for some cruel or disrespectful words I let fall in my passionate delirium. It's not in the disarray of fever that one can form a coherent idea and express it appropriately. It's not my fault if I'm not a god, if in your presence I can't control the seething ardour of my blood, if I lose my head, if I go crazy. Perhaps I'd have the right to complain of the steely composure with which you condemned me to frightful tortures without taking any pity on me. But it's not your fault either. You were too perfect to play the same part as we commonplace creatures subject to human passions, slaves of our unrefined constitutions. I've often told you, Indiana, you're not a woman, and when I think about it, reflecting calmly, you're an angel. I worship you in my heart like a divinity. But alas! When I'm with you the old Adam has often resumed his rights. Often, as I felt the sweet breath that comes from your lips, my own were consumed by a burning fire. Often, when my hair brushed against yours as I leaned towards you, a tremor of indescribable delight ran through all my veins, and then I would forget that you were an emanation from heaven, a dream of eternal bliss, an angel come from God's bosom to guide my steps in this life and to tell me of the joys of another existence. Why, O pure spirit, did you assume the tempting shape of a woman? Why, O angel of light, were you clothed in the seductions of hell? I often thought I was holding happiness in my arms, and you were only virtue.

'Forgive these culpable regrets, my dear. I wasn't worthy of you and perhaps, if you had agreed to descend to my level, we should both have been happier. But my inferiority brought you constant suffering and you have turned your virtues into my crimes.

'Now that you pardon me—as I'm sure you do, for perfection implies mercy—let me raise my voice again to thank and bless you . . . Oh no, my life, that's not the word, for my heart is more rent than yours by the courage that snatches you from my arms. But I admire you, and even as I weep I congratulate you. Yes, my Indiana, this heroic sacrifice, you have found the strength to carry it out. It snatches away my heart and my life; it makes my future desolate; it ruins my existence. But I still love you enough to endure it without complaint, for my honour is of no consequence, it is yours which is all-important. As for my honour, I would sacrifice it a thousand times for you, but yours is more precious to me than all the happiness you would have given me. Oh no, I would not have enjoyed such a sacrifice. I would have tried in vain to be distracted by ecstatic raptures, in vain you would have tried to intoxicate me with celestial delights, remorse would have come to seek me out; it would have poisoned all my days and I would have been more humiliated than you by men's scorn. Oh God! To see you degraded and destroyed by me! To see you fallen from the state of veneration which surrounds you! To see you insulted in my arms and not to be able to wipe out the offence! For even if I had spilt all my blood for you, it would have been of no use. I might have avenged you, but I could never have justified you. My zeal in defending you would have been a further accusation against you; my death an irrefutable proof of your crime. Poor Indiana, I would have ruined you. Oh, how unhappy I would be!

Go, then, my beloved. Go and gather under another sky the fruits of virtue and religion. God will reward us for such an effort, for God is good. He will reunite us in a happier life and perhaps even . . . but this thought is still a crime. Yet I cannot forbid myself the hope. Farewell, Indiana, farewell. You see clearly that our love is sinful. Alas! My heart is broken. Where would I find strength to bid you farewell?'

Raymon himself took this letter to Madame Delmare's house, but she shut herself up in her room and refused to see him. So he left the house after slipping the letter into the hand of the servant and cordially embracing the husband. As he left the last step of the staircase behind him, he felt more light-hearted than usual. The weather was milder, the women were more beautiful, the shops more sparkling. It was a happy day in Raymon's life.

Madame Delmare put the letter away with its seal unbroken in a box which she would not open till she was in Bourbon Island. She wanted to say good-bye to her aunt; Sir Ralph, very determinedly opposed her doing so. He had seen Madame de Carvajal. He knew she intended to overwhelm Indiana with scornful reproaches. He was furious at this hypocritical severity and could not bear the idea of Madame Delmare's exposing herself to it.

The following day, just as Delmare and his wife were about to go into the coach, Sir Ralph said to them in his usual casual way:

'I've often indicated, my friends, that I wished to accompany you, but you refused to understand me or to give me an answer. Will you allow me to go with you?'

'To Bordeaux?' asked M. Delmare.

'To Bourbon,' answered M. Ralph.

'You mustn't think of it,' replied M. Delmare. 'You can't move your household like this to suit a couple in a precarious situation and with an uncertain future. It would be taking an unworthy advantage of your friendship to accept the sacrifice of your whole life and the abnegation of your social position. You are rich, young, and free. You ought to marry again, found a family.'

'That's not the question,' Sir Ralph replied coldly. 'Since I don't know how to wrap up my ideas in words which change their meaning, I'll tell you frankly what I think. It seemed to me that over the last six months the friendship of both of you has cooled towards me. Perhaps I've done something wrong that my lack of discernment has prevented me from noticing. If I'm mistaken, one word from you will be enough to reassure me. Allow me to go with you. If I've lost your esteem, now is the time to tell me. In leaving me behind, you ought not to leave me with the remorse of not having made amends for my mistakes.'

The Colonel was so moved by this frank and generous approach that he forgot all the wounds to his *amour propre* which had alienated him from his friend. He held out his hand to him, swore to him that his friendship was more sincere than ever and that he had refused his offers only out of tact.

Madame Delmare said nothing. Ralph made an effort to extract a word from her.

'And you, Indiana,' he said in a choking voice, 'do you still feel friendship for me?'

These words revived all the filial affection, all the childhood memories, all the habits of intimacy which united their hearts. They fell weeping into each other's arms and Ralph almost fainted, for in that strong body, in that calm, reserved personality, seethed powerful emotions. He sat down so as not to fall and remained silent and pale for a few moments. Then he grasped the Colonel's hand in one of his and Indiana's in the other.

'At this moment of a separation which may last for ever, be frank with me,' he said. 'You are refusing my proposal to accompany you on my account and not on yours?'

'I swear to you on my honour that in refusing you, I am sacrificing my happiness to yours,' said Delmare.

'For my part', said Indiana, 'you know that I would never want to leave you.'

'God forbid that I should doubt your sincerity at such a moment,' replied Ralph. 'Your word is enough for me. I am pleased with you both.'

And he left them.

Six weeks later the brig *Coraly* set sail from Bordeaux. Ralph had written to his friends that he would be in the town towards the end of their stay there, but in his usual way his style was so laconic that it was impossible to know whether he intended to bid them a last farewell or to go with them. They waited for him in vain till the last moment, and when the captain gave the signal for departure Ralph still had not appeared. Ominous forebodings added to the dull pain which oppressed Indiana's heart when the last houses of the port disappeared amongst the foliage of the coast. She shuddered at the thought that henceforth she was alone in the world with a husband she hated, that she would have to live and die with him, without a friend to comfort her, without a relative to protect her against his brutal domination.

But when she turned round, she saw on the deck behind her Ralph's calm, kindly face smiling at her.

'So you are *not* deserting me?' she said, her face bathed in tears, and throwing her arms round his neck.

'Never!' replied Ralph clasping her to his heart.

XXIII

Letter from Madame Delmare to M. de Ramière

From Bourbon Island, 3 June 18.

'I had resolved to weary you no more with my memory, but on arriving here and reading the letter you sent me the day before my departure from Paris, I feel that I owe you a reply, for in the throes of dreadful distress I went too far. I was mistaken about you and ought to make amends to you not as a *lover* but as a *man*.

Forgive me, Raymon. At that terrible moment of my life, I took you for a monster. One single word, one single look from you, banished for ever all trust, all hope, from my heart. I know I can no longer be happy but I still hope not to be reduced to despising you. That for me would be the final blow.

'Yes, I took you for a deceiver, for the worst possible kind of man, for an *egoist*. I detested you. I was sorry that Bourbon Island wasn't further away so that I could fly further from you, and indignation gave me the strength to drain my cup of misery to the dregs.

But since I've read your letter, I feel better. I don't regret you but I don't hate you any more and I don't want to leave your life in remorse for having destroyed mine. Be happy, be carefree. Forget me. I'm still alive and perhaps I'll live a long time.

'In fact you're not to blame. It's I who was out of my mind. Your heart was not unfeeling but it was closed to me. You didn't lie to me, it's I who was mistaken. You didn't commit perjury nor were you insensitive, you just didn't love me.

'Oh, good God! You didn't love me! How then should one love you? But I'll not stoop to complain. I'm not writing to you to poison the calm of your present life with an odious memory. Nor am I writing to implore your compassion for ills which I have the strength to bear alone. Now that I know your proper role better I write, on the contrary, to absolve and pardon you.

'I shan't amuse myself by refuting your letter; that would be too easy. I shan't reply to your remarks about my duties. Don't worry, Raymon. I know what they are and I didn't love you little enough to transgress them unthinkingly. You don't need to tell me that mankind's contempt would have been the price of my sin; I knew that very well. I was not unaware that the stain would be deep, indelible, and extremely painful, that I would be rejected on all sides, cursed and covered with shame, and that I wouldn't find a single friend left to pity and comfort me. My only mistake was to have confidence that you would open your arms to me and that, there, you would help me to forget the scorn, the distress, and the desertion of my friends. The only thing I didn't foresee was that you might refuse my sacrifice after letting me complete it. I had imagined that was impossible. I went to your house thinking you would repulse me at first out of principle and duty, but with the conviction that when you learned the inevitable consequences of the step I had taken, you would feel bound to help me bear them. No, I never really thought you would abandon me alone to the consequences of such a dangerous decision, and would let me harvest its bitter fruits instead of gathering me to your heart and giving me the protection of your love.

'Then, how I would have defied them, those distant murmurings of a world powerless to harm me! Strong in your love, how I would have braved hatred! How weak my remorse would have been, and how the passion you inspired would have stifled its voice! With my mind filled entirely with thoughts of you, I would have forgotten myself. Proud in the possession of your heart, I wouldn't have had the time to blush for mine. One word, one look, one kiss from you, would have been enough to absolve me, and the memory of men and laws could have found no place in such a life. The fact is that I was mad, that, as you cynically said, I had learned about life in novels written for ladies' maids, in those optimistic, childish fictions in which the heart becomes interested in the success of crazy enterprises and impossible joys. That remark of yours, Raymon, was horribly true. What frightens and devastates me is that you are right.

'What I can't explain so well is that the impossibility was not the same for both of us, that I, a weak woman, drew strength from my exalted feelings to put myself alone in an improbable fictional situation, and that you, a generous-hearted man, didn't find in your will the strength to follow me there. Yet you shared the dreams of the future, you assented to these illusions, you nourished in me a hope that could not be realized. For a long time, you had listened to my childish plans, to my pygmy's ambitions, with a smile on your lips and joy in your eyes, and your words were all love and gratitude. You, too, were blind, lacking in foresight, boastful. How is it that your reason didn't return till you saw the danger? I thought that danger charmed the eyes, stimulated one's resolve, made fear impotent! But there, you trembled at the crucial moment! Have you men, then, only the physical courage which faces death? Aren't you capable of the moral courage which accepts misfortune? You, who explain everything so admirably, explain to me, please.

'Perhaps it's because your dream wasn't the same as mine, for with me courage was love. You had imagined you loved me and you woke up surprised at such a mistake on the day I came trusting in mine. Good God! What a strange illusion yours was, since you didn't then foresee all the obstacles which struck you at the moment of action, since you only mentioned them to me for the first time when it was too late.

'Why should I reproach you now? Is one responsible for the fluctuations of one's feelings? Did it depend on you to love me for ever? Definitely not. My fault was not to have been able to make you feel affection for me longer and more seriously. I seek the reason for this and cannot find it in my heart, but none the less it exists apparently. Perhaps I loved you too much; perhaps my affection was demanding and tiring. You were a man; you loved independence and pleasure. I was a burden to you. Sometimes I tried to control your life. Alas! Those were very petty faults to explain such a cruel desertion!

'So enjoy the liberty you have reclaimed at the expense of my whole life. I shall not disturb it again. Why didn't you give me this lesson earlier? I would have been hurt much less, and you, too, perhaps.

'Be happy; that's the last wish of my broken heart. Don't urge me any more to think of God; leave that to the priests, whose task it is to touch the hardened hearts of the guilty. As for me, I have more faith than you have. I serve the same God but I serve Him better and with a purer heart. Yours is the god of men, the king, the founder, and protector of your race; mine is the God of the universe, the creator, the support, and hope of all creatures. Yours has made everything for you alone; mine made all species for each other. You think yourselves masters of the world; I think you are only its tyrants. You think God protects you and authorizes you to usurp the empire of the earth; but *I* think He allows it for a short time and the day will come when His breath will scatter you like grains of sand. No, Raymon, you don't know God, or rather, let me repeat what Ralph said to you one day at Lagny: it's that you believe in nothing. Your education, and your need for an irrefutable authority with which to oppose the brutal power of the masses, have made you adopt without scrutiny the beliefs of your fathers. But the feeling of the existence of God has never reached your heart; perhaps you've never prayed to Him. *I* have only one belief, probably the only one you don't have; I believe in Him. But the religion you have invented, I reject. All your morality, all your principles, are but the interests of your society that you have erected into laws and that you claim emanate from God Himself, just as your priests have set up the rites of church worship to establish their power and wealth over the nations. But all that is lies and blasphemy. I who invoke God, I who understand Him, I know very well that there is nothing in common between Him and you and that it is by clinging to Him with all my strength that I can detach myself from you who continually strive to overturn His works and sully His gifts. It ill becomes you, you know, to invoke His name to crush the resistance of a weak woman, to stifle the lament of a broken heart. God doesn't want the creatures of His hands to be oppressed and crushed. If He deigned to descend so far as to intervene in our petty concerns, He would break the strong and raise up the weak. He would spread His large hand out over our unequal heads and make them level like the surface of the sea. He would say to the slave: "Cast aside your chain and flee to the mountains, where I have placed water, flowers, and sunshine for you." He would say to the king: "Throw your purple robes to the beggars for them to use as mats, and go and sleep in the valley, where I have spread out carpets of moss and heather for you." He would say to the powerful: "Bend the knee and carry the burden of your weaker brethren, for henceforth you will need them and I shall give them strength and courage." Yes, these are my dreams; they are all of another life, of another world, where the ruffian's law will not bear down on the head of the peace-lover, where at least resistance and flight will not be crimes, where man can escape man as the gazelle escapes the panther, without the chain of the law being stretched out round him to force him to come and throw himself beneath his enemy's feet, without the voice of prejudice being raised in his distress to insult his suffering and say to him: "You are a base coward because you would not bend the knee and crawl."

'No, don't speak to me of God, you, of all people, Raymon. Don't invoke His name to send me into exile and reduce me to silence. In submitting, it is to the power of man that I am yielding. If I listened to the voice that God has placed at the bottom of my heart, and to the noble instinct of a strong, bold nature which is perhaps the real conscience, I would flee to the desert, I would be able to do without help, protection, and love. I would live for myself alone in the heart of our beautiful mountains. I would forget the tyrants, the unjust, and the ungrateful. But alas! Man cannot do without his own kind, and even Ralph cannot live alone.

'Farewell, Raymon! May you live happily without me. I forgive you the harm you have done me. Speak of me sometimes to your mother, the best woman I have ever known. Be assured that there is no anger or desire for vengeance against you in my heart. My grief is worthy of the love I had for you.

Indiana.'

The unfortunate woman was boasting. Her deep, calm grief was merely the feeling for her own dignity when she was addressing Raymon. But when she was alone, she gave herself up freely to her consuming, impulsive passion. At times, however, vague gleams of blind hope appeared in her troubled eyes. Perhaps she never entirely lost all confidence in Raymon's love, in spite of the cruel lessons of experience, in spite of the terrible thoughts which, every day, indicated his coldness and indolence when his interests or pleasures were no longer concerned. I think that if Indiana had been willing to appreciate the bare truth, she would not have dragged out the exhausted, blighted remnant of her life for so long.

Woman is naturally foolish. To counterbalance the outstanding superiority which her sensitive perceptions give her over us men, it seems that heaven has intentionally placed in her heart a blind vanity, a stupid credulity. Perhaps to gain a hold over so subtle, flexible, and perceptive a creature, it's a matter only of knowing how to praise her and of flattering her *amour propre*. At times, men who are the most incapable of gaining any kind of ascendancy over other men, exercise absolute dominion over the minds of women. Flattery is the yoke which makes those ardent, frivolous heads bow so low. Woe betide the man who wants to be frank in love! He will have Ralph's fate.

That would be my reply if you told me that Indiana is an exceptional character and that the ordinary woman has neither her cold stoicism nor her exasperating patience in conjugal resistance. I would tell you to look at the other side of the coin and to see the pitiful weakness, the clumsy blindness, she shows in her relationship with Raymon. I would ask you where you've found a woman who wasn't as ready to be deceived as to stay deceived, who couldn't bury in the depths of her heart the secret of a hope she so thoughtlessly ventured to entertain on a day of passionate excitement and who, in the arms of one man, again became as childishly weak as she could be strong and invincible in the arms of another.

XXIV

MADAME Delmare's home had, however, become more peaceful. Many of the difficulties which had been aggravated formerly by the officious zeal of her false friends had disappeared with these eager mediators. Sir Ralph with his silence and apparent non-intervention was more skilful than all of them in letting fall those little nothings of private life which are blown up with the help of the breeze of gossip. Moreover, Indiana lived almost always alone. Her house was in the mountains above the town, and every morning M. Delmare, who had a warehouse at the port, went there for the whole day to attend to his trade with India and France. Sir Ralph, who had no other home than theirs but found ways of making it materially comfortable without his gifts being noticed, was busy with natural-history study or supervised work on the plantation. Indiana resumed the indolent habits of Creole life, and spent the heat of the day in her Indian chair and the long evenings in the solitude of the mountains.

In truth, Bourbon is simply an enormous cone, with a base whose circumference measures about one hundred miles, and with gigantic peaks which rise to a height of ten thousand feet. From nearly every point of that impressive mass, the eye can discern in the distance, behind the steep rocks, behind the narrow valleys and the tall, straight trees, the unbroken horizon enclosed by the blue girdle of the sea. From the windows of her room, Indiana could see the white sails on the Indian Ocean between two rocky peaks of a wooded mountain opposite the one where her house was situated. During the silent hours of the day, this sight attracted her and gave a tinge of permanent, steady despair to her melancholy. That splendid view, far from casting its poetic influence over her thoughts, made them bitter and gloomy. Then she would lower her raffia window-blind and retreat even from the daylight to shed bitter, scalding tears in her secret heart.

But when, towards evening, the land breeze began to rise and bring her the scent of the flowering rice-fields, she would

go out into the savannah, leaving Delmare and Ralph on the
verandah to enjoy the aromatic *faham** infusion and slowly
puff out their cigar smoke. Then, from the top of some access-
ible peak, the extinct crater of a former volcano, she would go
and watch the declining sun, which set the red vapours of the
atmosphere aglow and scattered, as it were, a dust of gold and
rubies over the rustling tops of the sugar cane and the gleaming sides of the reefs. She rarely went down into the gorges of
the Saint-Gilles river* because, although it pained her, the
sight of the sea had fascinated her with its magnetic mirage. It
seemed to her that beyond those waves and that distant haze
the magic vision of another land would be revealed to her. At
times the coastal clouds assumed strange shapes for her; at
times she would see a white breaker rise up from the ocean
and form a long line which she took for the façade of the
Louvre; at times two square sails, emerging suddenly from
the mist, aroused the memory of the towers of Notre-Dame de
Paris when a dense fog rises from the Seine and surrounds the
bases of the towers and makes them look as if suspended in
the sky; at other times it was wisps of pink cloud which, with
their changing shapes, assumed all the capricious architectural
forms of a very large town. Indiana's mind was lulled in the
illusions of the past and she would begin to quiver with joy at
the sight of that imaginary Paris whose realities had marked
the most unhappy time of her life. A strange giddiness would
then take hold of her. Poised at a great height above the coast
and seeing the gorges that separated her from the ocean disappear beneath her eyes, it seemed to her that she was being
thrust swiftly into space and was making her way through the
air towards the marvellous city of her imagination. In this
dream, she clung to the rock which was her support, and for
anyone who might have seen her eager eyes, her breast panting with impatience, and the terrifying expression of joy on
her face, she would have shown all the symptoms of madness.
Yet, this was her happy time and the only moments of con-
tentment on which the hopes of her day were centred. If a
whim of her husband's had disallowed these solitary walks,
I don't know what thoughts would have sustained her, for,
in her, everything was linked to a certain ability to create

delusions, to an ardent aspiration towards something that was not memory, nor expectation, nor hope, nor regret, but desire in all its consuming intensity. She lived thus for weeks and months beneath the tropical sky, loving, knowing, cherishing only a shadow, going only more deeply into a dream.

As for Ralph, in his walks, he was attracted towards dark, enclosed places where the winds from the sea could not reach him, for the sight of the ocean had become distasteful to him, as well as the idea of crossing it again. In his heart's memory, France had only an accursed place. It was there that unhappiness had brought him to the brink of despair, a man who was used to misfortune and bore his ills patiently. He tried with all his might to forget it, for however weary of life he was, he wanted to live as long as he would feel himself necessary. So he took care never to say one word connected with his stay in that country. What he would have given to tear its horrible memory away from Madame Delmare! But he had such a poor opinion of his own ability, he felt so clumsy and so lacking in eloquence, that he shunned her rather than tried to take her mind off it. In his excessive, sensitive reserve he continued to assume all the appearance of coldness and selfishness. He went far afield to suffer alone, and to see him determinedly combing the woods and mountains in pursuit of birds and insects, one would have said he was a naturalist hunter absorbed in his innocent passion and completely detached from the emotional interests all around him. And yet hunting and nature-study were only the pretexts with which he covered his long, bitter reveries.

This conical island is split all round its base and conceals in the gaps deep gorges, where the pure waters of turbulent rivers flow. One of these gorges is called Bernica. It is a picturesque place, a kind of deep, narrow valley, hidden between two perpendicular walls of rock, whose surface is clothed with clumps of saxatile shrubs* and tufts of ferns.

A stream flows in the groove formed by the junction of the two sides. At the point where they meet, it hurtles down into terrifying depths and at the spot where it falls, it forms a little pool surrounded by reeds and by a damp mist. Around its banks and at the edges of the trickle of water fed by the overflow from the pool, grow litchi, banana, and orange trees, whose dark, luxuriant green covers the interior walls of the gorge. It was there that Ralph retreated from the heat and from company. All his walks brought him back to this favourite spot. The fresh, monotonous sound of the waterfall lulled his melancholy to sleep. When his heart was troubled by his secret anguish so long harboured and so cruelly misunderstood, it was there that, in unseen tears, in silent laments, he expended his unused emotional energy and the pent up activity of his youth.

To enable you to understand Ralph's character, perhaps I should tell you that at least half his life had been passed in the heart of this ravine. It was there that, from his earliest childhood, he would come to strengthen his courage against the injustices of which he was a victim in his family. It was there that he would strive with all his might against the arbitrariness of his destiny, and that he had acquired the habit of stoicism to such an extent that it had become second nature to him. There too, in his adolescence, he had carried little Indiana on his shoulders. He had set her down on the river bank while he fished for camarous* in the clear water or tried to scale the cliff to look for birds' nests.

The only inhabitants of that solitude were the seagulls, the petrels, the coots, and the sea swallows. These seabirds could continually be seen flying up and down in the gorge, hovering overhead, or circling round, for, to rear their wild broods, they had chosen the holes and clefts in those inaccessible walls. Towards evening, they would collect in uneasy flocks and fill the echoing gorge with their fierce, raucous cries. Ralph liked to follow their majestic flights and listen to their melancholy voices. He pointed out to her the beautiful Madagascar teal with its orange breast and emerald back. He taught her to admire the flight of the red-winged tropic bird which sometimes loses its way on the coasts and flies in a few hours from Mauritius to Rodriguez where, after a journey of two hundred miles across the sea, it returns every evening to sleep under the *veloutier** which conceals its nestful of young. The black-backed gull, forerunner of storms, would also come and spread its tapering wings over these cliffs. And the queen of the sea, the magnificent frigate bird with its forked tail, its slate-coloured coat, and its finely chiselled beak, which alights so rarely that it seems as if the air is its natural habitat and perpetual motion its nature, would raise its cry of distress above all the others. These wild inhabitants had evidently become used to seeing the two children wandering around their dwellings, for they hardly deigned to take fright at their approach, and when Ralph reached the rock where they had just settled, they arose in black whirling clouds and alighted a few feet above him. Indiana would laugh at their twistings and turnings, and then carefully bring back in her rice-straw hat the eggs that Ralph had managed to steal for her and that often he had to fight bravely for against strong blows from the wings of the great amphibious birds.

These memories crowded back into Ralph's mind, but with extreme bitterness, for times had greatly changed and the little girl who had been his constant companion was no longer his special friend, or at least, no longer with all her heart as in the past. Although she returned his affectionate care and devotion, there was one point which stood in the way of trust between them, a memory on which all the emotions of their lives turned like a pivot. Ralph felt that he could not touch on it. On one day fraught with danger, he had dared to do so on a single occasion, and that courageous act had been to no purpose. To return to it now would have been cold-blooded barbarity and Ralph would have decided to forgive Raymon, the man for whom he had less esteem than anyone in the world, rather than add to Indiana's sorrows by condemning him as he thought justice demanded.

So Ralph said nothing and he even avoided her. Although they lived under the same roof, he had managed hardly ever to see her except at meal times, and yet, like a mysterious providence, he watched over her. He left the house only when the heat confined her to her hammock but, in the evening, when she had gone out, he would find a way of leaving Delmare on the verandah and go to wait for her at the foot of the cliffs where he knew she usually sat. He would stay there for hours on end, sometimes looking at her through the branches which were beginning to look white in the moonlight, but respecting the small space which separated them and not venturing to shorten by a moment her sad reverie. When she came down into the valley again, she always found him by the bank of a little stream which flowed alongside the path to the house. Some large, flat stones, surrounded by silvery ripples of water, served him as a seat. When Indiana's white dress was visible on the bank, Ralph would get up in silence, offer her his arm, and bring her back to the house without saying a word to her, unless, more sad and depressed than usual, she herself began the conversation. Then, when he had left her, he would retire to his room and, before going to bed, would wait until everyone in the house was asleep. If Delmare raised his voice to scold her, Ralph, under the first pretext that occurred to him, would go to the Colonel and manage to calm him down or divert his thoughts without ever letting him suspect that that was his purpose. This house, as it were transparent compared to those in our climate, this continual necessity of always being in each other's presence, forced the Colonel to exercise more restraint in his outbursts. The unavoidable person of Ralph, who, at the least sound, would come and place himself between Delmare and his wife, forced him to control himself, for he had enough self-respect to master his temper before that strict though silent censor. And so, to give vent to the bad mood which his business worries had intensified in him during the day, he would wait until bedtime had delivered him from his judge. But it was in vain; the hidden influence was keeping watch with him and at the first bitter word, at the first sound of a raised voice which would resound through the thin walls of his house, a sound of moving furniture, or of someone walking about, coming by chance from Ralph's room, seemed to impose silence on him and tell him that Indiana's discreet, patient, solicitous protector was not falling asleep.

PART 4

XXV

Now, it so happened that the ministry of 8 August,* which caused so many upsets in France, dealt a hard blow to the security of Raymon's position. M. de Ramière was not one of those blindly vain individuals who were triumphant over one day's victory. He had made politics the life-blood of all his thoughts, the basis of all his dreams of the future. He had flattered himself that the King, by pursuing a policy of shrewd concessions, would, for a long time to come, maintain the balance which assured the existence of the noble families. But the arrival on the scene of the Prince de Polignac* destroyed that hope. Raymon saw too far ahead, he was too well known in the *new* society, not to be on his guard against the momentary victory. He realized that his whole future was at risk with the monarchy's and that his fortune, perhaps his life, was hanging by a thread.

He found himself then in a delicate and embarrassing position. He was in honour bound, in spite of all the risks of such devotion, to devote himself to the family whose interests until then had been closely tied to his own.* In this matter, he could hardly deceive his conscience and the memory of his kinsfolk. But this new order, this tendency towards absolutism, shocked his prudence, his reason, and, he said, his deep convictions. It compromised his whole existence; it was worse than that, it made him look ridiculous, him, a famous publicist who had dared to promise so many times, in the name of the crown, justice for all and fidelity to the sworn agreement. Now, all the government did gave the lie officially to the young eclectic's imprudent assertions. All the tranquil and lazy-minded, who, two days earlier, asked only to attach themselves to the constitutional monarchy, began to rush into the opposition and to treat the efforts of Raymon and his fellows as deceitful tricks. The most courteous accused them of lack of foresight and incapacity. Raymon felt that it was humiliating to be considered a dupe after playing such a brilliant part in the political game. Secretly he began to curse and despise that royalty which was debasing itself and dragging him down in its fall. He would have liked to be able to detach himself from it without shame before the hour of battle. For some time he made incredible mental efforts to win the confidence of both camps. The opposition groups of that period were not difficult about the admission of new adherents. These groups needed recruits and, thanks to the few credentials that were required, they enlisted a fair number. Moreover, they did not despise the support of great names and, every day, flattery which they skilfully slipped into their newspapers tended to detach the brightest jewels from the worn-out crown. Raymon was not duped by these demonstrations of esteem, but he did not reject them, convinced as he was of their usefulness. On the other hand, the champions of the monarchy showed more intolerance as their situation became more desperate. They drove from their ranks, thoughtlessly and without consideration, their most useful defenders. They soon began to show their displeasure and mistrust to Raymon. He, for his part, embarrassed, deeply attached to his reputation as the principal advantage he possessed in life, was very conveniently attacked by a bout of acute rheumatism, which forced him to give up every kind of work for the time being and retreat to the country with his mother.

In this isolation, Raymon really suffered at finding himself discarded like a corpse amid the frenetic activity of a society on the brink of dissolution, at feeling prevented, as much by the embarrassment of choosing a colour* as by illness, from being enrolled under the warlike banners which were waving on all sides to summon the most obscure and incapable to the great fight. The acute pain of his illness, solitude, boredom, and fever imperceptibly gave his ideas a different direction. He wondered, perhaps for the first time, if society deserved all the care he had taken to please it, and, at seeing it so indifferent towards him, so forgetful of his talents and his glory, he passed judgement on society. Then he consoled himself for having been its dupe by assuring himself that he had only sought in it his personal well-being and had found it there, thanks to himself. Nothing confirms us in selfishness as much as reflection. From it Raymon drew the conclusion: as a social being, man needs two kinds of happiness, the happiness of public life and that of private life, social triumphs and family joys.

His mother, who looked after him assiduously, fell dangerously ill. It was his turn to forget his ills and take care of her, but his strength was not adequate. Ardent, passionate souls acquire enduring, miraculous health in dangerous days, but placid indolent souls do not endow the body with supernatural bouts of strength. Although Raymon was a good son, as these words are understood in society, he succumbed physically under the weight of fatigue. Stretched out on his bed of pain, having at his bedside only paid servants or, occasionally, friends impatient to return to the excitement of social life, he began to think of Indiana; he sincerely regretted her, for at this time she would have been a great help to him. He recalled the dutiful care he had seen her take of her old, bad-tempered husband and he imagined the soothing attentions and the comforts which she would have had the skill to lavish on her lover.

'If I had accepted her sacrifice,' he thought, 'she would be dishonoured, but what would that matter to me in my present plight? Abandoned by a frivolous, selfish society, I would not be alone. The woman scornfully rejected by everyone would be lovingly at my feet. She would weep over my suffering; she would know how to alleviate it. Why did I turn that woman away? She loved me so much that she would have been able to console herself for the insults of others by spreading some happiness over my domestic life.'

He resolved to get married when he was better and he went over in his mind the names and faces that had struck him in the salons of the two sections of society.* Charming visions passed through his dreams, hair piled with flowers, snow-white shoulders wrapped in swansdown, supple bodices encased in muslin or satin; these attractive phantoms fluttered their gauze wings beneath Raymon's heavy, burning gaze, but he had seen these peris* only in the perfumed whirlwind of the ballroom. When he woke up, he wondered if their rosy lips had other smiles than those of coquetry, if their white hands could dress the wounds of grief, if their subtle, brilliant minds could descend to the painful task of consoling and entertaining an invalid laden with worries. Raymon was a man with a clear head and, more than other men, he mistrusted feminine coquetry; more than others, he hated selfishness because he knew that there was nothing to be gained there for his own happiness. And then Raymon found it as difficult to choose a wife as to choose a political colour. The same reasons imposed deliberation and prudence. He belonged to an aristocratic, exclusive family which would not tolerate a misalliance, but nevertheless, wealth was to be found with certainty only in plebeian families. According to all appearances, that class was going to rise on the ruins of the other, and to remain in the forefront of public life one had to be the son-in-law of an industrialist or a stockbroker. So Raymon thought it was wise to wait and see which way the wind would blow before embarking on a course of action that would decide his whole future.

These practical reflections showed him clearly the coldness of heart that presides over marriages of convenience, and the hope of having one day a companion worthy of his love only entered by chance into his prospects of happiness. Meanwhile his illness might be a long one and the hope of better days does not wipe out the acute feeling of present pain. He returned to the painful thought of his blindness on the day he had refused to elope with Madame Delmare and he cursed himself for having so little understood his own real interests.

Meanwhile, he received the letter that Indiana wrote to him from Bourbon Island. The grim, inflexible strength she retained, in the midst of misfortunes which ought to have broken her spirit, made a strong impression on Raymon.

'I judged her wrongly,' he thought. 'She truly loved me; she loves me still. For me she would have been capable of those heroic efforts which I thought were beyond a woman's strength. And now I would perhaps only have to say a word to attract her, like an irresistible magnet, from one end of the world to the other. If six months, perhaps eight months, were not needed to achieve that aim, I would like to try!'

He fell asleep with this thought in his mind, but he was soon woken up by a great bustle in the room next door. He got up with difficulty, put on a dressing-gown, and dragged himself to his mother's room. She was very ill indeed.

Towards morning, she recovered enough strength to talk to him. She had no illusion about the short space of time that remained to her to live; she was concerned about her son's future.

'You are losing your best friend,' she said. 'May heaven replace her with a companion worthy of you. But be prudent, Raymon, and don't risk the peace of your whole life for an ambitious day-dream. I only knew one woman, alas, whom I would like to have called my daughter, but heaven had disposed of her. But listen, my son. M. Delmare is old and broken. Who knows if that long journey has not exhausted what strength remained to him? Respect his wife's honour as long as he is alive; but if, as I believe, he is called to follow soon after me to the grave, remember that there is still one woman in the world who loves you almost as much as your mother has loved you.'

In the evening, Madame de Ramière died in her son's arms. Raymon's grief was bitter and deep. In the face of such a loss, there could be neither false emotion nor cold scheming. His mother was really necessary to him; with her he lost all the moral well-being of his life. On her pale brow and lifeless eyes he shed tears of despair; he cursed his destiny; he wept, too, for Indiana. He called God to account for the happiness He owed him; he reproached Him for treating him like any other man and snatching everything away from him at once. Then he doubted the existence of this God who chastised him. He preferred to deny Him rather than submit to His decrees. He lost all his illusions and all his perception of the realities of his life, and he went back to his bed of fever and suffering, broken like a fallen king, like a cursed angel.

When he was almost recovered, he looked around at the situation in France. Things were getting worse; on all sides, people were threatening to refuse to pay taxes. Raymon was amazed at his party's foolish confidence and, thinking it judicious not to throw himself into the fray just yet, he shut himself up at Cercy with the sad memory of his mother and Madame Delmare.

By dint of reflecting on the idea that he had not taken very seriously at first, he became used to thinking that Indiana was not lost to him if he wanted to take the trouble to ask her to come back. He saw many drawbacks to this course of action, but still more advantages. It was not in his interest to wait till she was a widow in order to marry her, as Madame de Ramière had thought. Delmare might live for another twenty years and Raymon did not want to give up for ever the chance of a brilliant marriage. His optimistic, fertile imagination thought of something better than that. By taking a little trouble, he could exercise an unbounded influence over his Indiana. He felt his mind was skilful and crafty enough to make of that passionate, sublime woman a submissive, devoted mistress. He could remove her from the wrath of public opinion, conceal her behind the impenetrable wall of his private life, keep her like a treasure in the depths of his country retreat, and use her to spread the happiness of a pure, generous affection over his moments of solitary meditation. He would not have to make much effort to avoid her husband's anger; the Colonel would not come three thousand miles to look for his wife when his business interests pinned him down irrevocably in another world. Indiana would not demand much in the way of pleasure and liberty after the harsh trials which had bent her neck to the yoke. She was ambitious only for love, and Raymon felt he would love her out of gratitude as soon as she was useful to him. He recalled too, her constancy and gentleness during the long days of his coldness and neglect. He promised himself to preserve his liberty skilfully so that she would not dare to complain. He flattered himself that he would take sufficient control over her thoughts to make her agree to everything, even to seeing him married, and he supported this hope with the numerous examples of intimate liaisons he had seen survive, in spite of the laws of society, because of the prudence and skill which had enabled them to avoid the judgements of public opinion.

'Moreover,' he added to himself, 'she will have made an irrevocable, total sacrifice for me. For me, she will have travelled across the world and left every means of existence, all possibility of pardon, behind her. Society is severe only on petty commonplace faults. An unusual bold deed surprises it, a striking misfortune disarms it. It will pity her; perhaps it will admire the woman who will have done for me what no other would dare to attempt. It will blame her but it will not mock her, and I'll not be blameworthy for taking her in and protecting her after such a signal proof of her love. Perhaps, on the contrary, I'll be praised for my courage. At least I'll have defenders and my reputation will be subjected to a glorious and inconclusive trial. Sometimes society likes to be defied. It does not bestow its admiration on those who crawl along the beaten track. At the present time, public opinion must be driven by a whip.

Under the influence of these thoughts, he wrote to Madame Delmare. His letter was what was to be expected from the hand of such a skilful, experienced man. It gave the impression of love, grief, and, above all, of truth. Alas! What a pliable reed truth is, to bend thus at every breath!

Yet Raymon was wise enough not to express explicitly the purpose of his letter. He pretended to look on Indiana's return as an unhoped for happiness, and this time he spoke vaguely of his duties. He told her his mother's last words. He depicted vividly the despair to which his loss reduced him, the miseries of his solitude, and the danger of his political situation. He painted a sombre, terrible picture of the revolution which was developing on the horizon in France, and while pretending to rejoice that he was alone to withstand its blows, he hinted to Indiana that the moment had come to put into practice the enthusiastic fidelity, the perilous devotion, of which she had boasted. Raymon blamed his fate and said that virtue had cost him very dear, that his yoke was very harsh, that he had held happiness in his hand, and that he had had the strength to condemn himself to eternal solitude.

'Don't tell me any more that you have loved me,' he added. 'That makes me so weak and disheartened that I curse my courage and hate my duty. Tell me that you are happy, that you are forgetting me, so that it will be within my power not to snatch you away from the bonds that separate us.'

In a word, he said he was unhappy: that was to tell Indiana he was waiting for her.

XXVI

DURING the three months which elapsed between the sending of this letter and its arrival at Bourbon Island, Madame Delmare's situation had become almost intolerable after a domestic incident of the greatest importance for her. She had acquired the sad habit of writing down every evening an account of the day's sorrows. The diary of her suffering was addressed to Raymon, and although she had no intention of sending it to him, she talked to him, at times passionately, at times bitterly, of the sorrows of her life and of the feelings she could not suppress. These papers fell into Delmare's hands; that is to say, he broke open the box where they, as well as Raymon's old letters, were kept, and he read them eagerly with furious jealousy. In his first access of anger, he lost the power of self-control and, with beating heart and clenched fists, he went outside to wait for her return from her walk. Perhaps if she had been a few minutes later, the unhappy man would have had time to regain his self-possession, but the evil stars of both of them decreed that she should appear before him almost immediately. Then, without being able to say a word, he grabbed her by the hair, threw her down, and kicked her on the forehead with the heel of his boot.

He had no sooner imprinted the blood-stained mark of his brutality on a weak creature than he was horrified by his own deed. He fled aghast at what he had done and shut himself up in his room, where he loaded his pistols to blow his brains out. But just as he was about to do so, he saw Indiana beneath the verandah; she had picked herself up and, calmly and coldly, was wiping away the blood which covered her face. Since he thought he had killed her, his first feeling was of joy at seeing her on her feet, but then his anger blazed up anew.

'It's only a scratch,' he cried, 'and you deserve a thousand deaths! No, I shan't kill myself, for you would go and rejoice over my death in your lover's arms. I don't want to assure the happiness of both of you. I want to live to make you suffer, to see you waste away from dreary boredom, to dishonour the scoundrel who tricked me.'

He was struggling against his torturing, jealous fury when Ralph came in by another verandah door and found Indiana in the dishevelled state in which this horrible scene had left her. But she had not shown the least sign of fear, she had not uttered one scream, she had not raised a hand to ask for mercy. Tired of life, she seemed to have had the cruel desire to give Delmare time to commit murder by calling no one to help her. It is clear that when this incident took place, Ralph was twenty paces away and had not heard the slightest sound.

'Indiana!' he cried, drawing back in horrified surprise. 'Who has hurt you like that?'

'You may well ask!' she replied with a bitter smile. 'Who else but *your friend* has the *right* and the desire to do it?'

Ralph threw away the cane he was holding. He needed no weapons other than his large hands to strangle Delmare. In two strides he reached the door and broke it open with his fist . . . But he found Delmare stretched out on the ground, his face purple, his throat swollen, a prey to the suffocating convulsions of apoplexy.

He picked up the papers scattered over the floor. When he recognized Raymon's writing and saw the remains of the box, he understood what had happened. Carefully collecting the incriminating documents, he hurried to give them to Madame Delmare, urging her to burn them immediately. Delmare had probably not taken time to read them all.

Then he urged her to retire to her room while he would call the servants to look after the Colonel. But she did not want either to burn the papers or hide her injury.

'No,' she said haughtily. 'I'm not willing to do that. In the past he didn't deign to hide my flight from Madame de Carvajal. He rushed to make public what he called my dishonour. I want to show everyone this stigma of his own dishonour that he took care to stamp on my face himself. It's a strange justice that requires one person to keep secret another's crimes, when that other assumes the right to condemn one without pity.'

When Ralph saw the Colonel in a fit state to listen to him, he overwhelmed him with reproaches more energetically and fiercely than one would have thought him capable of doing. Then Delmare, who was certainly not a bad-natured man, wept like a child over the crime he had committed. But he wept over it without dignity, as one is prone to do when one reacts to the feeling of the moment without rational consideration of its causes and effects. Quick to rush to the opposite extreme, he wanted to call his wife and ask her pardon. But Ralph was opposed to the idea and tried to make him understand that such a childish reconciliation would compromise the authority of the one without wiping out the insult to the other. He knew very well that there are unpardonable insults and unforgettable woes.

From that moment, the husband became an odious person in his wife's eyes. Everything he did to atone for the wrong he had done deprived him of the little consideration he had been able to retain till then. His fault had been enormous, to be sure. The man who does not feel strong enough to be cold and implacable in his vengeance must forgo all show of impatience and resentment. There is no possible role between that of the Christian who forgives and that of the man of the world who repudiates. But Delmare too had his share of selfishness. He felt old; his wife's attentions were becoming more necessary to him every day.

He was developing a terrible fear of solitude, and if, in the crisis of his wounded pride, he returned to his soldier's habits in ill-treating her, reflection soon brought him back to the old man's weakness of being terrified of being left alone. Too weakened by age and hardships to aspire to become a father, he had remained an old bachelor in his household and he had taken a wife as he would have taken a housekeeper. So it was not out of affection for her that he forgave her for not loving him, it was out of self-interest. And if he was sad not to reign over her affections, it was because he was afraid he would be less well looked after in his old age.

For her part, when Madame Delmare, deeply wounded by the laws of society, stiffened all the sinews of her heart to hate and despise them, there was also, at the bottom of her thoughts, a quite personal feeling. But perhaps this consuming need for happiness, this hatred of injustice, this thirst for liberty, which disappear only with life, are all constituent parts of *egotism*, the word the English use for love of self, considered as a human right and not as a vice. It seems to me that the individual selected from amongst all others to suffer from institutions beneficial to his fellows must, if he has any spiritual energy, fight against such an arbitrary yoke. I also think that, the greater the nobility of his soul, the more it must be outraged by the blows of injustice. If he had dreamed that happiness should reward virtue, into what terrible doubts, into what desperate bewilderment, must he be cast by the disappointments experience brings!

So all Indiana's reflections, all her activities, all her sorrows, were linked to nature's terrible, great struggle against civilization. If the island's deserted mountains had been able to hide her for long, she would certainly have taken refuge there on the day she was assaulted. But Bourbon was not extensive enough to conceal her from search parties, and she resolved to put the sea, and uncertainty about her hiding-place, between herself and her tyrant. After she had made that decision, she felt more at ease and seemed almost carefree and cheerful at home. Delmare was so surprised and delighted at this that, with a bully's reasoning, he thought it a good thing to make women feel the law of the strongest occasionally.

After this incident, Indiana dreamt only of flight, solitude, and independence. In her wounded, grief-stricken mind, she turned over a thousand plans for settling romantically in the desert lands of India or Africa. In the evening, her eye followed the flight of the birds as they went to their rest on Rodrigue Island.* This abandoned island promised her all the delights of solitude, the first need of a broken heart. But the same reasons which prevented her from going into the interior of Bourbon made her give up the idea of the restricted refuge of the neighbouring islands. At her home she often saw wealthy traders from Madagascar who had business dealings with her husband, stolid, bronzed, coarse individuals, who were shrewd and tactful only in their trading interests. Nevertheless, their tales aroused Madame Delmare's attention. She

liked questioning them about the wonderful products of
Madagascar, and what they told her about nature's marvels in
that island kindled more and more her desire to go and hide
there. The extent of the area and the small amount of territory
occupied by Europeans led her to hope that there she would
never be discovered. So she settled on this plan and fed her
unoccupied mind with dreams of a future that she aimed to
create quite alone. She was already building her solitary hut in
the shelter of a virgin forest on the bank of a nameless river;
she was seeking refuge in the protection of those peoples who
have not been debased by the yoke of our laws and prejudices.
Ignorant as she was, she hoped to find there the virtues banished from our hemisphere, and to live in peace, away from all
organized society. She imagined she could escape the dangers
of isolation and resist the devastating diseases of the climate.
She was a weak woman who could not endure one man's
anger, yet thought she could defy the rigours of the state of
nature.

In the midst of these romantic preoccupations and extravagant plans, she forgot her present ills. She made for herself
a world apart, which consoled her for the one in which she
was forced to live. She became used to thinking less about
Raymon, who was soon to have no place in her solitary,
reflective existence. By building a future according to her own
fancy, she let the past rest a little, and already, through feeling
her heart freer and braver, she imagined she was reaping in
advance the fruits of her hermit's life. But Raymon's letter
arrived and the structure of daydreams vanished like a puff of
wind. She felt, or thought she felt, she loved him more than in
the past. For my part, I like to think she never loved with all
the strength of her heart. It seems to me that an ill-placed
affection differs from a mutual affection as much as error
differs from truth. It seems to me, too, that if the exaltation
and fervour of our feelings deceive us to such an extent as to
make us believe that that is love in all its power, we learn later
when we experience the joys of a real love, how much we
deceived ourselves.

But Raymon's situation, as he described it, rekindled in
Indiana's heart the generous impulse which was a need of her

nature. Learning he was alone and unhappy, she felt in duty bound to forget the past and not to foresee the future. The day before, she wanted to leave her husband out of hatred and resentment. Now, she was sorry she did not esteem him so that she could make a real sacrifice to Raymon. Such was her enthusiasm that she was afraid of doing too little for him, in escaping from an ill-tempered master at the risk of her life and in undergoing the awful conditions of a four-month voyage. She would have given her life, and think she had not paid enough for one smile from Raymon. That's how women are.

So it only remained for her to leave the island. It was very difficult to get round Delmare's mistrust and Ralph's perspicacity. But that was not the principal obstacle; she had to avoid the announcement which, according to law, all passengers are obliged to put in the newspapers about their departures.

Among the few vessels anchored in the dangerous roadstead at Bourbon, the ship *Eugène* was about to leave for Europe. For a long time, Indiana looked for an opportunity to speak to the captain without being seen by her husband, but every time she expressed a wish to go for a walk by the harbour, he affected to put her under Sir Ralph's protection, and his eyes followed them with a maddening persistence. However, by noting with scrupulous care all the signs favourable to her purpose, Indiana learned that the captain of the ship bound for France had a relative at the village of La Saline* in the interior of the island and that he often walked back to his ship to spend the night on board. From that moment she kept constant watch at the rock which she used as an observation post. To allay suspicions she would go by roundabout paths and return by the same route when, at nightfall, she had not seen the person she wanted on the path to the mountains.

She had only two more days of hope left, for the land wind was already blowing on the roadstead. The anchorage was threatening to be no longer secure and Captain Random was impatient to sail out to sea.

Finally, she prayed ardently to the God of the weak and the oppressed, and went and installed herself right on the road to La Saline, braving the danger of being seen and risking her last hope. She had been waiting for less than an hour, when Captain Random came down the path. He was a real sailor, always rough and cynical, whether he was in a cheerful or gloomy mood. His look made the melancholy Indiana freeze with terror. However, she plucked up all her courage and, resolute and dignified, went to meet him.

'Monsieur,' she said, 'I have come to put my life and honour in your hands. I want to leave the colony and go back to France. If, instead of granting me your protection, you betray the secret I am entrusting to you, there is nothing left for me but to throw myself into the sea.'

The Captain replied with an oath that the sea would refuse to sink such a pretty schooner and that, since she came of her own accord to seek refuge from the wind, he undertook to tow her to the end of the world.

'So you agree, Monsieur,' she replied, holding back the angry tears that glistened on her long eyelashes. 'The step I am taking in approaching you gives you leave to insult me, and yet, if you knew how detestable my life is in this country, you would have more pity than contempt for me.'

Indiana's noble, touching expression impressed Captain Random. Those who don't make too much use of their sensibility sometimes rediscover it safe and unimpaired when it is called for. He immediately recalled the odious figure of Colonel Delmare and the reaction that his violent behaviour had aroused in the colony. As his eyes lingered amorously on the frail, pretty creature, he was struck by her frank, innocent look. Above all, he was keenly moved at seeing on her forehead a white mark which stood out against her flushed face. He had had business dealings with Delmare, which left him with resentment against a man who was so rigid and tight-fisted in business matters.

'Damn it all!' he cried. 'I have nothing but contempt for a man capable of kicking such a pretty woman in the face. Delmare's a pirate and I wouldn't mind playing such a trick on him. But be prudent, Madame; you must realize that in doing so I risk my good name. You must escape unobserved when the moon has set, and fly away like a poor petrel from the foot of some hidden reef.'

'I know, Monsieur, that you can't do me this important service without breaking the law,' she replied. 'You may run the risk of having to pay a fine. That's why I'm giving you this casket, which is worth at least twice the cost of the voyage.'

The Captain took the casket with a smile.

'This is not the moment to settle our accounts,' he said. 'I'm quite willing to take charge of your little fortune. In the circumstances, you presumably haven't much luggage. On the night we are to sail, go to the rocks at Lataniers creek. You'll see a boat, manned by two good oarsmen, come towards you and you'll be brought aboard between one and two in the morning.'

XXVII

THE day of departure went by like a dream. Indiana was afraid of finding it long and painful, but it passed like a moment. The silence of the countryside and the calm of the house contrasted with the agitated feelings which consumed Madame Delmare. She locked herself in her room to prepare the few things she intended to take with her. Then she hid them under her clothes and carried them one by one to the rocks at Lataniers Creek, where she packed them in a bark basket buried in the sand. The sea was rough and the wind grew stronger every hour. As a precaution the *Eugène* had left the harbour and Madame Delmare saw her white sails in the distance puffed out by the breeze, while the crew made her tack about in order to keep her in place. Indiana's fast-beating heart then went out to the vessel, which seemed to paw with impatience like a fiery charger about to go. But when she went back into the interior of the island she found in the mountain gorges a calm, gentle atmosphere, bright sunlight, the song of birds, the humming of insects, and the activity of work going on like the day before, indifferent to the violent emotions that were torturing her. Then she had doubts about the reality of her situation and wondered if her imminent departure was not the illusion of a dream.

Towards evening, the wind dropped. The *Eugène* came nearer to the coast and, at sunset, Madame Delmare, from the top of her rock, heard cannon echoing through the island. It was the departure signal for the following day at the return of the sun which was then sinking below the horizon.

After supper, M. Delmare did not feel well. His wife thought that all was lost, that he would keep the household awake all night, and that her plan would fail. And then he was in pain, he needed her; this was not the moment to leave him. It was then that remorse entered her heart and she wondered who would take pity on the old man when she had deserted him. She shuddered at the thought that she was going to commit what was a crime in her own eyes, and that the voice of conscience would perhaps rise louder than society's to condemn her. If, as usual, Delmare had demanded her attentions harshly, if he had been impervious and capricious in his suffering, resistance would have seemed sweet and legitimate to the oppressed slave. But for the first time in his life, he bore his pain good-temperedly and was grateful and affectionate to his wife. At ten o'clock, he announced that he felt quite well, insisted that she should retire to her room, and forbade any further anxiety about him. Ralph, indeed, confirmed that all symptoms of illness had disappeared and that a good sleep was the only further remedy required. When eleven o'clock struck, everything was silent and peaceful in the house. Madame Delmare fell on her knees and prayed, weeping bitterly, for she was going to burden her soul with a grievous sin, and henceforth the only pardon she could hope for would come from God. She went quietly into her husband's room. He was sleeping deeply; his face was calm, his breathing regular. Just as she was about to withdraw, she noticed in the darkness another person asleep on an armchair. It was Ralph, who had got up without a sound to watch over her husband in his sleep, in case there should be another accident.

'Poor Ralph!' thought Indiana. 'What an eloquent and cruel reproach to me!'

She longed to wake him up, to confess everything to him, to beseech him to save her from herself, and then she thought of Raymon.

'One more sacrifice,' she said to herself, 'and the cruellest of all, that of my duty.'

Love is a woman's virtue. It is for love that she glories in her sins, it is from love that she derives the heroism to defy her remorse. The more it costs her to commit the crime, the more she will have deserved from the man she loves. It is like the fanaticism which puts the dagger in the hands of the religious maniac.

She took from her neck a gold chain that her mother had given her and that she had always worn. She put it gently round Ralph's neck as the last token of sisterly affection and turned her lamp on to her old husband's face to assure herself that he was no longer ill. He was dreaming at the moment and said in a faint, sad voice:

'Beware of that man, he will ruin you . . .'

Indiana trembled from head to foot and fled to her room. She wrung her hands in painful indecision. Then suddenly she seized upon the idea that she was not acting in her own interest but in Raymon's, that she was not going to him in search of happiness but to bring happiness to him, and that, even if she were to be accursed to all eternity, she would be compensated enough if she embellished her lover's life. She rushed out of the house and quickly reached Lataniers creek, not daring to turn round and look at what she was leaving behind her.

She immediately set about digging up her bark basket and sat on it, silent and trembling, listening to the whistling wind, the splash of the waves which were breaking at her feet, and the shrill moan of the *satanite** in the great bunches of sea-weed hanging from the walls of the cliffs. But above all these sounds the beating of her heart rang in her ears like a funeral bell.

She waited for a long time. She looked at her watch and saw that the appointed hour had passed. The sea was so rough, and navigation in all weathers is so difficult round the coast of the island, that she was beginning to despair of the willingness of the oarsmen ordered to take her aboard, when she espied on the gleaming water the dark outline of a piragua* which was trying to come towards the land. But the swell was so strong and the waves so high that the frail boat kept disappearing and being buried, as it were, in the dark folds of a shroud studded with silver stars. She got up and replied several times to the signal which was made to her, but her shouts were carried away by the wind before they could reach the oarsmen. At last, when they were near enough to hear her, they rowed towards her with great difficulty. Then they stopped to wait for a breaker. As soon as they felt it raise the skiff, they redoubled their efforts, and the wave, as it broke, cast them up with the boat on to the shore.

The land on which Saint-Paul is built was made from sea-
sand and mountain rubble, which the current of the River
des Galets brought down from far above its mouth. These
heaps of rounded pebbles around the coast form underwater
mountains, which the swell drags along, overturns, and re-
builds as it pleases. Their instability makes collision with them
unavoidable and the pilot's skill is of no use as a guide
amongst these reefs, which are constantly being re-formed.
The big ships in the harbour of Saint-Denis are often
wrenched from their anchors and smashed on the shore by the
violent currents. All they can do, when the land wind begins to
blow and makes the sudden retreat of the waves dangerous, is
to make for the open sea as quickly as possible, and that is
what the *Eugène* had done.

The rowing-boat carried off Indiana and her fortune amidst
the wild waves, the howling of the stormy wind, and the oaths
of the two oarsmen, who did not restrain themselves from
loudly cursing the danger to which they were exposed for
her. The ship should have weighed anchor two hours ago,
they said, and it was because of her that the Captain had
obstinately refused to give the order. Thereupon they added
cruel, insulting remarks, to which the unhappy fugitive,
swallowing her shame, made no reply. And, as one of the two
men remarked that they might be punished if they were lacking in the consideration they had been ordered to show for the
Captain's mistress, the other replied with an oath:

'Don't bother me about that. It's the sharks we have to
reckon with tonight. If ever we see Captain Random again, he
won't be more vicious than them, I hope.'

'As for sharks,' said the first man, 'I don't know if that's one
on our scent already, but I can see in our wake a face which
isn't a Christian's.'

'Fool! You're taking a dog's face for a sea-wolf's. Halt
there, my four-legged passenger; you were left on the shore.
But I'm blowed if you're going to eat the crew's biscuit. Our
orders referred only to a young lady; there's no mention of the
lapdog . . .'

At the same time he raised his oar to hit the animal on the
head, but Madame Delmare, looking distraughtly and tear-

fully at the sea, recognized her beautiful dog Ophelia, who had found her scent on the island rocks and was swimming after her. Just as the sailor was about to strike her, the wave she was struggling against with difficulty carried her away far from the boat and her mistress could hear her whining with distress and impatience. Indiana begged the oarsmen to take the dog on board and they pretended to get ready to do so, but just as the faithful animal was coming near them, they broke her skull with loud guffaws and Indiana saw the dead body of a creature who had loved her more than Raymon floating on the water. At the same time a violent breaker dragged the boat down as it were to the bottom of a waterfall and the sailors' laughs turned to curses and cries of distress. But thanks to its lightness and flatness, the canoe bounced up again like a diving bird on the water, quickly rising again to the top of the wave to be hurled down into another ravine and rise yet again onto the foaming crest of the water. As the coast receded the sea became less rough and soon the boat moved swiftly and without danger towards the ship. Then the two oarsmen regained their good humour and with it their rationality. They made efforts to make up for their insulting behaviour to Indiana but their compliments were more insulting than their anger.

'There now, young lady,' said one of them. 'Take heart. I'm sure the Captain will give us a drink of the best wine in the ship's store for the pretty package we've fished up for him.'

The other one pretended to be sorry that the waves had wet the young lady's clothes, but, he added, the Captain was waiting for her and would look after her well. Without moving, Indiana listened to their words in silent terror. She understood how awful her situation was and saw no other way of avoiding the insults that awaited her than to throw herself into the sea. Two or three times she almost jumped out of the boat. Then she regained courage, a sublime courage, with the thought:

'It's for him, it's for Raymon that I'm enduring all this suffering. I must live, even if I'm overwhelmed with shame!'

She put her hand on her troubled heart and found the blade of a dagger that she had hidden there in the morning with a

sort of instinctive foresight. The possession of this weapon
restored all her confidence. It was a short, pointed stiletto that
her father used to carry, an old Spanish weapon that had
belonged to a Medina-Sidonia,* whose name was engraved on
the steel blade with the date 1300. That good weapon had no
doubt been red with noble blood; it had probably avenged
more than one insult, punished more than one insolent fellow.
With it in her possession, Indiana felt she became Spanish
again and she went resolutely on to the ship, telling herself
that a woman incurred no risk as long as she had the means of
taking her own life before accepting dishonour. She avenged
her guides' harshness only by rewarding them handsomely for
their fatigue. Then she retired to her quarters on deck and
waited anxiously for the hour of departure.

At last day broke and the sea was covered with small craft
bringing the passengers on board. Indiana, hidden behind a
porthole, looked with terror at the faces of the people leaving
the boats. She trembled lest she should see her husband's face
as he came to claim her. At last the echoes of the gun which
signalled the departure died away on the island which had
been her prison. The ship began to churn up torrents of foam,
and as the sun rose in the sky, it cast a cheerful, pink glow on
the white summits of the Salazes mountains, which began to
sink on the horizon.

Several miles out to sea, a kind of comedy was enacted on
board to evade an admission of trickery. Captain Random
pretended to discover Madame Delmare on his vessel; he
feigned surprise, questioned the sailors, pretended to get
angry, then to calm down, and finally drew up a report on the
finding of a stowaway on board. That's the technical term
used in such situations.

Allow me to end here the account of the voyage. To do
Captain Random justice, it will be enough for me to tell you
that, in spite of his rough career, he had enough natural good
sense to understand Madame Delmare's character quickly. He
made few attempts to take advantage of her solitary state, and
finally was touched by it and acted as her friend and protector.
But this good man's honourable behaviour and Indiana's dignified bearing did not prevent the crew's comments, the mock-

ing looks, the insulting suspicions, and the coarse, biting jests. These were the real tortures of this unfortunate woman during the voyage, for I say nothing of the fatigue, the privations, the perils of the sea, the discomforts, and the seasickness; she herself counted them as nothing.

XXVIII

THREE days after the letter had been sent to Bourbon Island, Raymon had completely forgotten both the letter and its purpose. He had felt better and ventured to pay a visit in the neighbourhood. The Lagny estate, which M. Delmare had sold to pay his creditors, had just been bought by a rich industrialist, M. Hubert, a capable and worthy man, not in the way all rich industrialists are but like a small number of the newly-rich. Raymon found the new owner settled in the house which held so many memories for him. To start with, he was happy to give free rein to his emotion as he crossed the garden, where Noun's light steps still seemed imprinted in the sand, and the huge rooms which still seemed to ring with the sound of Indiana's gentle voice; but soon the presence of a new host changed the course of his thoughts.

In the large drawing-room, in the place where Madame Delmare usually sat at her work, a tall, slender young woman, with a penetrating glance that was both friendly and teasing, was sitting in front of an easel and amusing herself by copying the unusual wainscoting of the walls in water colours. The copy was quite charming, a subtle caricature clearly marked by the mocking yet courteous personality of the artist. She had amused herself by exaggerating the pretentious elegance of the old frescoes; she had captured the false, glittering spirit of Louis XV's century* on those stilted figures. By restoring the colours faded by time, she had given them back their affected graces, their atmosphere of courtiership, their costumes of the boudoir and of the shepherd's hut, so curiously identical. Beside this work of historical mockery, she had written the word *pastiche*.

She slowly raised her long eyes with their wheedling, ironic, attractive but treacherous look to Raymon's face; for some reason it reminded him of Shakespeare's *Anne Page*.* In her demeanour, there was neither shyness, nor boldness, nor the fashionable affectation, nor lack of self-confidence. Their conversation turned on the influence of fashion on the arts.

'Don't you think, Monsieur, that the moral tone of the period was in that paint-brush?' she said, pointing to the wooden panelling covered with rustic cupids in the style of Boucher.* 'Isn't it true that those sheep don't walk, sleep, or graze like sheep today? And that pretty landscape, so artificial and well-groomed, those rose bushes with a hundred leaves, in the middle of woods where only wild rose hedges grow in our day, those tame birds of a species that seems to have disappeared, those pink satin dresses unfaded by the sun, don't you think that in all that there was poetry, thoughts of ease and happiness, the feeling of a whole pleasant, useless, and harmless life? No doubt these ridiculous fictions were just as good as our gloomy political lucubrations! Why wasn't I born in those days?' she added with a smile. 'Frivolous and limited woman that I am, I'd have been much better suited to painting fans or expertly unpicking thread-work than to commenting on the newspapers or understanding the debates in the Chambers.'

M. Hubert left the two young people together and gradually their conversation strayed till it came to the subject of Madame Delmare.

'You were a very close friend of our predecessors in this house,' said the girl, 'and it's certainly generous on your part to come and see new faces. They say Madame Delmare was a remarkable woman,' she added with a penetrating look at him. 'She must have left memories for you here which are not to our advantage.'

'She was an excellent woman,' Raymon replied unconcernedly, 'and her husband was a good fellow.'

'But it seems to me that she was something more than an excellent woman,' continued the heedless girl. 'If I remember rightly, there was a charm about her which deserves a more lively, poetic description. I saw her two years ago at a ball at the Spanish embassy. She was lovely, that evening. Do you remember?'

Raymon started at the memory of that evening when he had spoken to Indiana for the first time. At the same time he recalled that at this ball he had noticed the interesting face and intelligent eyes of the young woman to whom he was speaking at that moment. But he had not then asked who she was.

It was only on leaving and when he was congratulating M. Hubert on his daughter's charms, that he learned her name.

'I haven't the good fortune to be her father,' replied the industrialist, 'but I have made up for that by adopting her. Don't you know my story then?'

'I've been ill for several months,' replied Raymon. 'All I know of you is the good you've already done in the district.'

'There are people who give me great credit for adopting Mademoiselle Nangy,' replied M. Hubert, smiling. 'But you, Monsieur, who have a noble heart, you will see whether I did anything more than decency required. A childless widower, I found myself the owner of a considerable capital, the result of my work, which I was seeking to invest. In Burgundy I found for sale the estate and château of Nangy, which were national property* and suited me very well. I had been the owner for some time, when I learned that the former owner of this estate was living in seclusion in a cottage with his seven-year-old granddaughter in conditions of extreme poverty. The old man had duly received his indemnity* but he had devoted it to paying off scrupulously debts incurred during the emigration. I wanted to ameliorate his lot and offered him a home in my house. But in his misfortunes he had retained all the pride of his rank. He refused to return to his ancestral home, as if on charity, and died shortly after my arrival without being willing to accept any help from me. Then, I took in his child. The little patrician was proud already and accepted my care against her will. But at that age prejudices are not deep-seated and resolutions don't last long. She soon became used to looking on me as her father and I brought her up as my own daughter. She has rewarded me well by the happiness she brings to my old age. So, to make sure of my happiness, I adopted Mademoiselle de Nangy and my only ambition now is to find her a husband worthy of her and capable of skilful management of the property I'll leave her.'

Little by little, the excellent man, encouraged by Raymon's interest in his confidences, let him unpretentiously into the secret of all his affairs. His attentive listener realized that M.

Hubert had a fine, large fortune administered with the most minute care; to be displayed in all its splendour, it was only awaiting a younger and more fashionable user than its worthy proprietor. Raymon felt that he might be the man called to that agreeable task and he thanked his ingenious destiny which reconciled all his interests by offering him, with the help of romantic incidents, a wife of his own rank in possession of a fine, plebeian fortune. It was a stroke of fate not to let slip, and he exercised all his skill to take advantage of it. In addition, the heiress was charming. Raymon became a little more reconciled to his providence. As for Madame Delmare, he did not want to think about her. He banished the fears aroused in him from time to time by his letter. He tried to persuade himself that poor Indiana would not grasp its meaning or would not have the courage to respond to it. Finally, he managed to deceive himself and not to think he was at fault, for Raymon would have been horrified to think he was selfish. He was not one of those frank scoundrels who come on to the stage to make a naïve confession of their vices to their own hearts. Vice does not see itself in its own ugliness, for it would frighten itself, and Shakespeare's Iago,* a character so true to life in his deeds, is false in his words, forced as he is by our dramatic conventions to reveal, himself, the deep secret recesses of his tortuous heart. Man rarely tramples his conscience underfoot in cold blood. He turns it over, squeezes it, pulls it this way and that, distorts it, and when he has perverted it, enfeebled it, and worn it out, he carries it about with him as an indulgent and easy-going guardian, who gives in to his passions and his interest, but whom he always pretends to consult and to fear.

So M. de Ramière often returned to Lagny, and M. Hubert welcomed his visits; for, as you know, Raymon had the art of making himself liked, and soon the rich plebeian's only wish was to call him his son-in-law. But he wanted his adopted daughter to choose Raymon herself and he allowed the young people complete freedom to get to know, and to form an opinion about, each other.

Laure de Nangy was in no hurry to reach a decision about Raymon's happiness. She kept him perfectly balanced between fear and hope. Less generous than Madame Delmare but more skilful, detached but flattering, proud but attentive, she was the woman to get the better of Raymon, for her skill outdid Raymon's as much as his outdid Indiana's. She soon realized that her admirer was in pursuit of her fortune as much as of herself. Her rational imagination had hoped for nothing better from suitors. She had too much good sense, too much knowledge of the real world, to have dreamed of love side by side with two million. Calmly and philosophically, she had accepted the situation and did not blame Raymon. She did not dislike him for being calculating and materialistic like the age he lived in, only she knew him too well to love him. She prided herself on not being below the cold rational standard of the age. Her *amour propre* would have suffered had she retained the naïve illusions of an ignorant girl at boarding school. She would have blushed at a disappointment as if it were a blunder. In a word, she made her heroism consist in avoiding love as Madame Delmare placed hers in yielding to it.

Mademoiselle de Nangy had therefore quite made up her mind to submit to marriage as a social necessity, but she took a malicious pleasure in making use of the liberty she still had and in imposing her authority for a while on the man who aspired to deprive her of it. No youth, no sweet dreams, no brilliant, deceptive future, for this girl who was condemned to undergo all the miseries of wealth. For her, life was a stoical calculation and happiness a childish illusion, against which she must defend herself as against a weakness and an absurdity.

While Raymon was working at building up his fortune, Indiana was approaching the shores of France. But how surprised and alarmed she was when on disembarking, she saw the tricolour flag flying on the walls of Bordeaux! A violent disturbance was disrupting the town; the prefect had been almost murdered the night before; on all sides the populace was rising; the garrison seemed to be preparing for a bloody struggle and the outcome of the revolution in Paris* was still unknown.

'I've come too late!' was the thought that struck Madame Delmare like a lightning blow.

In her fear, she left the little money and few clothes she possessed on the boat, and began to walk about the town in a kind of daze. She looked for a coach going to Paris, but the public conveyances were laden with fugitives or with profiteers from the spoils of the conquered. It was not till the evening that she found a place. Just as she was getting into the coach, a patrol of the improvised national guard opposed the travellers' departure and asked to see their papers. Indiana had none. While she was struggling against the fairly absurd suspicions of the triumphant victors, she heard it firmly stated around her that the monarchy had fallen, the King had fled, and the ministers with all their supporters had been murdered. This news, proclaimed with laughter, stamping feet, and shouts of joy dealt Madame Delmare a mortal blow. In all this revolution, only one item was of personal interest to her; in all France she knew only one man. She fell in a faint on the pavement and only recovered consciousness in a hospital ... several days later.

Without money, clothes, or possessions she left hospital two months later, weak, tottering, and exhausted by an inflammatory brain fever which had nearly cost her life several times. When she found herself in the street, alone, barely able to stand, with no support, resources, or strength, and when, making an effort to recollect her situation, she realized she was lost and friendless in the great city, she had an indescribable feeling of terror and despair; for she thought that Raymon's fate had probably been decided long since and there was not a single person around her who could put an end to her frightful uncertainty. The horror of being deserted weighed down upon her broken spirit with all its might, and the apathetic despair aroused by utter misery gradually deadened all her faculties. In the moral numbness that she felt was coming over her, she dragged herself to the harbour and, shivering with fever, sat down on a bollard to warm herself in the sun, gazing idly at the water flowing at her feet. She stayed there for several hours, without energy, hope, or will-power. Then at last she remembered her clothes and money that she had left on the *Eugène* and that she might be able to retrieve. But night had fallen and she dared not venture amongst the sailors, who were leaving their work with boisterous cheerfulness, to ask them for information about the ship. On the contrary, she wanted to avoid the attention she was beginning to attract, and so she left the harbour and hid in the ruins of a demolished house behind the huge esplanade of Les Quinconces.* Huddled in a corner, she spent the night there, a cold October night filled with terrors and bitter thoughts. At last day dawned; hunger, biting and implacable, made itself felt. She decided to beg. Although in a fairly bad condition, her clothes still indicated more comfortable circumstances than is normal for a beggar. People looked at her with curiosity, suspicion, or mockery, but gave her nothing. She dragged herself back to the harbour and, asking for news of the *Eugène*, learned from the first boatman she met that it was still in the Bordeaux roadstead. She had herself rowed out to the ship and found Random having breakfast.

'Well, my lovely passenger,' he cried. 'So you're back from Paris already? You've come just in time, for I'm sailing back tomorrow. Do you want to be taken back to Bourbon?'

He informed Madame Delmare that he had had a search made for her everywhere so that he could return her belongings. But when Indiana was taken to hospital, she had no document on her which could indicate her name. She had been entered as *unknown* on the admissions register and on the police records; the Captain had therefore been unable to obtain any information.

The next day, in spite of her weakness and fatigue, Indiana left for Paris. Her anxiety should have been lessened when she saw the turn political events had taken.* But anxiety does not reason and love is fertile in childish fears.

The very evening of her arrival in Paris, she hurried to Raymon's house. She questioned the porter anxiously.

'Monsieur is well,' he replied. 'He's at Lagny.'

'At Lagny! Do you mean Cercy?'

'No, Madame, at Lagny. He's the proprietor there now.'

'How kind Raymon is!' thought Indiana. 'He has bought the estate to provide a refuge for me, where malicious gossip cannot touch me. He was quite sure I would come.'

Beside herself with happiness, light-hearted and filled with new life, she took a room in a hotel without delay and spent the night and a part of the next day resting. It was such a long time since the unfortunate young woman had had a peaceful sleep! Her dreams were delightful, yet deceptive, but when she awoke she did not regret their illusions, for she found hope at her bedside. She dressed with care; she knew that Raymon cared about all the details of dress, and the evening before she had ordered a pretty, new dress that was brought to her when she got up. But when she wanted to do her hair she looked in vain for her long, magnificent tresses: during her illness they had fallen under the nurses' scissors. She noticed this for the first time, for her preoccupations had been so great that they had distracted her from trivialities.

Nevertheless, when she had arranged her short black hair in curls on her melancholy, white brow and put on her pretty head a little hat in the English style (called then a *three per cent** by allusion to the recent slump in dividends), when she had fixed in her belt a bunch of the flowers whose scent Raymon liked, she hoped he would still find her attractive; for she had become pale and delicate-looking again, as on the days when he had first known her, and the effects of illness had removed the traces of the tropical sun.

In the afternoon she hired a carriage, and about nine o'clock in the evening she reached a village on the edge of the Forest of Fontainebleau. There she ordered the driver to unharness the horse and to wait for her till the next day; then she set off alone on foot along a path in the wood which led her in less than a quarter of an hour to the grounds at Lagny. She tried to push the little gate open but it was locked on the inside. Indiana wanted to go in secretly, to evade the servants' eyes and to surprise Raymon. She skirted the wall of the grounds. It was old; she remembered it had many broken sections, and fortunately she found one which she climbed over without too much difficulty.

As she set foot on land which belonged to Raymon and which from now on was to be her refuge, her sanctuary, her fortress, and her home, she felt her heart leap for joy. Light-footed and triumphant, she sped along the winding paths she knew so well. She reached the English garden, so dark and isolated on that side. The clumps of trees had not changed but the bridge, whose painful sight she was dreading, had disappeared; even the river had altered it course. Only the places which would have recalled Noun's death had become different.

'He wanted to remove that cruel memory from me,' thought Indiana. 'He was wrong; I could have borne it. Wasn't it for my sake that he brought this remorse into his life? From now on we are quits, for I too have committed a crime. I have perhaps caused my husband's death. Raymon can open his arms to me. We will take the place of innocence and virtue for each other.'

She crossed the river on planks which were lying there till a planned bridge was built, and walked through the flower garden. She was forced to stop, for her heart was beating as if it would burst. She looked up at the window of her old room. Oh joy! Light was shining through the blue curtains; Raymon was there. Could he occupy another room? The door of the secret staircase was open.

'He's expecting me at any time,' she thought. 'He'll be happy but not surprised.'

At the top of the staircase she stopped again to draw breath. She felt less strong to cope with joy than with sorrow. She bent down and looked through the keyhole. Raymon was alone; he was reading. It was really him; it was Raymon full of strength and vitality. Sorrows had not aged him; political upheavals had not removed a hair from his head. He was there, calm and handsome, his forehead resting on his white hand, which was buried in his black hair.

Indiana eagerly pushed the door, which opened without difficulty.

'You were expecting me,' she cried, falling on her knees and leaning her head, almost fainting, on Raymon's breast. 'You had counted the months and the days! You knew the time had passed but you also knew I couldn't fail to answer your call . . . It was you who asked me to come. Here I am, here I am, I feel faint!'

Her thoughts became confused in her mind. She remained silent for some time, breathless, unable to speak or think.

Then she opened her eyes, recognized Raymon as if she were emerging from a dream, uttered a cry of frantic joy, and pressed her lips to his, passionately, wildly happy. He was pale, silent, motionless, as if thunderstruck.

'Recognize me, then,' she cried. 'It's me; it's your Indiana; it's your slave, whom you recalled from exile and who has come a thousand miles to love and serve you. It's your chosen companion, who has left everything, risked everything, braved everything, to bring you this moment of joy. Tell me, are you happy, are you pleased with her? I'm waiting for my reward; one word, one kiss, will repay me a hundredfold.'

But Raymon made no reply; his remarkable presence of mind had deserted him. He was overwhelmed with surprise, remorse, and terror at seeing this woman at his feet. He hid his head in his hands and longed for death.

'My God! My God! You don't speak to me, you don't kiss me, you don't say a word to me!' cried Madame Delmare, pressing Raymon's knees against her breast. 'Aren't you able to speak then? Happiness is painful; it kills people; I'm well aware of that! Oh, you feel ill; you're suffocating; I surprised you too suddenly. But try to look at me. See how pale I am, how I have aged, how I have suffered. But it was for you, and you'll only love me the better for it. Say one word to me, Raymon, just one.'

'I'd like to weep,' said Raymon in a choking voice.

'And so would I,' she said, covering his hands with kisses. 'Oh, yes, that would do you good. Weep, weep then, on my heart. I'll wipe your tears away with my kisses. I've come to bring you happiness, to be whatever you want, your companion, your servant, or your mistress. I was very cruel before, very unreasonable, very selfish. I made you suffer a lot and I didn't want to understand that I was demanding more than your strength could bear. But since then, I've thought about it, and as you're not afraid to brave public opinion with me, I've no longer the right to refuse to make any sacrifice for you. Do what you like with me, with my blood, with my life. I am yours, body and soul. I've travelled three thousand miles to belong to you, to tell you that. Take me, I am your property, you are my master.'

I don't know what infernal idea suddenly crossed Raymon's mind. He lifted his head from his clenched hands and looked at Indiana with diabolical calm; then a terrible smile hovered on his lips and made his eyes gleam for Indiana was still beautiful.

'First of all, we must hide you,' he said, getting up.

'Why hide me here?' she asked. 'Aren't you the master who can welcome and protect me; for I have no longer anyone but you in the world and without you, would be reduced to begging on the public highway? Why, even society can no longer make it a crime for you to love me . . . It is I who have taken everything on my own shoulders . . . I alone! . . . But where are you going?' she cried as she saw him walk towards the door.

She clung to him with the terror of a child who doesn't want to be left alone for a moment, and dragged herself along on her knees to follow him.

He wanted to lock the door, but it was too late. It opened before he could touch it, and Laure de Nangy came in. She seemed less surprised than shocked, didn't utter a sound and bent down a little, blinking, to look at the half-fainting woman on the floor. Then, with a bitter, cold, contemptuous smile, she said:

'Madame Delmare, it seems to me you enjoy putting three people in a strange situation. But I thank you for giving me the least ridiculous role, and this is how I fulfil it. Would you please go.'

Indignation restored Indiana's strength. She rose and, in a high and mighty tone, said to Raymon:

'Who is this woman? And what right has she to give me orders in your house?'

'You are in my house,' replied Laure.

'But say something, Monsieur!' cried Indiana, shaking the unhappy man's arm furiously. 'Tell me if she's your mistress or your wife!'

'She's my wife,' replied Raymon with a dazed look.

'I forgive your uncertainty,' said Madame de Ramière with a cruel smile. 'If you had stayed where your duty lay, you would have received a card announcing Monsieur's marriage. Come, Raymon,' she said with ironic amiability, 'I pity your embarrassment; you're rather young; I hope you will realize that more prudence is required in life. I leave to you the task of putting an end to this absurd scene. I would laugh at it if you didn't look so unhappy.'

With that speech, she withdrew, fairly satisfied with the dignity she had just displayed and secretly triumphant at the inferior, dependant position in which this incident had put her husband with regard to her.

When Indiana recovered the use of her senses, she was alone in a closed carriage and being driven rapidly towards Paris.

XXIX

AT the city boundary, the carriage stopped. A servant, whom Madame Delmare recognized as having seen in the past in Raymon's service, came to the carriage door to ask where he should take *Madame*. Without thinking, Indiana gave the street and the name of the hotel where she had spent the previous night. When she arrived, she collapsed on to a chair and stayed there till the next morning without thinking of going to bed, longing for death, but too broken, too exhausted, to have the strength to kill herself. She thought it was impossible to live after such terrible sorrows and that death would surely come of itself to seek her out. So she stayed in this state the whole of the following day, without having anything to eat and without replying to the few offers of service that were made to her.

I'm not sure that there's anything more horrible than staying in a furnished room in Paris, especially when, like this one, it is in a narrow, dark street and only a damp, murky daylight creeps reluctantly about the smoky ceiling and dirty windows. And then there's something in the appearance of the unaccustomed furniture, to which your idle glance turns in vain in search of a memory and a fellow-feeling, something freezing and repellent. All these objects belong, as it were, to nobody, by dint of belonging to all comers; no one has left any trace of being there, except for an unknown name sometimes left on a card in the frame of the mirror; this bought refuge has sheltered so many poor travellers, so many lonely strangers, but was hospitable to none of them; it has seen the passage of so many agitated human beings but cannot say anything about them; the discordant, continuous noise from the street doesn't even let you sleep to escape from grief or boredom; these are all grounds for disgust and depression, even for someone who doesn't come here in Madame Delmare's horrible state of mind. Poor provincial, who have left your fields, your expanse of sky, your green places, your home, and your family, to come and shut yourself up in this prison cell of the mind and the heart; look at Paris, the beautiful Paris that you had dreamed of as being so marvellous! Look at it stretched out there, black with mud and rain, noisy, foul, and swift as a torrent of mud! There is the perpetual revelling, always brilliant and perfumed, that you had been promised; there are the intoxicating pleasures, the gripping surprises, the treasures of sight, hearing, and taste, which were to vie for your limited senses and faculties unable to appreciate them all at once. Look over there at the Parisian who had been described to you as friendly, courteous, and hospitable, rushing along, always in a hurry, always careworn. Tired out before you have mingled with this ever-moving population or entered this inextricable maze, overcome with fear, you fall back into the cheerful precincts of a furnished hotel room, where, after you have hastily taken up residence, the only servant in a house that is often huge, leaves you to die alone in peace, if fatigue or sorrow deprives you of the strength to attend to the thousand needs of life.

But to be a woman and to find oneself in such a place, a thousand miles from every human affection, to be there with no money, which is much worse than being abandoned in a vast desert without water, not to have in the whole course of one's life one happy memory that is not poisoned or faded, in all one's future not one hope of a possible existence to distract one's mind from the emptiness of the present situation, that is the last degree of misery and hopelessness. So Madame Delmare did not try to struggle against a fulfilled destiny, against a broken, ruined life; she let hunger, fever, and grief gnaw at her without uttering one complaint, without shedding one tear, without making one effort to die one hour sooner, to suffer one hour less.

They found her on the ground, the morning after the second day, stiff with cold, with blue lips and lifeless eyes, but she was not dead. The landlady looked carefully in the drawer of the writing desk and, seeing so little in it, considered whether she should send the stranger to hospital, since she certainly had not the means to pay the cost of a long, expensive illness. However, as she was a woman *full of human kindness,* she had Indiana put to bed and sent for a doctor so as to find out from him if the illness would last more than two days. One appeared who had not been sent for.

When Indiana opened her eyes, she found him at her bedside. I don't need to tell you his name.

'Oh, it's you, it's you!' she cried, throwing herself half-fainting on his breast. 'It's you who are my good angel! But you come too late; I can't do anything more for you than to die blessing you!'

'You won't die, my dear,' Ralph replied with emotion. 'Life can still smile at you. The laws which opposed your happiness will no longer shackle your affection. I'd have liked to destroy the invincible charm cast over you by a man I neither like nor esteem. But that is not in my power and I am weary of seeing you suffer. Your life has been appalling up to now; it can't become more so. In any case, if my sad expectations are realized, if the happiness you've dreamed of is not to last long, at least you'll have experienced it for a while; at least you won't die without having a taste of it. So I sacrifice all my dislike. The destiny which thrusts you, all alone, into my arms imposes on me the duties of a guardian and father. I come to tell you that you are free and that you can unite your lot with M. de Ramière's. Delmare is no more.'

Tears flowed slowly down Ralph's cheeks as he was speaking. Indiana suddenly sat up in bed and cried, wringing her hands in despair:

'My husband is dead! It's I who killed him! And you speak to me of the future and happiness as if any remained for a heart which detests and despises itself! But know that God is just and that I am cursed. M. de Ramière is married.'

She fell back exhausted into her cousin's arms. They could not resume their conversation till several hours later.

'Your conscience is rightly disturbed, but set it at rest,' said Ralph solemnly, but gently and sadly. 'Delmare was dying when you left him. He never knew of your flight and he died without cursing you or mourning for you. Towards morning, as I emerged from the doze into which I had fallen at his bedside, I found that his face was purple and his sleep heavy and feverish. He had already had an apoplectic fit. I ran to your room; I was surprised not to find you there. But I hadn't time to enquire into the reasons for your absence. I only became seriously alarmed after Delmare's death. All that medical skills could do was of no avail; the disease progressed with frightening speed. An hour later he died in my arms without regaining the use of his senses. Yet, at the last moment his dulled, inert mind seemed to make an effort to revive. He looked for my hand, which he took for yours, for his own were already stiff and numb. He tried to press it and died stammering your name.'

'I heard his last words,' said Indiana mournfully. 'Just as I was leaving him for ever, he spoke to me in his sleep: "That man will destroy you," he said. Those words are there,' she added, putting one hand on her heart and the other to her head.

'When I had the strength to lift my eyes and thoughts from the dead man,' continued Ralph, 'I thought of you, of you, Indiana, who were free from now on and could mourn your master only out of kindness and religious feeling. I was the only one who was deprived of something by his death, for I was his friend, and even if he wasn't always sociable, at least I had no rival in his heart. I feared the effect on you of breaking the news too suddenly, and I went to wait for you at the front door, thinking you wouldn't be long in coming back from your morning walk. I waited for a long time. I won't tell you of my anxiety, my searches, my fear when I found Ophelia's blood-stained dead body, which had been broken on the rocks. The waves had thrown it on to the shore. Alas! I looked for a long time, thinking I'd soon discover yours; for I thought there'd be nothing left on earth for me to love. There's no point in telling you of my grief; you must have foreseen it when you deserted me.

'However, the rumour soon spread in the colony that you had fled. A ship which was coming into the roadstead had crossed the *Eugène* in the Mozambique channel; the crew had come alongside your vessel. A passenger had recognized you and in less than three days the whole island knew about your departure.

'I'll spare you the absurd and insulting rumours which resulted from the coincidence of these two events on the same night, your flight and your husband's death. I wasn't spared in the charitable conclusions that people were happy to draw from it, but I didn't bother about them. I had still one duty to fulfil on earth, that of making sure you were still alive and of helping you if it were necessary. I left soon after you, but the voyage was awful and I've only been in France for a week. My first thought was to hurry to M. de Ramière's house to get news of you. But, by chance, I met his servant Carle, who had just driven you here. I only asked him your address and came with the conviction that I wouldn't find you alone.'

'Alone, alone! Shamefully deserted!' cried Madame Delmare. 'But let's not talk about that man; let's never talk about him. I don't want to love him any more, for I despise him. But you mustn't tell me that I have loved him; that would remind me of my shame and my crime. It would cast a terrible reproach on my last moments. Oh, be my consoling angel, you who come at every crisis in my lamentable existence to hold out a friendly hand to me. Fulfil your last mission to me with compassion. Speak to me words of affection and forgiveness, so that I may die in peace and hope for the pardon of the judge who awaits me above!'

She hoped she would die, but sorrow rivets the chains of our lives instead of breaking them. She was not even seriously ill; she was not strong enough for that. But she lapsed into a state of languor and apathy which resembled imbecility.

Ralph tried to distract her. He took her away from everything which might remind her of Raymon. He took her to Touraine. He surrounded her with all the comforts of life; he devoted every moment of his own life to making some moments of hers bearable; and, when he had no success, when he had exhausted all the resources of his skill and affection without being able to bring a single ray of pleasure to that sad, worn face, he deplored the impotence of his language and reproached himself bitterly for the clumsiness of his affection.

One day he found her more crushed and despairing than ever. He did not dare speak to her and sat down sadly beside her. Indiana then turned towards him and said, pressing his hand affectionately: 'I give you a lot of pain, my poor Ralph, and you must have a great deal of patience to put up with the sight of an unhappy, selfish creature like me. Your painful task has long since been fulfilled. The most unreasonable, demanding person could not ask more from friendship than you have given me. Now leave me to the pain which consumes me. Don't spoil a pure, saintly life by contact with an accursed one. Try to find elsewhere the happiness which cannot develop near me.'

'Indeed, I give up trying to cure you, Indiana,' he replied, 'but I'll never desert you, even if you tell me I'm a nuisance to you, for you still need care in material matters, and if you don't want me to be your friend, I'll at least be your servant. Yet, listen to me: I've an expedient to propose that I've reserved for the final period of your pain but which is certainly infallible.'

'I know only one remedy for grief,' she replied, 'and that is forgetfulness; for I've had the time to convince myself that reason is of no use. So let's pin our hope on time. If my will could obey the gratitude you arouse in me, I would be as calm and cheerful from now on as in our childhood days. Believe me, my dear, I take no pleasure in making the most of my pain and rubbing salt into my wound. Don't I know that all my suffering rebounds on to your heart? Alas, I'd like to forget, to be cured. But I'm only a weak woman, Ralph. Be patient and don't think me ungrateful.'

She burst into tears. Sir Ralph took her hand.

'Listen, dear Indiana,' he said. 'It's not in our power to forget. I don't blame you. I can suffer patiently, but to see you suffer is more than I can bear. Besides, why should we, feeble creatures that we are, struggle like this against an iron destiny? We've carried this millstone round our necks for long enough. The God whom you and I worship has not destined man to suffer so much misery without giving him the instinct to deliver himself from it, and what, in my opinion, constitutes the main superiority of men over animals is that they understand where the remedy lies for all their ills. The remedy is suicide; that's the one I propose, that I advise.'

'I've often thought of it,' replied Indiana after a short silence. 'In the past, I was strongly tempted by it, but a religious scruple held me back. Since then, my ideas developed in my solitude. By clinging to me, misfortune gradually taught me a different religion from the one taught by men. When you came to my assistance, I was determined to let myself die of hunger, but you begged me to live and I hadn't the right to refuse you that sacrifice. Now it's your life, your future, that holds me back. What will you do alone in the world, my poor Ralph, without family, without passions, without affections? Since these terrible blows, which have cut me to the heart, I'm no longer any use to you, but perhaps I'll recover. Yes, Ralph, I'll try as hard as I can, I swear to you. Be patient a little longer; soon I'll be able to smile . . . I want to become calm and cheerful again, so as to devote to you the life that you've worked so hard to rescue from misfortune.'

'No, my dear, no,' replied Ralph. 'I don't wish for such a sacrifice; I'll never accept it. In what respect is my life more precious than yours? Why must you impose a hateful future on yourself to give me a pleasant one? Do you think I could possibly enjoy it while feeling that your heart did not enjoy it too? No, I'm not as selfish as all that. Believe me, let's not try to be impossibly heroic. It's presumptuously arrogant to hope to renounce all self-love in this way. Anyway, let's look at our situation calmly, and let's treat our remaining days as common property which neither of us has the right to monopolize at the expense of the other. For a long time, from the day I was born I might say, life has wearied and been a burden to me. Now I feel I have no longer the strength to endure it without bitterness and impiety. Let us go together, Indiana; let us return to God, who banished us to this world of trials, to this *vale of tears*, but will surely not refuse to open His arms to us when, weary and bruised, we go to ask for His mercy and pity. I believe in God, Indiana, and it was I who first taught you to believe in Him. So have confidence in me. An upright heart cannot deceive a man who questions it with sincerity. I feel we have both suffered enough on this earth to be absolved from our sins. The baptism of misfortune has purified our souls quite enough; let us return them to Him who gave them to us.'

This idea occupied the minds of Ralph and Indiana for several days, at the end of which they decided to commit suicide together.

'It's a matter of some importance,' said Ralph, 'but I had already given it some thought and this is what I have to suggest to you. Since the deed we are about to commit isn't the result of a momentary aberration, but the reasoned objective of a decision taken in a feeling of calm, thoughtful piety, it is important that we should bring to it the meditative attitude of a Catholic towards the sacraments of his church. For us, the universe is the temple where we worship God. It is in the heart of beautiful, unspoilt nature that we rediscover an awareness of His power, pure of all human profanation. So let us go back to the desert in order to be able to pray. Here, in this country teeming with men and vice, in the heart of this civilization which rejects or deforms God, I feel I'd be ill at ease, distraught, saddened. I'd like to die joyfully, my brow serene, my eyes raised to heaven. But where can I find such a place here? So I'm going to tell you the place where suicide appeared to me at its most noble and solemn. It was at the edge of a precipice on Bourbon Island; it was at the top of the waterfall which, transparent and topped by a brilliant rainbow, rushes forth into the lonely ravine of Bernica. It was there that we spent the happiest hours of our childhood; it was there that, later, I wept at the bitterest sorrows of my life; it was there that I learned to pray and to hope; it's there that, on a beautiful, tropical night, I should like to submerge myself in those pure waters and go down into the cool, flower-decked grave that lies in the depths of the verdant abyss. If you have no preference for any other place in the world, grant me the satisfaction of carrying out our double sacrifice at the spot which witnessed the games of our childhood and the sorrows of your youth.'

'I agree,' replied Madame Delmare, putting her hand in Ralph's to indicate a compact. 'I've always been attracted to the water's edge by an invincible feeling, by the memory of my poor Noun. To die as she did will be pleasing to me; it will be my atonement for her death, which I caused.'

'And then,' added Ralph, 'a new voyage, undertaken this time with feelings other than those which have troubled us up to now, is the best imaginable preparation for reflecting and detaching ourselves from earthly affections, for raising ourselves, pure and unsullied, to the feet of the Supreme Being. Isolated from the whole world, ready at any moment to leave life gladly, we shall delight in seeing the storm arouse the elements and reveal before us its magnificent spectacles. Come, Indiana, let us go, let us shake from our feet the dust of this heartless land. To die here, under Raymon's eyes, would look as if it were a petty, cowardly revenge. Let us leave the task of punishing him to God; let us rather ask Him to open the treasures of His mercy to that barren, ungrateful heart.'

They left France. The schooner *Nahandove*, swift and light as a bird, took them to their twice-deserted native land. Never was a passage so quick and pleasant. It was as if a favourable wind had been given the task of leading to port these two unfortunate beings who had been tossed about on the rocks of life. During those three months, Indiana reaped the reward of her docile obedience to Ralph's advice. The bracing, penetrating, sea air restored her fragile health; calm returned to her weary heart. The certainty of soon seeing an end to her troubles produced on her the effect of a doctor's promises on a credulous patient. Forgetting her past life, she opened her soul to the profound emotions of religious hope. All her thoughts became impregnated with a mysterious charm, with a heavenly perfume. Never had the sea and sky seemed to her so beautiful. It was as if she were seeing them for the first time, so many rich and splendid beauties did she discover in them. Her brow became serene again and it was as if a ray of the Divine had passed into her gentle, melancholy, blue eyes.

A no less extraordinary change took place in Ralph's soul and appearance; the same causes produced almost the same effects. His heart, long steeled to pain, softened in the reviving warmth of hope. Heaven also descended into that bitter, wounded heart. His words reflected his feelings and, for the first time, Indiana came to know his true character. The sacred, filial intimacy which brought them close to each other, cured the one of his painful shyness and the other of her unfair prejudices. Every day removed some of Ralph's natural awkwardness and one of Indiana's errors of judgement. At the same time, the poignant memory of Raymon became dulled, faded, and gradually fell away before Ralph's unknown vir-

tues and absolute sincerity. As Indiana saw the good qualities
of the one grow and develop, the other fell in her esteem.
Finally, by dint of comparing the two men, every spark of her
blind, disastrous love was extinguished in her heart.

XXX

It was last year, on an evening of the eternal summer which prevails in that part of the world, that, three days after landing, two passengers from the schooner *Nahandove* went deep into the mountains of Bourbon Island. These two people had given the intervening time to resting, a precaution apparently very alien to the purpose which brought them to the island. But presumably they did not think so; for after taking *faham* together on the verandah, they dressed with special care as if they had intended to spend the evening in town, and, taking the road to the mountains, after an hour's walk they reached the Bernica ravine.

By chance, it was one of the most beautiful of tropical, moonlit nights. That heavenly body, just emerged from the dark waves, was beginning to spread a long band of quicksilver over the sea, but its rays did not reach the gorge, and the borders of the lake mirrored only the trembling reflection of a few stars. Even the lemon trees on the higher slopes of the mountain were not covered with the pale diamonds that the moon scatters on their polished, brittle leaves. The ebony and taramind trees were murmuring in the darkness; only the clusters of leaves at the top of a few gigantic palm trees, whose slender trunks rose a hundred feet from the ground, were tinged with a greenish, silvery gleam.

The seabirds in the crevices of the cliff were silent and only the sad, passionate voices of a few blue pigeons, hidden behind the mountain ledges, could be heard in the distance. Gorgeous beetles, like living jewels, hummed faintly in the coffee shrubs or, buzzing, skimmed over the surface of the lake, and the continuous sound of the waterfall seemed to exchange mysterious words with the echoes on its banks.

By taking a long, steep, winding path the two lonely walkers reached the top of the gorge at the spot where the torrent gushes out in a thin white column of vapour and plunges to the bottom of the precipice. Then they stood on a little platform perfectly suited to the fulfilment of their plan.

At this spot a few tropical creepers, hanging on stalks of raffia grass, formed a natural cradle half-suspended over the water-fall. With wonderful self-possession, Sir Ralph cut off a few branches which might have impeded their leap; then he took his cousin's hand and sat her down on a moss-covered rock where, by day, the charming view of the place could be seen in all its wild, vigorous grandeur. But at that moment, the darkness of the night and the condensed vapour of the water-fall enveloped everything and made the deep abyss seem immeasurable and terrifying.

'My dear Indiana,' said Ralph, 'I must tell you that we need the greatest self-possession for the success of our undertaking. If you jump hastily in the direction which, in the thick dark-ness, looks empty to you, you are bound to hurt yourself on the rocks and your death will be slow and painful, but if you take care to throw yourself on to the white line marked by the waterfall, you will go down into the lake with it and the waterfall itself will ensure that you reach the bottom. If, however, you are willing to wait an hour longer, the moon will be high enough in the sky to give us its light.'

'I'm all the more willing to wait, as we ought to devote our last moments to religious thoughts,' replied Indiana.

'You're right, my dear,' continued Ralph. 'I think our last hour is one of reflection and prayer. I don't say we ought to make our peace with the Eternal; that would be to forget the distance which separates us from His sublime power. But I think we ought to make our peace with the men who have made us suffer, and entrust to the wind, that blows towards the north-east, words of pity for people from whom we are separated by three thousand miles.'

Indiana accepted this suggestion without surprise or emotion. For several months her thoughts had became more exalted in proportion to the change that had taken place in Ralph. She no longer listened to him merely as a phlegmatic adviser; she followed him silently as a good spirit who had been given the task of taking her away from the earth and delivering her from her woes.

'I agree,' she said. 'I am happy to feel that I can forgive without an effort, that I have no hatred, no regret, no love, no

resentment in my heart. As my last hour approaches, I can
barely remember the sorrows of my sad life and the ingratitude of the people who surrounded me. Almighty God! Thou
seest into the depths of my heart; Thou knowest that it is pure
and calm and that all my thoughts of love and hope are turned
towards Thee.'

Then Ralph sat down at Indiana's feet and began to pray in
a strong voice louder than the sound of the waterfall. It was
perhaps the first time since he had been born that all his
thoughts came to his lips. The hour of death had struck. His
soul was no longer bound by fetters or shrouded in secrets; it
belonged only to God; the chains of society no longer weighed
upon it. His fervour was no longer a crime; he could freely
make a leap towards heaven which was awaiting him. The veil
that concealed so much virtue, nobility, and power fell away
completely and his mind rose at its first bound to the level of
his heart.

As a burning flame shines among swirls of smoke and
scatters them, the bright light of the sacred fire which lay
dormant and unknown in the depths of his being shot up. The
first time his strict conscience was freed from its fears and
restrictions, words came spontaneously to the help of his
thoughts and, in his last hour, the ordinary man who, in all his
life, had uttered only banalities became more eloquent and
persuasive than Raymon had ever been. Don't expect me to
repeat to you the strange speech that he confided to the echoes
of that solitary place. He himself couldn't repeat it if he were
here. There are moments of exaltation and ecstasy when our
thoughts become, in a way, more pure, more subtle, more
ethereal. These rare moments raise us up so high, carry us
so far out of ourselves, that when we fall back to earth we
lose the consciousness and the memory of that intellectual
intoxication. Who can understand the anchorite's mysterious
visions? Who can relate the dreams of the poet before his
emotion has cooled so that he can write them down for us?
Who can tell us of the wonders that are revealed to the soul of
the righteous man at the moment when heaven opens to
receive him? Ralph, apparently a very ordinary man, yet an

exceptional one, for he firmly believed in God and consulted daily the book of his conscience, at that moment Ralph was settling his account with eternity. It was the moment to be himself, to lay bare his whole moral being, to lay aside before his Judge, the disguise that men had imposed upon him. In casting aside the hair shirt that grief had attached to his bones, he rose up, sublime and radiant, as if he had already entered the dwelling of divine rewards.

As she listened to him, it did not occur to Indiana to be surprised; she did not wonder if it was really Ralph who was talking like that. The Ralph she had known no longer existed, and the man she was listening to now seemed to her to be a friend, whom she had seen formerly in her dreams and who at last became a reality for her on the brink of the grave. She felt her own pure soul soar up in the same flight. A profound religious sympathy led her to experience the same emotions; tears of enthusiasm fell from her eyes upon Ralph's hair. Then the moon rose above the top of the tall cabbage-palm, and its rays, shining through the gaps in the creeper, clothed Indiana in a pale, moist light which made her, in her white dress and with her long braided hair falling over her shoulders, look like the shade of some maiden lost in the desert.

Sir Ralph knelt before her, saying:

'Now, Indiana, you must forgive me all the harm I've done you so that I can forgive myself.'

'Alas!' she replied, 'what have I to forgive you, my poor Ralph? On the contrary, ought I not to bless you on my last day, as you have forced me to do on all the unhappy days that have marked my life?'

'I don't know to what extent I was blameworthy,' continued Ralph, 'but it is impossible that, in such a long, terrible struggle with my destiny, I was not at fault many times without realizing it.'

'What struggle are you talking of?' asked Indiana.

'That's what I must reveal to you before dying; that's my life's secret. You asked me to tell you on the boat that brought us back here, and I promised to do so on the shore of Lake Bernica, the last time the moon would rise on us.'

'The moment has come,' she said. 'I am listening.'

'Be patient, then, for I have a long story to tell, Indiana, and that story is mine.'

'I thought I knew it, for I've hardly ever been separated from you.'

'You don't know it; you know not a day, not an hour of it,' said Ralph sadly. 'For when could I have told it to you? Heaven willed that the only fitting moment for this confidence should be the last of your life and of mine. But it is as innocent and legitimate today as it would formerly have been crazy and criminal. It is a personal satisfaction that no one has the right to reproach me with at the present hour, and you will grant it me in order to complete the task of patience and gentleness that you have performed towards me. So bear to the end with the weight of my misfortunes, and if my words weary you, listen to the sound of the waterfall which sings the hymn of the dead over me.

'I was born to love; none of you were willing to believe it and this mistake determined my character. It is true that in giving me a loving heart nature made a strange mistake. It had put a stony mask on my face and an immovable weight on my tongue; it denied me what it grants to the most uncivilized beings, the power to express my feelings in looks or words. That made me selfish. The moral being was judged by the outer shell and, like a sterile fruit, I had to harden myself beneath the rough husk that I couldn't discard. I had barely been born when I was rejected by the heart I needed most. My mother sent me away from her breast with disgust because my infant face could not respond to her smile. At an age when one can hardly distinguish a thought from a need, I was already blighted by the odious name of egoist.

'Then it was decided that no one would love me, because I couldn't express my affection to anyone. They made me unhappy; they said I didn't feel it; I was almost banished from my father's house; they sent me to live on the cliffs like a poor bird from the shore. You know what my childhood was like, Indiana. I spent my long days in the wilds with no anxious mother coming to look for my footprints, with no friendly voice crying out in the silent ravines to tell me that night was calling me home. I grew up alone, I lived alone, but God has not permitted me to be unhappy to the end, for I shall not die alone.

'But, even then, heaven sent me a present, a consolation, a hope. You came into my life as if you had been created for me. Poor child! Abandoned like me, cast like me into life without love and without protection, you seemed destined for me; at least I flattered myself with the thought. Was I presuming too much? For ten years you were mine, mine alone, without rivals, without worries. At that time I hadn't yet understood what jealousy is.

'That was the least unhappy period of my life, Indiana. I made you my sister, my daughter, my companion, my pupil, my social group. Your need of me made my life something more than that of a wild animal. For you I emerged from the depression into which the contempt of my family thrust me. I began to have a good opinion of myself by becoming useful to you. I must tell you everything, Indiana. After accepting for your sake the burden of life, my imagination placed in that the hope of a reward. I became accustomed (forgive the words I'm going to use; even today I can't pronounce them without trembling), I became accustomed to thinking you would be my wife. Even though you were still a child, I looked on you as my fiancée. My imagination already embellished you with the charms of a young woman; I was impatient to see you grown up. My brother, who had usurped my share of family affection and who enjoyed domestic tasks, cultivated a garden on the hill which, in the daytime, can be seen from here and which new planters have turned into a rice-field. The care of his flowers occupied his happiest moments, and every morning he went to inspect their progress with an impatient eye and was surprised, child that he was, that they hadn't been able to grow in one night according to his expectations. As for me, Indiana, you were my sole occupation, my sole joy, my sole wealth. You were the young plant that I was cultivating, the bud that I was impatient to see flower. In the morning, I, too, noted the effect of one more day's sun passing over your head; for I was already a young man and you were still only a child. Already, passions whose name was unknown to you were stirring in my heart. My fifteen years were playing havoc with my imagination and you were surprised to see me often sad, taking part in your games without enjoying them. You didn't understand that a fruit or a bird were no longer riches for me as they were for you, and already I seemed to you cold and strange. Yet you loved me as I was, for, in spite of my melancholy, there wasn't a moment I didn't devote to you. My sufferings made you dearer to my heart. I nurtured the crazy hope that one day it would fall to you to change them into joys.

'Alas! Forgive me the sacriligious thought which kept me alive for ten years. If it was a crime for the ill-starred child to place his hopes in you, a beautiful, simple daughter of the mountains, God alone is guilty for giving him that bold thought as his only nourishment. On what could that wounded, misunderstood heart exist, a heart which found needs everywhere and refuge nowhere? From whom could he expect a look, a loving smile, if not from you, with whom he was in love almost as soon as he was your father?

'But don't be alarmed that you grew up under the wing of a poor bird consumed by love. No impure adoration, no guilty thought ever endangered the virginity of your soul; never did my mouth pluck from your cheeks the bloom of innocence that covered them as fruit is covered in the morning by a moist vapour. My kisses were a father's, and when your innocent, playful lips met mine they did not find the burning flame of a man's desire. No, it wasn't you, the little blue-eyed girl, I was in love with. As I held you in my arms with your candid smile and your sweet caresses, you were just my child, or at most, my little sister. But I was in love with your fifteen years, and when left alone with the passions of my own age, I would greedily anticipate the future.

'When I read you the story of Paul and Virginie, you only half understood it. But you wept. You had seen only the story of a brother and sister, where I, perceiving the torments of two lovers, had quivered with sympathy. This book brought torture to me, whilst it brought joy to you. You enjoyed hearing me read of the attachment of the faithful dog,* of the beauty of the coconut palms, and of the songs of the negro

Domingue.* But I, when I was alone, reread the conversations between Paul and his beloved, the impulsive suspicions of the one, the secret sufferings of the other. Oh, how well I understood those first anxieties of the adolescent who seeks in his own heart an explanation for the mysteries of life and grasps enthusiastically the first object of love that comes his way! But do me justice, Indiana; I didn't commit the crime of hurrying on by a single day the peaceful course of your childhood. I didn't let slip a word which might have told you that there were anxieties and tears in life. I left you, at the age of ten, in all the ignorance, in all the security that you had when your nurse put you in my arms one day when I had resolved to die.

'Sitting on this rock, I would wring my hands in a frenzy as I listened to all the sounds of spring and love concealed in the mountains, as I looked at the sunbirds* chasing and teasing each other, at the insects sleeping in a voluptuous embrace in the calyxes of flowers, as I breathed in the burning dust the palm trees send to each other,—ethereal transports, subtle pleasures, for which the soft, summer breeze serves as a resting place. At such times, I was crazy, I was beside myself. I would ask the flowers, the birds, the voice of the torrent, for love. I would summon wildly that unknown happiness, of which the mere idea sent me out of my mind. I would see you, playful and laughing, running towards me on the path over there, so tiny in the distance and so clumsy at climbing over the rocks that, with your brown hair and white dress, you might have been taken for a penguin from the southern hemisphere. Then my blood would calm down, my lips would stop burning. In the presence of the seven-year-old Indiana, I would forget the fifteen-year-old Indiana of whom I'd just been dreaming. I would open my arms to you with a pure joy; your caresses would cool my brow. I was happy; I was a father.

'How many free, peaceful days have we passed in this ravine! How many times have I bathed your little feet in the pure water of this lake! How many times have I watched you sleeping among these reeds with a palm leaf for a sunshade! Sometimes, then, my tortures would begin again. I would grieve that you were so small; I would wonder if, suffering as

I did, I could live till the day when you would be able to understand me and respond to me. I would gently lift up your fine, silky hair and kiss it lovingly. I would compare it with other locks that I had cut from your brow in previous years and that I used to keep in my wallet. I would be happy to confirm that, every spring, your hair was a darker shade. Then I would look at various marks on the trunk of a nearby date-palm, which I had carved to indicate the progressive increase in your height over four or five years. The tree still bears those scars, Indiana; I found them again the last time I came and suffered here. Alas! You grew in vain; in vain did your beauty keep its promises; in vain did your hair become black as ebony! You didn't grow for me; it wasn't for me that your charms developed; it was for another that, for the first time, your heart beat faster.

'Do you remember how, light as two turtle-doves, we would slip along by the wild rose-bushes? Do you remember, too, that sometimes we would get lost in the savannas that lie above us. Once we decided to climb to the mist-covered peaks of the Salazes but had not foreseen that, as we climbed higher, fruit became more scarce, the waterfalls less approachable, the wind colder and more devastating.

'When we saw we were leaving the vegetation behind us, you wanted to go back. But when we had crossed the belt where maidenhair fern grows, we found lots of strawberry plants, and you were so busy filling your basket with their fruit that you no longer thought of leaving the place. We had to give up the idea of going further. We were now walking only on volcanic rock speckled with brown marks like biscuits and strewn with fleecy plants. Those miserable wind-beaten weeds made us think of the goodness of God, who seems to have given them a warm garment to enable them to resist the violence of the climate. And then the mist became so thick that we could no longer see where we were going, and we had to go down again. I carried you back in my arms. I carefully went down the steep mountain slopes. Darkness overtook us as we entered the first wood in the third vegetation belt. There, I picked pomegranates for you but was content to quench my own thirst with creeper, which, when its branches are crushed, provides a cold, pure water. Then we recalled the adventures of our favourite heroes* when they were lost in the woods of the Red River.* But we had no loving mothers, no solicitous servants, no faithful dog, to search for us. Well, I was happy and proud; I alone had the task of watching over you and I thought myself happier than Paul.

'Yes, it was a pure love, a deep, sincere love, that you were already inspiring in me. At the age of ten, Noun was a whole head taller than you. A Creole in the fullest meaning of the term, she was already developed; her glistening eyes were already quickening with a strange expression; her face and her character were those of an adolescent girl. But I didn't care for Noun, or rather, I cared for her only because of you, whose games she shared. It never occurred to me to wonder if she was beautiful already, or whether some day she would be more so. I never looked at her. In my eyes, she was more of a child than you. It was you I loved. I counted on you; you were my life's companion, the dream of my youth . . .

'But I had counted without the future. My brother's death condemned me to marry his fiancée. I won't say anything about that period of my life. There was worse to come, Indiana, and yet I was the husband of a woman who hated me and whom I couldn't love. I was a father, but I lost my son. I was widowed, but I heard that you were married!

'I won't tell you about those days of exile in England, that painful period. If I had wronged anyone, it wasn't you; and if anyone wronged me, I don't want to complain. In England I became more *selfish*, that is to say, more depressed and distrustful, than ever. By having no confidence in me, people had forced me to become proud and to rely only on myself. So, in those trials, I had only the testimony of my heart to support me. People turned it into a crime that I didn't love a woman who married me only because she was forced to, and who treated me only with contempt. Since then people have noticed my apparent aversion for children and regarded that as one of the principal characteristics of my egoism. Raymon teased me cruelly about that tendency, remarking that the care required for the education of children didn't fit in with the rigidly methodical habits of an old bachelor. I don't think he knew I'd been a father and that it was I who brought you up. But none of you could understand that, after many years, the memory of my son was as painful to me as on the day he died, and that my wounded heart swelled with emotion at the sight of blonde heads that reminded me of him. When a man is unhappy, people are afraid of not finding him blameworthy enough, because they are afraid of being obliged to pity him.

'But what no one will ever be able to understand, is the deep indignation, the grim despair, which gripped me, when I, a poor child of the desert at whom no one had ever deigned to cast a pitying glance, was dragged away from this land to undertake the obligations of society; when I was forced to occupy a vacant place in the world that had spurned me, when they wanted me to realize that I had duties towards men who had not recognized theirs towards me. And what's more, not one of my own family had been willing to help me, and now they all summoned me to the defence of their interests! They weren't even willing to let me enjoy in peace what they don't deny to pariahs—solitude! I had only one thing I valued, one hope, one thought in life, that of your belonging to me for ever. They took that away from me; they told me you weren't rich enough for me. What bitter mockery! I, whom the mountains had nourished and who had been rejected by my father's house! I, who had never been allowed to learn how to use wealth and on whom they now imposed the task of managing profitably the wealth of others!

'Yet I submitted. I hadn't the right to ask that my fragile happiness should be spared. I was despised enough; to resist would have made them hate me. Inconsolable for the death of her other son, my mother threatened to die herself if I didn't give in to my destiny. My father, who accused me of not knowing how to comfort him, as if it were my fault that he loved me so little, was ready to curse me if I tried to escape from his yoke. I bowed to my fate, but even you, who have also been very unhappy, wouldn't be able to understand what I suffered. If, persecuted, wounded, and oppressed as I have been, I have not rendered to mankind evil for evil, it should perhaps be inferred that I have not the cold heart I am reproached with.

'When I came back here and saw the man you had been married to . . . forgive me, Indiana; it was then I was really selfish. There is always egoism in love, since there was some even in mine. I experienced a kind of cruel joy at the thought that this legal sham gave you a master and not a husband. You were surprised at my showing a kind of affection for him; that was because I didn't regard him as a rival. I knew quite well that this old man could neither inspire nor feel love and your heart would emerge intact from your marriage. I was grateful to him for your coldness and your sadness. If he had stayed here, perhaps I should have become very guilty, but you left me alone and it wasn't in my power to live without you. I tried to conquer the uncontrollable love, which had revived as violent as ever when I found you again, beautiful and melancholy as I had dreamed of you in your childhood. But solitude only increased my suffering, and I gave in to my need of seeing you, of living under the same roof, of breathing the same air, of being enraptured at every moment by the harmonious sound of your voice. You know what obstacles I was to encounter, what suspicions I had to fight against. I realized then what duties I was imposing on myself; I couldn't link my life to yours without reassuring your husband by a sacred promise, and I've never known what it was to make light of my word. So I pledged myself with mind and heart never to forget my role of brother, and tell me, Indiana, have I been false to my oath?

'I realized, too, that it would be difficult, perhaps impossible, for me to carry out this demanding task if I abandoned the disguise which forbade me any intimate relationship, any deep feeling. I realized that I mustn't play with danger, for my passion was too fervent to emerge victorious from a struggle. I felt I must erect a triple wall of ice around myself, so as to alienate your interest in me, so as to rob me of your compassion which would have destroyed me. I told myself that the day you pitied me, I'd already be guilty, and I was willing to live under the weight of the frightful accusation of hard-heartedness and selfishness which, thanks to heaven, you didn't spare me. The success of my pretence surpassed my hopes. You lavished on me a kind of insulting pity, like the

kind one has for eunuchs. You denied me a heart and senses.
You trampled me underfoot and I hadn't the right to show
even the energy inspired by anger and the desire for revenge,
for that would have been to betray myself and tell you I was
a man.

'I complain of mankind and not of you, Indiana. *You* were
always kind and merciful. You put up with me under the
contemptible disguise I had assumed so as to be near you. You
never made me blush for my role; you compensated me for
everything and sometimes I thought with pride that, if you
looked on me kindly in the guise I'd assumed in order to be
misunderstood, perhaps you'd love me if, one day, you could
really know me. Alas! What woman other than you would not
have spurned me? What other woman would have stretched
out her hand to that unintelligent, dumb idiot? Except for
you, everyone turned their backs on the egoist with disgust.
Oh, the fact is that there was only one creature in the world
generous enough not to be put off by that futile association.
There was only one heart large enough to spread the sacred
fire which animated it on to the narrow, icy heart of the poor
abandoned one. It required a heart that was overflowing with
what I hadn't enough of. There was on earth only one Indiana
capable of loving a Ralph.

'After you, the person who showed me the most consideration was M. Delmare. You accused me of preferring him to
you, of sacrificing your comfort to my own in refusing to
intervene in your domestic quarrels. Unjust, blind woman!
You didn't see that I was of as much use to you as I could be,
and above all, you didn't realize that I couldn't raise my voice
in your favour without betraying myself. What would have
become of you if Delmare had turned me out of his house?
Who would have protected you, patiently and silently, but
with the firm perseverance of an undying love? Not Raymon.
And then, I admit that out of gratitude, I was fond of the
rough, coarse creature who had the power to deprive me of
my one remaining happiness and who didn't do so. His unhappiness was because you didn't love him and his misfortune
had a secret affinity with mine. I was fond of him too for the
very reason that he had never made me suffer the tortures of
jealousy . . .

'But now, I've reached the point of telling you about the most terrible sorrow of my life, of the fatal period when your love, which I'd so long dreamed of, belonged to another. It was then that I fully realized the nature of the feeling I had been suppressing for so many years. It was then that hatred poured poison into my heart and jealousy consumed the rest of my strength. Until then, you had remained pure in my imagination; my respect for you surrounded you with a veil that not even the innocent boldness of dreams dared to lift. But when I had the horrible thought that another was involving you in his life, was snatching you from my control, and was being intoxicated with long draughts of happiness that I didn't even dare dream of, I became mad with rage. I'd have liked to see that detested man at the bottom of this abyss so that I could smash his head with stones.

'But your woes were so great that I forgot my own. I didn't want to kill him, because you would have mourned him. Twenty times I even wanted—may heaven forgive me—to be odious and despicable, to betray Delmare and serve my enemy. Yes, Indiana, I was so out of my mind, so miserable at seeing you suffer, that I was sorry I had tried to enlighten you, and would have given my life to be able to leave my heart to Raymon. Oh, the scoundrel! May God forgive him the harm he's done me; may He punish him for the sorrows he has heaped on your head! It's for those that I hate him, for as far as I'm concerned, I don't bother about my own life any more when I see what he's done to yours. It's he on whose forehead society should have put a stigma from the day of his birth! It's he whom society should have cursed and rejected as the most hard-hearted and depraved of men. But, on the contrary, he was carried in triumph. Oh, I recognize mankind in that and I ought not to be indignant, for in adoring the deformed creature who virtually destroys the happiness and reputation of others, man only obeys his own nature.

'Forgive me, Indiana, forgive me! Perhaps it's cruel to complain in your presence, but it's the first and last time. Let me curse the heartless creature who is driving you to the grave. You needed this terrible lesson to open your eyes. A voice was raised in vain from Delmare's death-bed and from Noun's to cry out to you: "Beware of him; he will destroy you!" You were deaf. Your evil genius swept you along and, with your reputation tarnished, public opinion condemns you but absolves him. *He* has done all kinds of harm and no one bothered about it. He killed Noun but you forgot that; he ruined you but you forgave him. It's because he could dazzle people's eyes and deceive their minds; it's because his skilful, deceitful language made its way into people's hearts; it's because his viper's glance was fascinating; it's because nature would have made him complete if it had given him my wooden features and my sluggish intellect.

'Oh, yes, may God punish him, for he behaved savagely towards you; or rather may God forgive him, for perhaps he was more stupid than wicked. He didn't understand you; he didn't appreciate the happiness he could enjoy. Oh, you loved him so much! He could have made your life so beautiful. In his place I wouldn't have been virtuous; I would have fled with you into the furthest depths of the wild mountains; I would have snatched you away from society to have you all to myself and I would have had only one fear, that of not seeing you sufficiently accursed and abandoned that I could be everything to you. I'd have been jealous of your reputation but not in the way he was; I'd have wanted to destroy it so as to replace it with my love. I'd have suffered at seeing another man give you a scrap of happiness; that would have been to rob me, for your happiness would have been my responsibility, my property, my life, my honour. Oh, how this wild ravine for our only dwelling and these mountain trees for all our fortune would have made me proud and wealthy, if heaven had given them to me with your love! . . . Let me weep, Indiana; I'm weeping for the first time in my life. God has willed that I shouldn't die without experiencing that sad pleasure.'

Ralph was weeping like a child. It was, indeed, the first time that stoical heart had indulged in self-pity. Yet in those tears there was more grief for Indiana's fate than for his own.

'Don't weep for me,' he said, when he saw that she too was in tears. 'Don't pity me. Your pity wipes out all the past, and the present is no longer bitter. Why should I suffer now? You no longer love him.'

'If I'd really known you, Ralph, I'd never have loved him,' cried Madame Delmare. 'It was your virtue that ruined me.'

'And then,' said Ralph, looking at her with a melancholy smile, 'I've many other reasons for joy. Without realizing it, you confided something to me when we opened our hearts to each other during the crossing. You told me that Raymon was never as fortunate as he impudently claimed to be and so you relieved me of some of my torture. You freed me from the remorse of having protected you so badly, for I had the presumption to want to protect you from his seductive charms, and in that, I insulted you, Indiana. I didn't have faith in your strength. That's another of my crimes you must forgive me.'

'Alas!' said Indiana. 'You ask that I should forgive you, I who caused the unhappiness of your life, I who requited such a pure, generous love with incredible blindness and fierce ingratitude! It is I who should go on my knees to you and ask for forgiveness.'

'So my love doesn't arouse your aversion or your anger, Indiana! Oh, thank you, God! I'll die happy! Listen to me Indiana. Don't reproach yourself any more for my sufferings. At this moment I'm not sorry I've had none of Raymon's joys, and I think he ought to envy my fate if he had a man's heart. Now it is I who am your brother, your husband, your lover for all eternity. Since the day you swore to depart this life with me, I cherished the happy thought that you belonged to me, that you'd been given back to me never to leave me again; I began again to call you my fiancée under my breath. It would have been too great a happiness, or perhaps not enough, to possess you on earth. In God's bosom the joys of my childhood's dreams await me. It's there you will love me, Indiana; it's there your divine understanding, stripped of all the deceptive falsehoods of this life, will make up to me for a whole life of suffering, sacrifice, and self-denial; it's there you will be mine, my Indiana, for heaven is you, and I've deserved to be saved, I've deserved to possess you. It was with these thoughts in mind that I asked you to put on this white dress; it's your wedding-dress, and that rock jutting out over the lake is the altar that awaits us.'

He got up and plucked from a nearby grove a flowering orange branch and placed it on Indiana's black hair. Then, kneeling down, he said:

'Make me happy; tell me that your heart agrees to this marriage in the other life. Give me eternity; don't force me to ask for annihilation.'

If the tale of Ralph's inner life has had no effect on you, if you haven't come to love that good man, it's because I've been an incompetent narrator of his memories; it's because I haven't been able to exert over you the power contained in the voice of a man whose passion is deep and genuine. And then I've not the moon's melancholy influence to help me; the song of the waxbills,* the scent of the gilly-flowers, and all the lulling, intoxicating seductions of a tropical night don't invade your heart and head. Perhaps you don't know, either, from experience what powerful new sensations are aroused in the heart when confronted with suicide and how the things of this life appear in their true light just when we are about to put an end to them. This sudden, inevitable light flooded into the innermost recesses of Indiana's heart: the bandage which had been loosening for a long time, fell altogether from her eyes. Having realized the true nature of Ralph's heart, she saw it as it really was; she also saw his features as she had never seen them before, for the power of his extreme exaltation had had the same effect on him as an electric battery has on numbed limbs. It had delivered him from the paralysis which had enchained his hands and voice. Embellished by his frankness and his virtue, he was much more handsome than Raymon, and Indiana felt he was the man she should have loved.

'Be my husband in heaven and on earth,' she said, 'and let this kiss pledge me to you for all eternity.'

Their lips met. In a love which comes from the heart there is, no doubt, a more striking power than in the ardours of an ephemeral desire, for this kiss, on the threshold of another life, contained all their joys.

Then Ralph took his fiancée in his arms and carried her off to plunge with her into the torrent . . .

CONCLUSION
To J. Néraud*

On a hot sunny day last January, I left Saint-Paul to day-dream in the wild woods of Bourbon Island. I thought of you, my friend. These virgin forests had retained for me the memory of your expeditions and your studies. The ground had preserved your footprints. I found everywhere the marvellous things with which your magical tales had charmed my evenings in the past, and so as to admire them together I asked old Europe, where the modest benefits of obscurity surround you, to send you back to me. Happy man, whose intelligence and merit no treacherous friend has revealed to the world!

I had walked towards a deserted spot in the highest part of the island called the *Brûlé de Saint-Paul*.* The collapse of a large section of the main mountain in a volcanic disturbance has formed a long strip of sand studded with rocks arranged in the most magical disorder and in the most frightful confusion. In one place, a huge block of stone is balanced on some small fragments; in another, a wall of thin, light, porous rocks rises up, dentellated and ornamented with openwork like a Moorish building; in yet another a basalt obelisk, whose sides an artist seems to have carved and polished, rises up from a battlemented fortress; elsewhere a Gothic stronghold is crumbling away beside a formless, strange pagoda. There is the meeting place of all the draft outlines of artists, of all the rough sketches of architects. It seems as if the geniuses of all centuries and all nations have come to draw inspiration from this great work of chance destruction. There, no doubt, magical developments of ideas gave rise to the concepts of Moorish sculpture. In the heart of the forests, art has found one of its beautiful models in the palm tree. The *vacoa*,* which is anchored to the ground and clings to it with a hundred arms coming from its stem, must have been the first inspiration for the plan of a cathedral supported by light flying-buttresses. In the *Brûlé de Saint-Paul* all shapes, all beauty, all humour, all

bold conceptions, have been brought together, piled up, arranged, and constructed in one stormy night. The spirits of air
and fire must have presided over this diabolical piece of work;
they alone could give their first attempts the terrible, freakish,
unfinished character which distinguishes their works from
man's; they alone would have piled up these terrifying boul-
ders, moved these gigantic masses, made play with the mountains as with grains of sand, and scattered amongst creations
which man has tried to copy, those great artistic ideas, those
sublime, unrealizable contrasts which seem to defy the artist's
boldness, and say to him derisively: 'Try to repeat that.'

I stopped at the foot of a pile of crystallized basalt about
sixty feet high and cut in facets like a lapidary's work. At the
top of this strange structure it seemed as if an inscription had
been traced in large letters by an immortal hand. Volcanic
rocks of this kind often show the same phenomenon. In the
past, when their substance, softened by the action of the
flames, was still warm and malleable, it received the imprint of
the shells and creepers that stuck to it. These chance contacts
have resulted in some strange patterns, hieroglyphic marks,
mysterious characters, which look as if they had been cast
there like the seal of a supernatural being written in cabalistic
letters.

I stayed a long time, under the sway of the childish preten-
sion of finding a meaning in those mysterious marks. These
useless investigations made me fall into a profound meditation
during which I forgot that time was flying.

Thick mists were already piling up on the tops of the
mountains, coming down their sides, and quickly obscuring
their outlines. Before I had gone half-way across the plateau,
they bore down upon the area I was crossing and enveloped it
in an impenetrable curtain. A moment later, a fierce wind
arose and swept the mists away in a split second. Then the
wind dropped; then fog reformed, only to be driven away
again by a terrible gust.

I looked for refuge against the storm in a grotto which
provided shelter, but another scourge added to that of the
wind. Torrents of rain filled up the beds of the rivers, which all
start from the top of the mountain. In an hour, everything was

flooded and the mountain sides, streaming with water from all directions, were turned into a huge waterfall which rushed furiously down to the plain.

After two hours of a very difficult, dangerous journey, guided no doubt by Providence, I found myself at the door of a dwelling in an extremely wild spot. The simple but attractive house had withstood the storm since it was protected by a rampart of cliffs leaning over it and serving as an umbrella. A little lower down, a waterfall plunged madly to the bottom of a ravine and there it formed an overflowing lake with clumps of fine trees still lifting their battered, weary heads above it.

I knocked eagerly, but the face which appeared at the doorway made me step back. Before I had opened my mouth to ask for shelter, the owner of the house had silently and solemnly made a welcoming gesture. So I went in and found myself face to face with him, with Sir Ralph Brown.

It had been almost a year since the ship, the *Nahandove* had brought M. Brown and his companion back to the colony, but Sir Ralph had not been seen in the town three times. And as for Madame Delmare, her seclusion had been so complete that many of its inhabitants still doubted her existence. It was at about the same time that I had first landed at Bourbon, and this interview with M. Brown was the second in my life.

The first had left an ineffaceable impression on me. It was at Saint-Paul on the sea-shore. His features and bearing had at first only struck me slightly, but when, out of idle curiosity, I questioned the colonists about him, their answers were so strange and so contradictory that I examined the hermit of Bernica with more attention.

'He's a boor, a man with no breeding,' said one. 'There's absolutely nothing to him and he has only one good quality, that of keeping quiet.'

'He's a highly educated, thoughtful man,' said another. 'But he's too conscious of his own superiority, contemptuous and self-important, so that he thinks words he might happen to say to ordinary people are wasted.'

'He's a man who cares only for himself,' said a third, 'undistinguished but not stupid, and utterly selfish; he's even said to be completely unsociable.'

'But don't you know?' said a young man, brought up in the colony and completely imbued with provincial narrow-mindedness. 'He's a scoundrelly wretch who treacherously poisoned his friend so as to marry his wife.'

This reply bewildered me so much that I turned to another, older colonist, whom I knew had a certain amount of common sense.

As my look eagerly asked for the answer to these riddles, he replied:

'Sir Ralph was formerly a worthy man who was disliked because he wasn't communicative but whom everybody esteemed. That's all I can say about him, for since his unfortunate experiences, I've had nothing to do with him.'

'What experiences?' I asked.

He told me about Colonel Delmare's sudden death, his wife's flight on the same night, and M. Brown's departure and return. Judicial enquiries had not been able to throw light on the obscurities which surrounded all these events; nobody had been able to prove the fugitive's crime. The public prosecutor had refused to prosecute, but the partiality of the magistrates for M. Brown was well known and they were severely blamed for not having at least enlightened public opinion about an affair which left two people's reputations tarred with a vile suspicion.

The furtive return of the two accused and their mysterious establishment in the depths of the Bernica desert seemed to confirm the suspicions. It was said they had run away at first to hush up the affair, but public opinion had been so hostile to them in France that they had been forced to come back and take refuge in that lonely spot to satisfy their criminal attachment in peace.

But what made a nonsense of all these stories was a final assertion which seemed to me to originate with better informed people: Madame Delmare, they said, had always shown coolness and even aversion for her cousin M. Brown.

I had looked carefully then, I might say conscientiously, at the hero of so many strange tales. He was sitting on a bale of merchandise, waiting for the return of a sailor with whom he had been negotiating about some purchase or other. His eyes, blue as the sea, were gazing at the horizon with such a calm, candid, dreamy expression, all the lines of this face were in such complete harmony with each other, his nerves, his muscles, his blood, all seemed so tranquil, so well co-ordinated and regulated in this strong, healthy individual, that I could have sworn that he was the victim of a deadly insult, that he had not a crime in his memory, that he'd never had one in his thoughts, and that his heart and his hands were as pure as his brow.

But suddenly, the baronet's idle glance had fallen on me as I was studying him with eager, indiscreet curiosity. Embarrassed like a thief caught in the act, I had lowered my eyes in confusion, for Sir Ralph's contained a severe reproach. Since that moment, I had often thought of him involuntarily; he had appeared to me in my dreams. Whenever I thought of him, I experienced the vague anxiety, the indescribable emotion, which is like the magnetic fluid that surrounds an extraordinary destiny.

My desire to know Sir Ralph was then very real and very keen, but I should have liked to watch him from a distance and without his seeing me. It seemed to me that I had wronged him. His crystal-clear eyes froze me with fear. Such a man was bound to be so superior in virtue or in wickedness that I felt very insignificant and small in his presence.

His hospitality was neither ostentatious nor vulgar. He took me to his room, lent me clothes and clean linen, and then led me to his companion who was waiting for us to have supper.

On seeing her so young and beautiful (for she looked as if she were barely eighteen), and admiring her bloom, her grace, and her gentle voice, I experienced a painful emotion. I immediately thought that she was either very guilty or very unfortunate, guilty of a vile crime or injured by a vile accusation.

For eight days the overflowing river-beds, the flooded plains, the rain, and the wind kept me at Bernica. And then the sun came, but I no longer thought of leaving my hosts.

Neither of them was brilliant. I don't think they had much wit, perhaps they had none at all, but they had the gift of making impressive or delightful remarks; they had the wit that comes from the heart. Indiana is ignorant, but not with the narrow, vulgar ignorance that stems from laziness, indifference, or empty-headedness. She is eager to know what the occupations of her life have prevented her from learning; and then perhaps there was a little coquetry on her part in questioning Sir Ralph so as to show off her friend's immense knowledge before me.

I found her playful but not capricious. Her manners have retained something of the languid melancholy which is natural to Creoles but which, in her, seemed to contain a more fundamental charm. Above all, her eyes have an incomparable gentleness; they seem to speak of a life of suffering, and when her mouth smiles, there is still melancholy in her eyes but a melancholy which seems to express a reflection on happiness or an emotion of gratitude.

One morning, I told them that I was going to leave at last.

'Already!' they said.

The tone of this word was so sincere and touching that I felt encouraged. I had promised myself not to leave Sir Ralph without asking him for his story, but because of the terrible suspicion that had formerly been put into my mind, I felt an insurmountable timidity.

I tried to conquer it.

'I must tell you,' I said, 'men are great scoundrels. They've spoken ill of you to me. I'm not surprised now that I know you. Your life must be very beautiful since it has been slandered so much . . .'

I stopped short on seeing an expression of innocent surprise appear on Madame Delmare's face. I realized that she knew nothing of the atrocious nasty remarks spread abroad about her, and on Sir Ralph's face I met an unequivocal look of haughty displeasure. Ashamed and sad, I got up then to leave them, overawed by M. Brown's look, which reminded me of our first interview and the silent conversation of the same kind that we'd had together by the seashore.

In despair at having to leave for ever this excellent man in such a frame of mind, and sorry to have angered and hurt him in return for the happy days he had just given me, I felt my heart swell and I burst into tears.

'Young man,' he said, taking my hand, 'stay a day longer with us. I haven't the courage to let the only friend we have in the district leave us like this.'

Then, after Madame Delmare had left the room, he said:

'I understand you,' he said. 'I'll tell you my story, but not in front of Indiana. There are wounds which must not be reopened.'

In the evening we went for a walk in the woods. The trees, so fresh and beautiful a fortnight before, had completely lost their leaves but they were already covered with plump, resinous buds. The birds and insects had regained possession of their empire. The faded flowers had already been replaced by new buds. The streams were steadily washing away the sand which had filled their beds. Everything was returning to life, happiness, and health.

'Just look how amazingly quickly kind, fertile nature repairs its losses here!' Ralph said to me. 'Doesn't it look as if it was ashamed of the time wasted, and wanted, with its strength and sap, to restore in a few days the work of a whole year?'

'And it will succeed,' continued Madame Delmare. 'I remember last year's storms; after a month there was no trace of them.'

'It is the image of a heart broken by sorrows,' I said. 'When happiness comes back, it revives and regains its vitality very quickly.'

Indiana gave me her hand and looked at M. Brown with an indescribable expression of affection and joy.

When night fell, she retired to her room and Sir Ralph, making me sit beside him on a bench in the garden, told me his story up to the point where we left it in the previous chapter.

Then he paused for a long time and seemed to have forgotten my presence completely.

Impelled by my interest in his tale, I decided to interrupt his meditation with one final question.

He started like a man who is waking up. Then smiling good-naturedly, he said:

'My young friend, there are memories we take the shine off by recounting them. Let it suffice you to know that I had firmly decided to kill Indiana with myself. But, presumably, approval of our sacrifice had not yet been recorded in the archives of heaven. A doctor might tell you that very probably I was overcome by giddiness and mistook the direction of the path. As for me, who am not in the least a doctor in that sense, I prefer to think that the angel of Abraham and Tobias,* that beautiful, blue-eyed angel, in a white robe with a golden belt, whom you have often seen in your childhood dreams, came down on a moonbeam and, hovering in the trembling spray of the waterfall, spread his silvery wings over my sweet companion. All I can say with certainty is that the moon sank behind the great mountain peaks without any ominous sound disturbing the peaceful murmur of the waterfall, that the birds on the cliff didn't take their flight till a white streak stretched across the horizon, that the first crimson ray which lighted on the clump of orange trees found me there on my knees blessing God.

'But still I don't think that I immediately accepted the unhoped-for happiness which had just restored my destiny. I was afraid to make any judgement about the radiant future that was opening up before me, and when Indiana opened her eyes and smiled at me, I pointed to the waterfall and spoke of dying.

' "If you don't regret having lived till this morning," I said, "we can both affirm that we have tasted happiness to the full; that's an additional reason for leaving life, since perhaps my star will decline tomorrow. Who knows if, when I leave this spot and emerge from the ecstasy into which I have been thrust by thoughts of love and death, I won't once more become the hateful brute whom you despised yesterday? Won't you blush for yourself when you find me again as you knew me? . . . Oh, Indiana spare me such an excruciating pain; it would be the fulfilment of my destiny."

' "Do you doubt your own heart, Ralph, or does mine not offer you enough guarantees?" asked Indiana with an adorable expression of trusting affection.

'Shall I tell you? The first few days I wasn't happy. I didn't doubt Madame Delmare's sincerity but I was frightened of the future. I had been excessively mistrustful of myself for thirty years and it wasn't in one day that I could have a firm hope of pleasing and being loved. I had moments of uncertainty, of panic, of bitterness. Sometimes I regretted not having jumped into the lake when one word from Indiana had made me so happy.

'She too must have had recurrent attacks of melancholy. It was difficult for her to break the habit of suffering, for it takes root in the soul, which becomes used to unhappiness, and is detached from it only with difficulty. But I must do her heart the justice of saying that she never had a single regret for Raymon; she didn't even remember him to hate him.

'At last, as happens with deep, genuine attachments, time, instead of weakening our love, confirmed and sealed it. Each day made it stronger, because each day brought to both sides fresh reasons for esteeming and blessing. All our fears vanished one by one, and when we saw how easy it was to demolish these grounds for mistrust, we smilingly admitted to each other that we accepted our happiness like cowards and that we didn't deserve each other. From that moment we were secure in our love for each other.'

Ralph fell silent; then, after a few moments of solemn meditation in which we were both absorbed, he pressed my hand and said:

'I won't talk to you of my happiness. If there are sorrows which are never revealed and which envelop the soul like a shroud, there are also joys which remain buried in man's heart because an earthly voice cannot express them. Furthermore, if some angel from heaven were to alight on one of these flowering branches and tell you of them in the language of his own country, you wouldn't understand them, for you are a young man, not hurt by strong winds nor shattered by storms. Alas! What can the heart that has not suffered understand of happiness? As for our crimes . . .' he added smiling.

'Oh!' I cried, my eyes wet with tears.

'Listen to me, Monsieur,' he said, quickly interrupting me; 'you have lived only a few hours with the two Bernica criminals, but one single hour is enough for a knowledge of their whole life. All our days are the same; they are all calm and beautiful; they pass swiftly and purely like those of our child-hood. Every evening we praise God; every morning we pray to Him and ask Him for the sun and shade of the previous day. The major portion of our income is devoted to buying the freedom of poor, infirm blacks. That's the main reason for the bad things the colonists say about us. If only we were rich enough to free all who live in slavery! Our servants are our friends; they share our joys, we tend their ills. That is how our life is spent, without sorrows and without remorse. We rarely speak of the past, rarely too of the future; we speak of the latter without fear, of the former without bitterness. If, at times, we surprise each other with eyes moist with tears, it is because there must be tears in great happiness; there are none in great misery.'

'My friend,' I said after a long silence, 'if the world's accusations could reach you, your happiness would be sufficient answer.'

'You are young,' he replied. 'For your pure, guiltless conscience, our happiness is a sign of our virtue; for the world that constitutes our crime. You see, solitude is good and men are not worth any regrets.'

'They don't all accuse you,' I said, 'but even those who appreciate you blame you for despising public opinion, and those who acknowledge your virtue say you are proud and haughty.'

'Believe me,' replied Ralph, 'there's more pride in this reproach than in my alleged contempt. As for public opinion, Monsieur, if one looks at the people it rates highly, shouldn't one always hold out one's hand to those it tramples underfoot? They say its favour is essential to happiness; those who think so must respect it. As for me, I sincerely pity any happiness that is increased or diminished by its whims.'

'Some moralists blame your solitude. They claim that every man belongs to society, which requires his presence. They add that you set men an example which is dangerous to follow.'

'Society should demand nothing from a man who expects nothing from it,' replied Sir Ralph. 'As for being affected by my example, I don't believe it, Monsieur. Too much energy is required to break with the world, too many sorrows to acquire that energy. So let a private happiness, which costs nothing to anyone and hides itself for fear of making people envious, continue in peace. And so, young man, follow the course of your destiny, have friends, a profession, a reputation, a fatherland. As for me, I have Indiana. Don't break the chains which bind you to society; respect its laws if they protect you; value its judgements if they are fair to you. But if some day it slanders and spurns you, have enough pride to be able to do without it.'

'Yes,' I said, 'a pure heart can enable us to endure exile, but to enable us to love it, one needs a companion like yours.'

'Oh,' he said with an ineffable smile, 'if you knew how I pity this society which despises me.'

The next day, I left Ralph and Indiana; the former embraced me, the latter shed a few tears.

'Farewell,' they said, 'return to the world. If some day it banishes you, remember our Indian cottage.'*

EXPLANATORY NOTES

7   *Marmontel*: an eighteenth-century literary figure (1723–99) who wrote, amongst other things, agreeably told moral tales.

15 *Brie*: a region of France to the east of Paris.

17 *Argus*: in Greek mythology a creature with one hundred eyes, of which fifty remained always open. The name has come to be used as a symbol of relentless vigilance.

23 *Bourbon Island*: an island in the Indian Ocean to the east of Africa, now called Reunion Island.

28 *Rubelles*: a district not far from Melun, a town about forty kilometres south-east of Paris.

34 *Almaviva*: in Rossini's opera *The Barber of Seville* (based on Beaumarchais's play of that name). Count Almaviva disguises himself to gain access to the home of the heroine Rosine.

40 *Virginie wrote no more charming letter to Paul*: *Paul et Virginie* is a sentimental tale (1787) by Bernardin de Saint-Pierre of two young people brought up on an idyllic tropical island, the Ile-de-France (now called Ile Maurice) in the Indian Ocean, east of Madagascar.

41 *the scaffolds of '93*: a reference to the multiple executions of the Reign of Terror of 1793.

    vices of the Directory: the Directory was the government which ruled France towards the end of the Revolutionary period from 1798 to 1799. In reaction against the repressive Revolutionary regime it was a period of social license.

    the vanities of the Empire: General Bonaparte, who overthrew the Directory in 1799, became Emperor in 1801. His reign was marked by a certain amount of vain showmanship, e.g. elaborately decorated uniforms, glittering balls, pompous coronation.

    the grudges of the Restoration: the Monarchy was restored in France in 1814, when Louis XVIII became king. Many who had left France during the years of the Revolution and Empire returned, and grudges were felt by people who thought they had been insufficiently compensated for their losses.

eclectic salons: 'eclectic' was the name given to the philosophy of Victor Cousin, who tried to make a synthesis of what he thought were the most probable theories of former philosophers, discarding what was false or inadmissible. The eclectic salons were salons where Cousin's ideas and their political implications were accepted and discussed. In practice these salons supported the Restoration and the charter granted by Louis XVIII.

42 *Lovelace*: the seducer in Samuel Richardson's novel *Clarissa* (1749).

44 *Joseph Bonaparte*: (1768–1844) brother of Napoleon, who in 1808 was made Joseph, King of Spain, where he reigned till 1813.

48 *his great Emperor*: i.e. Napoleon. Colonel Delmare, like many former Napoleonic soldiers, is in favour of the Imperial regime.

the Restoration: i.e. the restoration to the French throne of the Bourbon monarchy in the person of Louis XVIII.

49 *reversi*: a card game of Spanish origin.

53 *Van Dyck*: Dutch painter (1599–1644), renowned especially for his portraits.

65 *Ixion*: in Greek mythology Ixion was a king to whom Jupiter gave refuge in Olympia. He was attached to a flaming wheel in perpetual rotation as a punishment for his lack of respect towards Juno.

66 *Deianeira's tunic*: in Greek mythology Deianira, the wife of Hercules, unwittingly gave him a poisoned tunic which caused his death.

84 *Martignac*: French Minister of the Interior, 1828–9. He tried to reconcile the aristocracy of the pre-Revolutionary regime with the liberal middle class. His main support in the Chamber of Deputies came from the *doctrinaires*, a moderate group with a left-wing tendency.

last revolution: the Revolution of 1830 in which Charles X was replaced by Louis-Philippe, who was more sympathetic to moderately liberal ideas.

absolute monarchy: the monarchy of Charles X, who was deposed in 1830.

the charter: Louis XVIII granted the charter in 1814. It gave legislative power to the Chamber of Peers and the Chamber of

Deputies, and tried to restore links with the old (i.e. pre-Revolutionary) regime, while maintaining some of the achievements of the Revolution and retaining the administrative structures of the Napoleonic Empire.

88 *Imperial cohorts*: Napoleon's armies.

the conquerors of Spain: Spain was conquered by the forces of Napoleon in 1809 with great loss of life.

89 *the King's forest*: the Forest of Fontainebleau, not far from Colonel Delmare's house at Lagny, belonged to the French crown.

117 *the Bourbons*: the royal house of France to which Louis XVIII, King of France from 1814 to 1830, belonged.

the Empire: the Napoleonic Empire which lasted from 1804 to 1814.

the Republic: the regime in France from 1792 to 1795.

England's intervention: England had been at war with the Napoleonic regime from 1804 till Napoleon's final defeat at Waterloo in 1815.

118 *a king proclaimed by foreign bayonets*: Louis XVIII became King of France in 1814, thanks to the victory of the allied armies of Britain, Prussia and Russia over the Napoleonic forces.

Constitutional Charter: the Charter granted by Louis XVIII in 1814.

the excesses of 1793: of the Reign of Terror.

1815: the date of Napoleon's final defeat at Waterloo.

119 *the Coblenz émigrés*: in 1792 aristocrats who had left France after the Revolution of 1789 gathered together at Coblenz to join forces fighting against the Revolutionary regime in France.

Fanchet: head of police during the reactionary ministry of Villèle (1822–7). He made use of informers and spies.

Fouché: Napoleon's clever but unscrupulous Minister of Police.

St Louis' sceptre: Louis IX of France (1218–70) was known as Saint Louis because of his great piety. He was greatly esteemed for his virtue.

at the foot of the Pyramids: Napoleon's victory in Egypt (1798) is known as the Battle of the Pyramids.

the oak of Vincennes: Louis IX was popularly envisaged as administering justice under the shade of an oak tree in the grounds of the royal château of Vincennes.

the white flag: the emblem of the Royalist supporters of the Bourbon monarchy.

the throne of 1815: the monarchy of Louis XVIII, whose reign in France was confirmed after the Battle of Waterloo in 1815.

his tricolour: the colours of the Revolutionary flag which were retained in the Napoleonic Empire.

Duc de Reichstadt: Napoleon's son.

desert sun: a reference to Napoleon's campaigns in the Middle East.

Moskva: the river in Russia near which Napoleon's forces gained a hard-won victory over the Russians, followed, however, by the French retreat from Moscow with great hardships.

120   *the Republic's day*: each of the three characters in this political discussion is representative of one of the different political views prevalent in France during the Restoration. Raymon presents the Royalist point of view, Delmare the Imperial, and Ralph the Republican.

the Hundred Days: after his defeat at Leipzig in 1813 and the signing of the Treaty of Fontainebleau (1814), Napoleon was forced to retire to the Island of Elba. But on 26 February 1815 he returned to France and on 20 March re-entered Paris. Louis XVIII fled but was restored to the French throne after Napoleon's defeat at the Battle of Waterloo, 18 June 1815. The period of Napoleon's brief second reign is known as the Hundred Days.

121   *Peau d'Ane*: a fairy-tale published in a collection of fairy-tales by Charles Perrault in 1697 over the name of his son aged 10.

122   *a pleasure-loving, frivolous age*: the eighteenth century, when, during the reign of the Regent, Philippe d'Orléans, and then of Louis XV, frivolity and licentiousness were prevalent in aristocratic society.

138   *the Elysian fields*: in classical mythology the shades of only the virtuous dead were permitted to enter the Elysian fields, where they dwelt in permanent happiness.

161   *the Regency type*: a reference to the lax moral standards of the period during the Regency of Philippe d'Orléans (1715–23).

161   *Madame du Barry*: the chief mistress of Louis XV from 1770
      till his death in 1774.

      the Dauphin's wife: Dauphin was the title given to the heir
      to the French throne. During the reign of Charles X (1824–30)
      the heir was the Duc d'Angoulême, who had married a daugh-
      ter of Louis XVI and Marie-Antoinette. She was a woman with
      harsh, anti-liberal opinions.

169   *the emigration*: after the French Revolution many French
      aristocrats left France. They became known as the *émigrés*.

      prosperity: after the restoration of the monarchy in 1814 the
      émigrés were able to return to France, and many recovered
      their former privileges.

172   *from the Institut as far as the Corps Législatif*: public
      buildings at some distance from each other on the left bank of
      the Seine; Indiana walked along the left bank until she reached
      the outskirts of Paris.

194   *faham*: a kind of wild orchid.

      Saint-Gilles river: a river in Bourbon Island near Indiana's
      home.

195   *saxatile shrubs*: shrubs which grow on stony ground.

196   *camaros*: large shrimps.

      veloutier: the name given in Bourbon Island to a plant of
      which there is a British version, borage, with bright blue
      flowers, and stem and leaves covered with prickly hairs.

199   *the ministry of 8 August*: the government which came to
      power in August 1829 and whose reactionary policies precipi-
      tated the 1830 Revolution which deposed Charles X.

      Prince de Polignac: the head of the ministry of 8 August.

      the family whose interests . . . had been closely tied to his own:
      the Royal family. Raymon, while supporting the Royal family,
      did not go along with the return to absolute monarchy of
      Charles X and the Polignac government.

200   *choosing a colour*: choosing a political party.

201   *the two sections of society*: the aristocracy and the rich
      bourgeoisie.

202   *peris*: fairy-like creatures in Persian tales which were fashion-
      able at the time.

210   *Rodrigue Island*: George Sand may not have realized that this island was as much as 800 kilometres east of Bourbon Island. Rodrigue Island was colonized in 1691, the colonists using slave labour to cultivate it, but when it became difficult to recruit slave labour the population declined, and in 1843 there were only 250 inhabitants.

212   *La Saline*: a village about ten kilometres from St Paul.

217   *satanite*: a Breton name for a petrel. Many Breton sailors came to Bourbon Island and left their mark on the local language.

     piragua: a long narrow canoe hollowed from the trunk of a single tree.

220   *Medina-Sidonia*: a noble Spanish family which took its name from a province of Cadiz. A Duke of Medina Sidonia was Commander of the Spanish Armada (1588–9).

222   *Louis XV's century*: the eighteenth century.

     Anne Page: one of the characters in Shakespeare's *Merry Wives of Windsor*.

223   *Boucher*: French painter (1703–70) of charming pastoral and mythological themes.

224   *national property*: property belonging to aristocrats which was confiscated at the Revolution became national property and then sold. At the restoration indemnity was paid to the previous owners.

     indemnity: see previous note.

225   *Iago*: the traitor in Shakespeare's *Othello*.

226   *revolution in Paris*: the 1830 Revolution, in which Charles X was deposed and Louis-Philippe came to the throne. The prefect of the Gironde Department, in which Bordeaux is situated, was opposed to the Revolution and loyal to Charles X. Consequently he was manhandled by the crowd and barely escaped with his life.

228   *Les Quinconces*: a large esplanade in Bordeaux, renowned for its size.

     the turn political events had taken: the disturbances of mob violence were soon brought under control and the Revolution took on a relatively conservative character with the accession of Louis-Philippe.

229   *three per cent*: since 1825 dividends on investments had greatly declined. At the same time, women's hats had decreased in size.

250   *the faithful dog*: the next few lines refer to incidents in Bernardin de St Pierre's novel *Paul et Virginie* (cf. note to p. 40 above).

251   *Domingue*: a character in *Paul et Virginie*.

       sunbirds: birds which live in the sugar-canes. There is a variety peculiar to Bourbon Island.

253   *favourite heroes*: Paul and Virginie.

       Red River: in *Paul et Virginie*, the river is Black River. George Sand seems to have misremembered. The lines which follow refer to incidents in Bernardin de St Pierre's novel.

260   *waxbills*: a kind of sparrow common in parts of Asia and Africa, including Bourbon Island.

261   *J. Néraud*: Jules Néraud was a friend of George Sand's who taught her botany.

       Brûlé de Saint-Paul: Indiana and Ralph had a long steep climb to the Brûlé de Saint-Paul, which is 2,000 metres high and twelve kilometres from Saint-Paul.

       vacoa: a kind of palm-tree found in the African islands of the Indian ocean.

268   *the angel of Abraham and Tobias*: in Gen. 22, God tests Abraham's faith by commanding him to sacrifice his son, Isaac, but just as he is about to kill the boy an angel calls on Abraham to stay his hand, his faith having been proved by his willingness to obey God's command. The story of Tobias is told in the Apocrypha in the Book of Tobit. An angel tells Tobias, son of Tobit, how to cure his father's blindness and guides him towards his future wife.

271   *Indian cottage*: a reference to Bernardin de St Pierre's novel *The Indian Cottage* (1791). In it a learned traveller in search of wisdom and truth finds them only in the cottage of an Indian pariah.

THE WORLD'S CLASSICS

A Select List

HANS ANDERSEN: Fairy Tales
Translated by L. W. Kingsland
Introduction by Naomi Lewis
Illustrated by Vilhelm Pedersen and Lorenz Frølich

ARTHUR J. ARBERRY (Transl.): The Koran

LUDOVICO ARIOSTO: Orlando Furioso
Translated by Guido Waldman

ARISTOTLE: The Nicomachean Ethics
Translated by David Ross

JANE AUSTEN: Emma
Edited by James Kinsley and David Lodge

Northanger Abbey, Lady Susan, The Watsons,
and Sanditon
Edited by John Davie

Persuasion
Edited by John Davie

WILLIAM BECKFORD: Vathek
Edited by Roger Lonsdale

KEITH BOSLEY (Transl.): The Kalevala

CHARLOTTE BRONTË: Jane Eyre
Edited by Margaret Smith

JOHN BUNYAN: The Pilgrim's Progress
Edited by N. H. Keeble

FRANCES HODGSON BURNETT: The Secret Garden
Edited by Dennis Butts

FANNY BURNEY: Cecilia
or Memoirs of an Heiress
Edited by Peter Sabor and Margaret Anne Doody

THOMAS CARLYLE: The French Revolution
Edited by K. J. Fielding and David Sorensen